THE ALASKA HIGHWAY

AN INSIDER'S GUIDE

"Ron Dalby has done a wonderful job of providing a real picture for the highway traveler. This book provides the kind of detailed information necessary to insure an enjoyable trip. A must for anyone planning to travel the Alaska Highway."

> Susan C. Kemp
> Executive Director
> The Great Alaska Highways Society

"Nobody, but nobody, knows Alaska's highways and byways like Ron Dalby, and he has done a five-star job of describing them."

> Mike Miller
> author of *Camping Alaska and Canada's Yukon*
> former majority leader of the Alaska House of Representatives

"Alaska highway insider Ron Dalby gives us a long overdue comprehensive guide to this beautiful wilderness highway. Whether you're a family of seasoned veterans or first timers, this guide is all you will need to make your trip up the highway the adventure of a lifetime. A must guide before, during and after your trip."

> Peter Sykas
> former publisher, *Alaska*™ magazine

"A must-have for the serious Alaska traveler ... takes you there and back, with detailed information on every facet of getting around in Alaska."

> Jay H. Cassell
> Senior Editor, *Sports Afield*

"A great book about a great highway. Even Sourdoughs will find new and helpful information here. One can always experience nostalgia and new adventures on the highway. NORTH TO THE FUTURE!"

> Ted Stevens
> U.S. Senator from Alaska

"The Alaska Highway can provide all the seeds for adventure you'll ever need without leaving your driveway. I like the way the book has been divided into one-day trips, with a length of highway that can be covered without pushing it."

— *Newsday*

"Ron Dalby is one of those few people who talks like they write ... a guidebook to driving the Alaska Highway that is no sterile set of maps and pointers ... with its meandering side trips and intentional focus away from cities, this might be considered an off-the-beaten track look at Alaska."

—*Los Angeles Daily News*

"*The Alaska Highway*, by Ron Dalby, is a great companion, covering just about any place and anything you may encounter along the Alcan."

—*Motorland*

"Dalby's insider tips are those of a seasoned Alaskan. He provides a host of practical tips."

—*Family Motor Coaching*

"Written by a native of the state, this paperback is a comprehensive guide for those interested in making the great driving adventure north."

—*Trailer Life*

"Dalby has been there. Just about anywhere in Alaska that you might choose to talk about. Dalby's trips along The Alaska Highway and his knowledge of his state give him the right to name his book, 'An Insider's Guide.'"

—*The Mature Traveler*

"Ron Dalby gives you all the information you need to prepare for the trip."

—San Diego *Tribune*

"Here is a book that will be enjoyed by the first-time visitor as well as the repeater."

—*Arizona Mobile Citizen*

The
ALASKA
Highway

The
ALASKA
Highway

An Insider's Guide
Revised Edition

Ron Dalby

Fulcrum Publishing
Golden, Colorado

Library of Congress Cataloging-in-Publication Data

Dalby, Ron, 1949–
     The Alaska highway / Ron Dalby. —Rev. ed.
          p.   cm.
     Includes index.
     ISBN 1-55591-171-4
     1. Alaska—Guidebooks. 2. Alaska Highway—Guidebooks.
3. Automobile travel—Alaska Highway—Guidebooks. 4. Northwest,
Canadian—Guidebooks. I. Title.
F902.D35 1993
917.9804'5—dc20   93-13870
                                                            CIP

Book design by Richard Firmage

Map by Patty Maher

Interior photographs by Ron Dalby

Front cover photograph of Glenn Highway and Chugach Moun-
tains/southcentral Alaska by Chris Arend, Alaska Stock Images

Back cover photographs by Ron Dalby

Printed in the United States of America

10   9   8   7   6   5   4   3   2   1

Fulcrum Publishing
350 Indiana Street
Golden, Colorado 80401-5093
800/992-2908

To Chris Dalby

who rests in the Yukon near our favorite fishing hole

CONTENTS

ACKNOWLEDGMENTS

This book, like most books, gives a single name on the cover as the author. However, just about anyone who has ever written a book will quickly tell you that an author has a lot of help. And without this help, there wouldn't be a book.

I would particularly like to thank Norman Jacobson at Lance Campers in Los Angeles. When he heard about the original project in early 1989, he volunteered the use of a Lance camper and a pickup.

For me, that made all the difference. I had, prior to then, driven the Alaska Highway with every other type of vehicle described herein, but never in a pickup camper. As the saying goes, I seemed to have saved the best for last. The combination of a four-wheel-drive pickup truck and camper allowed us all the comfort of a large motorhome, but provided a greatly enhanced ability to seek out the hidden places that were just too large or too rough to consider visiting in a motorhome or a large vehicle-and-trailer package. And, the Lance lived up to all the advance billing Norman provided—something along the line of its being the finest camper in the world.

Then, too, there was my original editor at Fulcrum, Pat Frederick. She knew just when to prod and just when to back off. Though I occasionally gave her fits—when my computer ate a chapter that wasn't backed up, for example—she stood with me to get this book from the idea to the finished product. Every writer needs an editor like Pat.

Subsequent editions of this book found me working with others on Fulcrum's talented staff. Key among them was managing editor Carmel Huestis, whose largest task was tying me down in one spot long enough to get everything done. Beyond Fulcrum's editorial staff, Linda Stark in marketing has been instrumental in making the original of this book a success, as has almost everyone in the sales and marketing departments. To say that I enjoy being a writer in Fulcrum's employ is an understatement.

It is a distinct pleasure to work with each and every person in their Golden, Colorado, offices.

My daughter Tiffany was also instrumental in the work that went into this project. She sat with me in the front seat for more than 6,000 miles, taking notes on everything I wanted written down but didn't have time to stop for. Her notes and logs provide the exact distances registered in this book, contributing greatly to its final form.

And, finally, there are those thousands of people I've met along the Alaska Highway since I began traveling it in 1972. Though I've forgotten many of their names and have not the space to list here those names I do remember, without these people the Alaska Highway would be just another road. The highlight of any travel experience is the people you meet; that alone makes my travels along the Alaska Highway the grandest experiences of my life.

PREFACE

I first saw the Alaska Highway—then almost universally known as the Alcan—in August 1950, from the back seat of a two-door, black Studebaker Champion. Being 13 months old at the time, I remember absolutely nothing of the trip, though over the years my mother has assured me that I had a great time.

Undoubtedly my great time came at her expense. Dad did the driving; Mother wrestled with my tantrums and diapers. This was before the advent of functional disposable diapers, so I suppose her chores were the toughest of the lot.

At any rate, we succeeded in reaching Nebraska so I could meet my grandparents—and in plenty of time for the birth of my brother. Yes, indeed, Mother must have had quite a trip, being eight months pregnant. In those days, doctors were even farther apart than gas pumps. Campgrounds were wide spots on the road or gravel pits created by the building of the highway, and help in the event of an emergency was usually a long distance away.

Significantly, I can't recall either of my parents mentioning many problems from that trip, not so much as a flat tire. To the end of his days, Dad looked upon it as one of the greatest adventures he'd ever had. Mother still grins when she spins a yarn about her 1950 trek from Alaska to Nebraska. Yet I'm certain they must have had a few tense moments or minor breakdowns.

I find myself acting much the same way. Certainly I've had my share of flat tires (seven in one trip), chipped windshields and loose bolts, but I have to force myself to remember these things. I've simply had too much fun driving back and forth on the Alaska Highway. When I think of the Alaska Highway, I think of friends from Whitehorse, Yukon, met by chance in the Squanga Lake Campground, or the largest lake trout I've ever seen surfacing at the end of my son's line after a 40-minute battle. Sunsets, vivid beyond belief, come to mind, as do mountain sheep grazing at roadside. Those are the things that make driving the Alaska Highway such an adventure, an adventure available to anyone with a driver's license and access to a vehicle.

Over the years I've learned to take a few simple precautions that will ensure a relatively trouble-free trip, save for an unpredictable accident. That's what part of this book is about. Driving to Alaska needn't be any more nerve-wracking than driving across the United States. It should, in fact, be a lot more relaxing because there's a lot less traffic. All it takes is a little planning and preparation.

The balance of this book describes some of the adventures promised by the words "Alaska Highway." Unfortunately, there's not room for all of them in a book of any size. Besides the nuts and bolts of where to go and what to see, anecdotes from my own experiences and those of others are included. Laugh with me, cry with me, even cuss with me as I detail some of the triumphs and problems overcome in nearly two decades of vacationing along the Alaska Highway.

And, for many people, once is not enough. Already we're planning next year's highway vacation, our fourteenth in 21 years. You see, I've been hearing rumors about these 40-pound lake trout right next to the road . . .

The
ALASKA
Highway

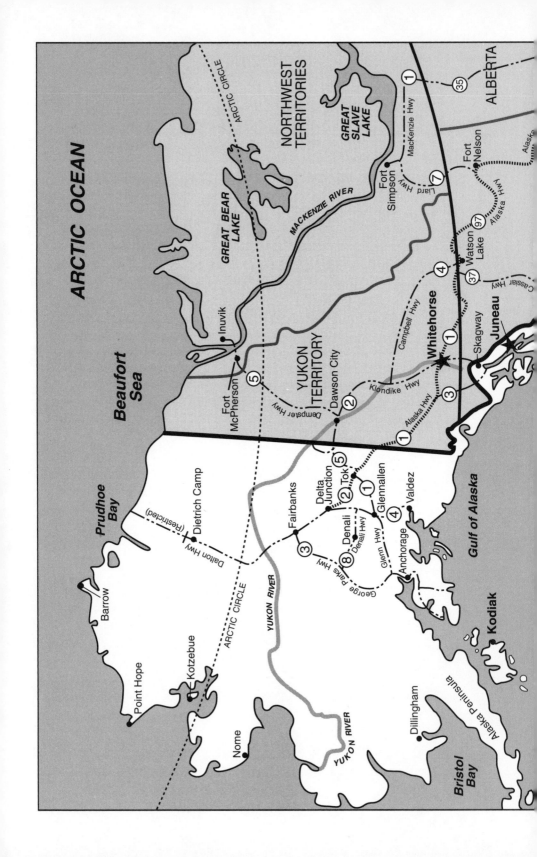

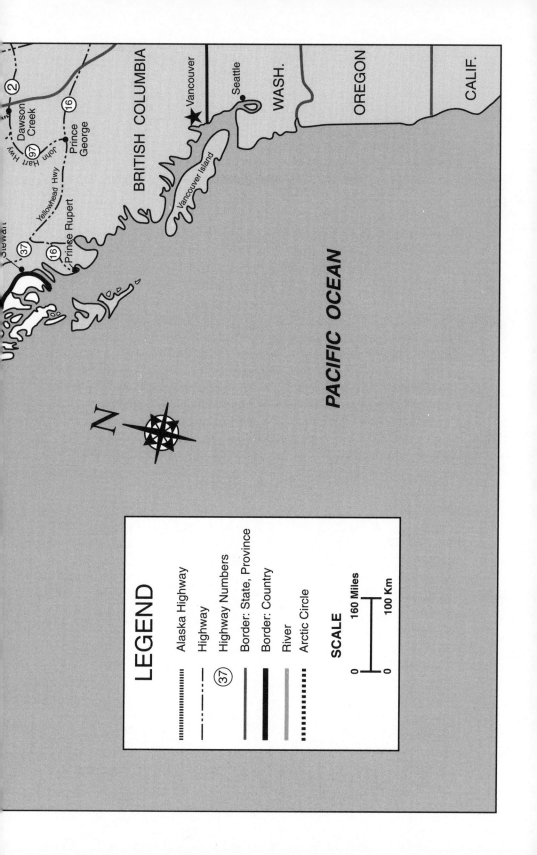

A ROAD TO ALASKA

The dust had barely settled over Pearl Harbor's sunken battleships in December 1941 when the U.S. government decided to build a road from Dawson Creek, British Columbia, Canada, through Yukon Territory, Canada, to the U.S. Territory of Alaska.

The connection between Japan's bombing the Pacific Fleet into rubble and a road to Alaska isn't immediately obvious—unless you're staring at the globe Adolph Hitler and his minions might have prepared in late 1941. Save for England, Hitler basically ruled Europe, his armies poised at the gates of Moscow. Hitler's Axis partner, Japan, was gobbling up Pacific islands and Asian mainland bases in Indochina and China. Japan and Germany, allied with Italy, looked all but unbeatable in late 1941 to many observers.

Only three countries of sufficient resources retained the independence necessary to prosecute World War II against one or both of the aggressors: England and its dominions, the Soviet Union and the United States.

The only place where two of these three diverse nations come close together is the Bering Strait, a narrow neck of water separating Alaska and Siberia. This distant but tenuous link in the Far North looked mighty good indeed to the Allied powers. Frankly, there weren't many other places to look at the time.

There was one immediate and pressing problem—in December 1941 there was no guarantee that Alaska could be supplied. Shipping was thought too dangerous because of the threat of Japanese naval forces. A road seemed the obvious answer, a road built far enough inland to be out of range of the airplanes carried by Japanese aircraft carriers. With few preliminaries, the U.S. Army Corps of Engineers was sent to build the Alcan Highway, the road known today as the Alaska Highway.

It being wartime and all, a few proprieties were initially overlooked. Canada and the United States are separate countries, and even though both were warring against the Axis, things were a bit strained when several

1

trains filled with U.S. soldiers and equipment began unloading in Dawson Creek one winter day, somewhat ahead of any agreement being signed granting the United States the right to build the road.

Both countries, though, took things in stride, having been friendly nations for more than a century. American soldiers just bulldozed ahead, figuring that the inevitable paperwork would catch up sooner or later, and the Canadians, while rushing to fill out the forms, politely allowed the Americans to get started. A few weeks later an agreement was announced, and the few ruffled feathers settled down. Ultimately, the Canadians won big; they were able to purchase most of the road from the Americans for about half its cost when the war ended—not a bad bargain by anyone's standards.

But the American GI who started overland from Dawson Creek in the middle of winter, generally heading northwest to Fairbanks, didn't think he had such a bargain. It gets right cold in that part of the world in winter. And winter lasts a long time. Not only that, but the officers running this show were in a hurry. As the surveyors walked along flagging a route across creeks, rivers, plains and mountains, they were rarely out of earshot of the bulldozers—often within sight of the big metal beasts.

Even as they pushed rapidly across this wilderness, it became evident that military-minded men had preceded them. Airstrips suitable for military interceptors and bombers were already operating in places like Fort Nelson, Watson Lake and Whitehorse; the new road just kind of linked them together. During the building of the road, this chain of airstrips provided vital links for communications and transportation.

Once the soldiers started northwest from Dawson Creek and southeast from Alaska, the road came together fast. Just 8 months and 12 days after they started, in November 1942, a celebration was held near Kluane Lake—about 150 miles northwest of Whitehorse—commemorating the completion of the project.

If that sounds a little fantastic for finishing a road across 1,500 miles of wilderness, it was. What was then called a road was described by men of great vision with limited functional eyesight. The Army had to station engineers with bulldozers along lengthy stretches of single-lane muddy trails, trails gradually sinking below ground level as the just-bared permafrost under the topsoil melted into mud the consistency of quicksand. The big tractors pulled trucks through these spots during the summer months.

Not much attention was paid to grades, either. If the surveyors hiked up or down a particularly steep hill, the bulldozers simply followed them. In fact, a sign just prior to a particularly steep and treacherous downhill stretch called Suicide Hill warned drivers to prepare to meet their maker, and not without reason. This plunge caused several major vehicle accidents before it was leveled out.

Civilian construction crews from Canada worked throughout 1943 and into 1944 straightening out hairpin curves, leveling grades and reinforcing muddy surfaces with gravel so that the word "road" could be a reasonable

Entrance to Alaska Highway at Dawson Creek, British Columbia.

description of this meandering path to Alaska. By then, though, they were working at a much lower priority than those who pioneered the route. By late 1943, Japanese forces were being chased out of Alaskan waters, and the perceived need for the road was markedly reduced.

As the war wound down in 1945, the Alcan actually became deserving of being described as a road. And what a road it was. Suddenly, large parts of the Canadian North were open to the people of North America. And the few people who lived in the region suddenly had access to the outside world, called the civilized world by those they met when they first ventured along the route. Tourists, first the heady adventurers, then later the calmer, saner folks, began looking north, north to the last great wilderness on the continent.

The Canadians took control of most of the road in 1946—about 1,200 miles of the 1,550 miles from Dawson Creek to Fairbanks are in Canada.

Still, though, it required the permission of the military to drive through to Alaska. This held for all of 1947 as well. In 1948, the road was opened briefly to the public but was soon closed again because of the number of vehicles pounded to pieces en route to Alaska. Not until 1949 was the road opened to the public on a year-round basis. Ever since, more and more facilities for travelers—gas stations, motels, restaurants and campgrounds—have opened every year. By the late 1970s, travelers were never more than 50 miles or so from at least a small service station. By 1992, the road was paved.

Spur roads began opening shortly after the highway was built. The first of these joined Haines, Alaska, near the northern end of the Alaska panhandle, to the Alaska Highway at a point about 100 miles northwest of Whitehorse, Yukon Territory. It was completed in December 1943. Soon after the war, it became possible to drive from Whitehorse to Dawson City, Yukon, the latter the scene of the Klondike gold rush of 1898. Yukon's capital moved from Dawson to Whitehorse in 1953, tacit recognition that Whitehorse had eclipsed Dawson as the territory's population and business center. The Alaska Highway played a major role in that switch.

In the last two decades, sufficient spur roads have opened to make it possible to drive from Canada to Alaska while driving on only about 10 miles of the actual Alaska Highway. Thus you could argue that there are two routes north. Additionally, the Liard Highway, running north from Fort Nelson, links the Alaska Highway to Northwest Territories, probably Canada's remotest province, certainly its largest. Another road near Dawson leads north to Inuvik, an Eskimo community at the apex of the Mackenzie River delta, well north of the Arctic Circle.

Gradually, but ever so steadily, villages throughout northwestern Canada are being connected to North America's road system. All these various roads increase the potential for adventure for those driving to Alaska. In fact, as Canadians will quickly tell you, you can spend the whole summer exploring northern British Columbia, Yukon and Northwest Territories without ever entering Alaska. That alone is as much fun or even more fun than driving to Alaska. Maybe you'd better plan to spend two summers up North so you can do both.

There is, without a doubt, a lot to see and do in Canada. The Alaska Highway, as it is officially known, provides a path to some of the most thrilling outdoor recreation opportunities in North America. Grizzly bears roam the tundra at roadside, black bears amble in the forests, Stone sheep feed on the road shoulder where it crosses the Rocky Mountains and grizzled trappers still wander the land in solitude, coming out only when necessary to buy supplies or to sell their furs.

The Alaska Highway leads you back in time, back to when the world was a simpler place, a wilder place and, to some, a more enchanting place. It gives you a glimpse of the way we were, and it shows the careful observer some of the steps we took to get where we are today.

· —— 2 —— ·

THE PEOPLE OF
THE AMERICAN NORTH

May 20, 1972; about 50 miles south of Fort Nelson. It was my third flat tire of the day. Luckily, there was a small gas station just a few miles up the road where I could get the punctured tire fixed to use as a spare for the miles ahead.

As I pulled in, I smelled something burning. A beat-up 1959 Ford sedan sat alongside the service station, faint wisps of smoke curling out from under the back. Before I could open the door of my stationwagon, the most grizzled old guy I'd ever seen leaned in my open window. I recoiled from his bad breath, then listened to his tale of woe.

"Northbound? Can you take us to Fort Nelson?" He pointed to his equally grizzled partner.

I started to stammer, not knowing whether or not to be scared, and he cut me off with an explanation.

"We're comin' out to sell our fur and burnt out the rear end in our car. Nearest Ford dealer's in Fort Nelson. We need a lift to town to get parts."

I couldn't help but like the old coot. I hesitated just long enough to tell him about getting a tire patched, and said I'd take them the 50 miles to Fort Nelson as soon as that was done.

While the gas station owner patched the tire, I looked inside the old man's car, scraping not just a little grime off the window to do so. The back seat was filled with raw furs: beaver, what looked to be marten and a wolverine hide or two, most of it in a hopeless jumble.

Tire fixed and car gassed up, I made room in the front seat for the three of us, and off we went. Turns out they were trappers who kept an old car by the road for annual trips to town to sell furs, whoop it up a little and buy supplies for the new season. Depending on the price of furs in a given year, the length of their stay in town—Fort Nelson—could be most of the summer.

5

"We always buy our grubstake before we spend the other money," the second man assured me.

Luckily it was a hot day and we could drive comfortably with the windows open. We had gone but a few miles when each pulled a flask from an inside pocket, which demonstrated the only disagreement between them during the entire trip. One had a fiery whiskey, the other an equally potent rum.

"Care for a snort?"

I did. I sampled each a couple of times in an hour and a half while they regaled me with tales of the winter of '48-'49 when it was ungodly cold, at least 70 below for days on end, or so they said. Then there was lots of speculation about how much money this year's catch would bring, the price of liquor in Fort Nelson and whatever else that was important in their world.

As we reached the outskirts of town, I saw a sign for a Ford dealer some distance ahead and asked if that's where they wanted to go. Looking outside, the one closest to the window spotted a tavern and pointed to it.

"Jes' let us out there," he said. "We'll work our way up the road."

I stopped, we shook hands for the third or fourth time, they went inside and I headed on shaking my head. I never did learn their names, and I counted three more bars between them and the Ford dealer.

A couple of hours later, nearing the summit of the Rocky Mountains, I came through a hairpin curve and stopped suddenly to avoid hitting a pickup truck with a camper broken down in the middle of the road. The truck had a flat, a bad one that bent the wheel. The license plates were from Louisiana.

The driver, an older fellow, was under the truck cussing in the finest Cajun style. His jack wasn't strong enough to lift the truck and camper combined. His wife was in the camper fixing dinner. I pulled out a jack and helped him change the tire. That earned me an invitation to supper—still in the middle of the road. There wasn't much traffic in those days. While we ate, I learned that they had recently retired as bakers in Shreveport, Louisiana, and were on their way north to spend the summer in Alaska, a lifelong dream.

We exchanged names and addresses. For the next several years, they regularly sent me a cake and a card at Christmas.

Those are just four people met in a single day along the Alaska Highway. Admittedly, things have changed since then. Though traffic isn't heavy yet by lower 48 standards, it's too heavy now to spend an hour sitting in the middle of the road changing a tire and eating dinner. And, there are still trappers in the wilderness bordering the highway, though I doubt the two guys I hauled to Fort Nelson are still alive. If they are, they're in their 80s.

And there are more people living and working along the highway these days. Last year in Fort Nelson, I couldn't even find the Ford dealer, much less the tavern where I let off my trapper friends. The road now runs alongside the town instead of through it.

Yet these are still special people, special people who live in a special place. When you break down along the Alaska Highway, the first car along will usually stop to help—if it's not another tourist or a long-haul trucker. Most of the tourists and the truckers these days are in too big of a hurry to get somewhere, and perhaps fearful that stopping to help along the Alaska Highway offers the same hazards that stopping at roadside in the lower 48 can bring. Significantly, though, most tourists eventually get into the mood of stopping to help by the time they're several hundred miles up the road. That's just the way things are done up here.

I like Canadians, something that should already be apparent. To me, they are a special part of an Alaska Highway adventure. Because of that, I find the best times to travel the highway are mid-May or September, just before and just after the summer's onslaught of tourists. Roadside businesses aren't so busy then and the people running them have time to talk. The road is less crowded as well.

Pulling into Fort St. John one May evening demonstrates what I mean. It was an unseasonably hot day, I was traveling alone and it had been a long, dry afternoon. By about 9 P.M., I was ready for a beer, a meal, a shower and sleep, in that order. I stopped at the first motel I saw.

The woman behind the counter was in her thirties; four or five kids of varying ages played in the yard out front. I filled out the form, she handed me a room key and I asked about a place for dinner. Her eyes lit up a little, she apologized that there was no restaurant close to the motel and then she asked me if I wanted a beer. "Absolutely."

She opened a small refrigerator behind the counter, pulled out two frosty bottles of good Canadian beer and said that should be enough to hold me until dinner. I started to pay for it and she stopped me. "We don't have our liquor license yet."

As for dinner, she said her husband would be home from his construction job in a half hour or so, then they and the kids were going to have a hot-dog roast and picnic in front of the motel. I was *told* to join them.

I did join them, eating hot dogs and potato chips and sampling more of that good beer until well past midnight. We watched the sun go down and talked throughout the lingering twilight that ultimately evolved into sunrise. I slept quite late the next morning, well past checkout time, and was sent on my way with a friendly wave from the whole family. There are times when being the only guest in a motel can be a wonderful experience.

The motel is still there, though I haven't stopped for years. It's the first one on your left as you approach Fort St. John from the south.

↪   This was not an isolated incident. Some years later, again driving north, this time with my wife and two very young children, we pulled into a gas station at Teslin, Yukon Territory. Again, a hot day, and we were pushing to get a few miles behind us.

We filled up a very thirsty pickup truck and paid the owner. Everybody climbed back in the truck, the kids less than eagerly, and I started the engine. Just as I was putting it in gear, out came the owner carrying four ice cream cones, one for each of us. Handing them through the window, he wished us a great trip and mumbled something about the ice cream being free because of the fill-up.

We now stop there on almost every Alaska Highway trip. The place, on the north side of Teslin, is called Halstead's, the name of the family that owns it. While their kids were growing up it was a family business in every sense of the word. Mom got up at 3 A.M. every summer morning to bake the doughnuts and pastries she was famous for; Dad sold gas and worked on the campgrounds and the rental boats. The kids were everywhere, helping out as needed.

The kids are grown now, though a couple of them still work there, and there's been a "For Sale" sign on the store for several years. But, as of 1993, the business hadn't been sold and the same faces kept showing up behind the counter, along with hired help added as the business has grown. It's a little bigger business these days, and the old-time homey feeling is some-what dampened, but I still consider it one of the best places to stop along the Alaska Highway—if for no other reason than the great rhubarb pie.

Each trip on the Canadian portion of the Alaska Highway provides telling anecdotes like these. Some unplanned meetings with Canadians lead to even more.

In 1979, a chance stop at the Squanga Lake Campground, about 50 miles south of Whitehorse, led to a long-lasting family friendship, thanks to our dog, a perky miniature dachshund we called Pretzel.

We had picked this spot as a place to meet my wife's parents on their drive to Alaska—a favorite fishing hole was nearby. We set up a tent to give the kids a place to nap and settled back to wait. A few minutes later, a Canadian family came over and introduced themselves.

Joe and Sheighla Pollock had been talking about getting a dog, and Sheighla really liked Pretzel. We showed off the dog, chatted for a while and they invited us to stop in Whitehorse for a slice of the apple pie Sheighla was planning to bake after their weekend was over. We sort of agreed, not knowing for certain which day we would be in Whitehorse, and left it at that. A few minutes later, my wife's folks pulled in and we left for Tagish Lake to set up camp and fish for lake trout.

In a grocery store in Whitehorse four or five days later, we bumped into Sheighla buying apples, the invitation was repeated and we headed over to their place.

Joe was the Yukon Territory engineer for Parks Canada, and at the time he was deeply involved in rebuilding the SS *Klondike II*, a sternwheeler that had plied the Yukon River several decades earlier. The boat is now the centerpiece of a riverfront park in Whitehorse.

After the pie, nothing less than an insider's tour of the boat would do, and we spent the afternoon crawling all over the boat as Joe pointed out everything involved with its construction. Truly an unbeatable experience, and one that I later turned into a couple of magazine articles. Over the years, we've shared many visits back and forth over the Alaska-Canada border, and still look forward to getting together as often as our schedules allow.

Obviously, the people we've met in the North over the years aren't exclusively Canadians. Alaskans, too, have provided memorable friendships and unique moments. Despite the presence of a national boundary, I think Alaskans are a lot more like northwestern Canadians than the people from other states. They live and work in the same kind of magnificent but often harsh environment.

If I have a favorite Alaskan—though he might better be described as a citizen of the world—it has to be a long-distance musher, Colonel Norman Vaughan, a fellow who enters the famed 1,049-mile Iditarod Trail Sled Dog Race from Anchorage to Nome each year. That in itself isn't so unusual; however, one must take into account that Norm is 86 years old, and his first great mushing adventure was struggling to the South Pole with Admiral Richard Byrd in 1928.

Norm has a cabin in the woods near Trapper Creek, a wide spot in the Parks Highway about 150 miles north of Anchorage. I've never been to his cabin and am not sure I could find it if I tried.

One of Norm's latest schemes is selling deeds to tiny pieces of the mountain in Antarctica that's named after him. He doesn't own it, of course, but he's trying to raise money to fund a huge dog-sled expedition to the South Pole. When he's not doing that or racing the Iditarod, he's spending his time these days trying to dig some World War II bombers out of the Greenland ice cap. He knows where they are because after the planes crashed in 1943, he mushed in to recover the top-secret bombsights carried aboard the bombers.

I was a guest at his third wedding a couple of years back on New Year's Eve, as was most of the Alaska press corps. It was done in typical Norm Vaughan style. The wedding was held at a backcountry lodge some seven or eight miles from the nearest road. Instructions on the invitation told guests to show up at the end of the road in the morning and hop a ride on the next dog sled or snow machine that came along. More than 150 of us did. Later I calculated that it took about 150 howling sled dogs, 13 dog sleds and 25 or 30 snow machines to get Norm married. It was an absolute riot of a day, just as Norm intended.

Norm Vaughan aside, long-distance mushers are a unique breed, though not as rare as they were a decade or so ago. With the Iditarod and later the Yukon Quest (another 1,000-miler between Fairbanks and Whitehorse), long-distance mushing has developed into quite a spectacular sport, embracing all kinds of people. And it's more than just mushers.

The Iditarod, for example, involves more than 1,200 volunteers from all walks of life, bringing them together for a couple of short weeks each March across a major portion of the Alaskan wilderness.

One of these volunteers is Don Burt, a short guy in his 50s with almost-white hair and a beard to match. A good friend once described Don as "a sawed-off Santa Claus gone bad." Don lives in a cabin off the Glenn Highway, again about 150 miles from Anchorage, this time to the northwest. You can spot his driveway by looking for the candy-apple-red mailbox next to the road.

Don led the Iditarod trail breakers on snow machines for several years. Four or five snow machines towing sleds leave a day or so ahead of the mushers to make certain the trail is clearly marked. They attempt to stay at least a day ahead of the leaders, though on a couple of occasions some fast-running mushers have actually caught up with the snow machines. It is, to say the least, a wild ride across Alaska's major mountain ranges and massive rivers, but breaking trail on the Iditarod is an unforgettable experience, made all the more so by Don's antics.

In 1989, at the bottom of one particularly steep hill, Don hung up a sign that said "Free Towing—Call 376-5155," the number for Iditarod headquarters. A couple years prior to that, he erected a plywood palm tree on a beach outside of Nome, a sandy beach blown clear of snow by the wind. If you didn't realize how cold it was outside, the tree perched on the sand dune looked almost like it belonged there. Nobody who has raced a trail marked by Don Burt has ever forgotten the experience.

His greatest claim to infamy in recent years was volunteering to be at the center of an explosion. At the Alaska State Fair, he lay in a wooden box and allowed an "expert" to detonate several sticks of dynamite all around him. He told me later that he had always wanted to do that. Living alone in the bush does strange things to people, I guess.

And, as bush dwellers go, he has lots of company. It does take a special breed to live alone in a snowed-in cabin for months on end, and we have more than our fair share of them in Alaska, mostly men. The "aura" that surrounds these supposedly macho individualists has been in the news a lot these days.

Back in 1986, an enterprising Anchorage woman started a magazine called *Alaska Men*. In it, she specialized in one-page stories with a photo of single Alaska men, heavily weighted to those supposedly rugged types living a romantic existence in the wilderness. She printed about 1,000 copies of the premier issue. The rest, as they say, is history, and it's been a phenomenal success story.

In 1988, a bunch of these men were flown to Chicago to appear on Oprah Winfrey's show, kind of a meat market in reverse where the women in the audience were obviously present as potential dates for these "wild-and-woolly" Alaskans.

Both the magazine and the men involved made much of the fact that Alaska is about the only place in the country where there are more men than women. However, in referring to these extra men, one Cordova woman told an Anchorage newspaper reporter, "Yes, the odds are good. But the goods are odd." I guess a subsistence lifestyle in the bush wasn't her idea of communal bliss.

Lest you get the wrong idea, not everybody in Alaska lives in a log cabin and ekes a living out of the fragile wilderness. By far, most Alaskans live in frame houses, condos or apartments in or near fairly substantial cities. Fully half the state's population, about a quarter-million people, lives within 50 miles of downtown Anchorage. Like people across the country, they have jobs in government and private business. As many say, though, "The only good thing about Anchorage is that it's just thirty minutes away from Alaska." The same can be said of Fairbanks or Juneau as well, though the time involved to get out of town would be less.

In that telling phrase is everything that explains why people live in Anchorage, or anywhere in Alaska. It is different up here. For instance, grizzly bears live within the municipal boundaries of Anchorage, which tends to inspire a certain amount of awe in city dwellers from other states.

In 1988, one of these bears got lost and wandered out of the mountains on the eastern side of town. Joggers on the coastal trail surrounding the city first spotted the bear near Cook Inlet on the west side of town. In the next couple of days the bear cut right through the heart of the city, crossing major highways, airports and parking lots as he headed back to his mountains. The last time he was seen, he was in the forest bordering an Army base on the edge of town and still making tracks for home.

Though grizzlies are rarely seen in town, moose are seen so frequently as to be almost an afterthought. Suburban gardeners go to great lengths to protect their succulent plantings, but nothing seems to work very well. After all, how do you tell 1,500 pounds of protoplasm what he can or can't eat? We just sort of gave up one night last summer after our resident moose came by and took a single big bite out of each head of cabbage. To our everlasting relief, he didn't know how to dig potatoes. To my son's delight, he also had a hearty taste for broccoli.

We're going to try a "new" technique next year for keeping moose away from the garden. We've been told that moose absolutely detest the smell of Irish Spring soap. So we're going to scatter several bars of it throughout the garden. Already there's a bar hanging from the scraggly chokecherry tree in the front yard, a tree whose leaves have been tasted several times by one or more moose.

Whether you consider bears in town and moose in the garden privileges or liabilities, these kinds of things make Alaska special. Most of us who live here would probably be quite bored living in more "normal" regions.

There are, I suppose, drawbacks, not the least of which are winter days with, at best, a couple of hours of daylight. Then, too, there's the cold, particularly in the interior around Fairbanks. It's not uncommon in Fairbanks to have weeks of bracing temperatures of 40 degrees below zero and colder—that's actual air temperature, not wind-chill temperature. We have on several occasions seen temperatures of 60 degrees below zero in Fairbanks.

Funny things happen to vehicles when the weather turns cold like that. Basically, they just don't like to run and do so only reluctantly. But, that's another part of the challenge accepted by people who live in the North.

It's challenges like the cold that make this a special place and the people who live here the kind that are equal to almost any occasion—like the local wag in McGrath during last year's Iditarod who told a national television reporter from New York, "If it gets any warmer, we could grow bananas." It was a balmy 24 degrees below zero at the time, and the reporter was doing a good bit of complaining. Most of McGrath was happy to see that particular reporter leave town to follow the race west.

Later that same day, after dark, a once-in-10-years display of the aurora borealis (northern lights) lit the night sky with reds, greens and purples. As the temperature grew ever colder, I joined a group of bundled-up people who stared at the heavens for hours. That was one of those moments when we really knew why we lived in Alaska, the cold and the dark notwithstanding.

Alaska is a special place and its residents special people. Only when you have met them and stayed with them will you know what I mean. Different writers have tried to describe these things for nearly a century now. The two who probably succeeded best are Jack London and Robert Service. Yet, you can get only so much from words, regardless of who writes them. Alaska is still the stuff of legends and dreams; you have to experience it to believe it. Only then can you bring these stranger-than-fiction, larger-than-life tales to your unbelieving friends.

WHY DRIVE TO ALASKA?

Ask any tourist you meet on the streets of Anchorage or Juneau or Fairbanks why he or she came to Alaska, and the answer isn't to see the city you're standing in. The response usually starts out firmly with words like glaciers, mountains, grizzlies and salmon, then the respondent's voice kind of trails off like he or she didn't understand the question. Either that or it suddenly seems like a ridiculous question.

With few exceptions, travelers venture to Alaska to see the wilderness for which this state is so justly famed. They want to touch that wilderness, to breathe its clean air—most claim they can "smell" the freshness in the air—and to experience this kind of place just one time in their lives. After all, this is as far as we can go in North America. Our centuries-old westward movement to the frontier has no place else to go. We've finally run out of continent.

That's not to say that this "last frontier" we call Alaska is in any great danger of disappearing soon, though certainly parts of it are jeopardized from year to year as miners, loggers and oil drillers think up new ideas for resource extraction.

This also is not meant to say that we shouldn't have miners, loggers and oil drillers. Alaska does harbor magnificent natural resources, resources that provide jobs for people and raw materials to build products. The major question is: Where do you draw the line?

Wilderness as a resource takes many forms. There's the obvious—a home for divergent species of wildlife in significant numbers, an unspoiled place for Alaska Natives to practice traditional lifestyles, expansive forests that can provide lumber and pulp and vast deposits of minerals. Then there's the less-than-obvious. The wilderness that is Alaska's natural depository of minerals and timber is also the wilderness that lures travelers to the North. Tourism in Alaska, though not an extraction industry per se, depends every bit as much on vast forests and untouched backcountry as do the loggers, the miners and the oil drillers. What travelers would venture to Alaska if every mountainside was clear-cut, if every inlet held an oil platform and if open pit mines scarred the broad vistas of the interior?

Arguments on this subject rage back and forth through every newspaper in the country, mostly because determined people on both sides refuse to seek compromise. All of the industries named here can exist in Alaska—do exist now, in fact. And all can be safely expanded without destroying the last great wilderness region in the United States. Significantly, many of the people voicing positions on either side have never seen or experienced the wilderness they are arguing about. Truly, they do not realize the scope—the vastness—of this land.

Thus, Alaskans and the people who visit Alaska often find themselves in the middle of a variety of emotional environmental debates, most of which could be settled via open discussion and education instead of through the courts, which is the usual avenue these days.

Take, for example, the grounding of the *Exxon Valdez* in Prince William Sound in March 1989. An absolutely inexcusable accident, no doubt about it. Sticky crude oil leached from the tanker blackened hundreds and hundreds of miles of pristine shoreline, killing tens of thousands of sea birds, scores of eagles and hundreds if not thousands of sea otters. That was industry at its worst, and the effects of this spill will be with us for a long time.

Yet, despite the devastation, Alaska, even Prince William Sound, is still a splendid destination for travelers. Much of the sound remains untouched by oil, including the two most visited parts of the sound, Columbia Glacier and College Fjord. Though crude oil damaged a lot of coastline, it still touched barely 2 percent of Alaska's shores, if that.

This is certainly not meant to dampen the outrage and liability Exxon must face or in any way lessen the seriousness of the spill, but it does demonstrate that Alaska can still offer an unparalleled wilderness adventure to travelers, even in the midst of such an industrial travesty. Those who drive to Alaska have the greatest opportunity to touch that wilderness and be a part of it for a brief interlude.

Essentially there are three ways to get to Alaska: drive, fly or take a cruise. Cruise ship passengers see a lot of wilderness passing by their windows, but they stay in a pampered, luxurious environment, with few options to actually experience the wilderness. Airliners fly 6 or 7 miles above the wilderness and deposit travelers in cities. Only drivers and their passengers, particularly those camping in either an RV or a tent, get firsthand experience actually living as part of the land. And only people driving to Alaska get a true feeling for the vastness of the American North. Alaska itself is only one part of that vastness. To put Alaska in its proper perspective, one must first cross Canada's seemingly endless horizons.

It's one thing to see a temperate rain forest from the deck of a cruise ship, and quite another thing to drive through it, shaded by towering trees with a misty rain dampening your windshield.

It's one thing to see a glacier from a ship and marvel at the size of it, and quite another thing to stop near a glacier, walk up to it and chip ice for the cooler. As glacier ice melts, it makes a faint fizzing or snapping sound, the release of tiny air bubbles locked in the ice for untold centuries.

It's one thing to be told by the pilot of an airliner that you are flying over the last great wilderness on the continent, and quite another thing to stop at roadside and wander briefly on the edge of the wilderness, perhaps picking a handful of tart blueberries for tomorrow morning's pancakes, all the while looking over your shoulder for a bear that might consider this *his* berry patch.

It's one thing to see a bear at great distance along the shoreline of a fjord, and quite another thing to have one dart across the road in front of your car or wander through your campground in the evening. And yes, being that close to a bear should certainly make you edgy. That, too, is part of the wilderness, the knowledge that you don't fully control all you survey.

It's one thing to see a bright, sparkling stream from the air and be told that it's the purest water on earth, and quite another thing to pull a glittering arctic grayling from that stream for your supper.

These differences and others of similar ilk but too numerous to mention are the reasons for overland travel to Alaska. To sail on a cruise ship or fly in an airliner is to miss out on the very experiences travelers seek in the North. And, most significantly, only those who drive can even begin to make an attempt at putting this majestic land in perspective.

·——— 4 ———·

WHAT KIND
OF VEHICLE?

Author's note: At different points in this chapter, I make specific recommendations for vehicles and campers I am familiar with. These recommendations are for those who may be thinking of purchasing a vehicle for an Alaska Highway trip. However, the strongest message I want this chapter to deliver is that a specialized vehicle is not necessary for the Alaska Highway. Virtually any vehicle sold in North America can handle the drive to and from Alaska, and each kind of vehicle offers different options for the trip.

Ultimately, the choice of a vehicle for an Alaska Highway adventure boils down to two deceptively simple but tough-to-answer questions: What do you want to do on the Alaska Highway, and how much money do you want to spend? One other factor, of course, is the vehicle you currently own.

The first question can get complicated, particularly if you're sitting at home several thousand miles away from the Alaska Highway and planning your first trip. Do you want to drive straight through to Alaska in the shortest possible time? Do you want to linger at places along the way, places you can either plan for in advance or those you won't know until you see them? Is money a major factor—do you have to get to Alaska and back cheaply? Who are your traveling companions—what do they want to do? Will you have a lot of luggage? Everybody who has ever planned a major driving trip has questions like these, which in this case all wrap neatly into the heading of what you want to accomplish on a trip to Alaska. Answers to these questions and others lead to the decisions made before the trip.

The money question is even more difficult, because it seems so straightforward. Unfortunately, it isn't. The cost of driving the Alaska Highway may actually be cheaper for someone driving a big motorhome with its lousy gas mileage than for someone in an economy car stopping at a hotel or lodge each evening and dining in restaurants. The purchase price of the vehicle involved may be the overriding difference in this situation.

As for what not to drive to Alaska, the list is pretty simple. Stay away from the exotic. Though the odds are pretty good that any car made today will make it to Alaska, some are pretty much functionless along the highway and you're in trouble if something goes wrong. Among these are things like Corvettes and other two-seat sports cars. At the other end of the scale are the Bentleys and Rolls Royces. Getting parts to repair these kinds of vehicles would prove almost impossible in northwestern Canada and most of Alaska outside of Anchorage and maybe Fairbanks.

Also, if you want to pull a trailer to carry extra equipment, avoid the small, single-wheel utility trailers that hold a couple of hundred pounds of gear. These things routinely end up in roadside junkyards, mostly after the tiny tire goes flat, an event unnoticed by most drivers until the trailer has destroyed itself bouncing down the road on its frame.

Is there a happy medium in terms of cost, experiences and comfort? Probably, though again the answer keeps coming back to your own aspirations for a driving trip to Alaska. A review of different categories of vehicles may offer some ideas when matched against your own wants and needs—and the vehicle you currently own.

ECONOMY CARS AND SMALL PICKUPS

People driving these kinds of vehicles have two options for overnighting—tent camping or motels. Both have advantages and disadvantages.

The motel option allows for the greatest amount of driving time in any single day—there's no unpacking and repacking of the car each day and no wrestling with the pots and pans and stoves necessary to cook in camp. However, staying in motels and eating in restaurants quickly eats up any cost savings derived from the great gas mileage offered by the vehicle. Staying in motels also reduces flexibility. You have to plan to be in a built-up area every night.

Tent campers won't go as far in a day as the motel stoppers, but the price will certainly be cheaper. Public campgrounds along the Alaska Highway run from $5 to about $12 a night. Private campgrounds—those with showers—are from $15 to $20 and usually require a handful of quarters for a shower. Motels, on the other hand, start at about $50 a night for a room and go up from there. You're probably safe to figure an average of $60 to $65 a night, if you're willing to do a little shopping around for cheaper places to stay. Without any shopping around, the average will be closer to $75 or $80 per night.

Remember, too, that a motel/hotel/lodge in Yukon Territory or rural Alaska is not likely to resemble a Holiday Inn at roadside in the lower 48. Away from the population centers, there is probably less than a 50-50 chance of having a television in your room. Bathrooms may be separate rooms down the hall shared by several guests—even outhouses in rare instances. You can, as a general rule, count on rooms being warm and reasonably clean. Don't expect more than that; then you'll be pleasantly surprised at whatever else an enterprising owner is able to provide.

As for those staying under canvas, the major argument against tent camping is time. It takes a fair amount of effort each evening setting up camp and preparing meals, then again in the morning for breakfast and putting things away. Tent campers, unless they get up very, very early, rarely get on the road before 10:30 or 11 A.M. This is particularly true if there are children in the party, which forces Mom and Dad to do a little extra "camping" for the youngsters—things like rolling up more sleeping bags, pitching the extra tent or a bigger tent, doing more dishes and so on.

But camping is almost always worth the extra effort. People venture to northwestern Canada and Alaska because it is wilderness, because it's unlike anything they've ever seen before. Camping puts you right in the middle of what most people travel the Alaska Highway to see and do; camping makes you a part of the wilderness you've come to experience. To that end, most people who tent camp find it worth the extra time and effort.

As for vehicles, any of the small, four-cylinder pickups on the market would be just fine for two adults either staying in motels or tent camping. Don't try to squeeze three people into one of these trucks, even if you routinely do so for buzzing around town back home. For a trip to Alaska, it's just too crowded for too long in the front seat of a mini-pickup with three adults crammed inside.

As for economy cars, a hatchback is better than a sedan and a stationwagon is better than a hatchback. A trip to Alaska is a long trek, and you'll want to carry extra gear, generally much more than can be carried in the trunk of a small sedan. Manufacturers whose small cars are popular in the North include Subaru, Nissan, Toyota and Ford (the Escort line). Small cars by other manufacturers will serve quite well, but these four brands are the ones most often seen around Fairbanks and Anchorage.

Besides clothing and other personal gear, drivers of small vehicles can carry along a car-top canoe or other small boat propelled by oars or paddles. Those with small pickups can also add a small outboard motor and the paraphernalia that goes along with it. Outboards and fuel tanks generally are best left out of the interiors of small automobiles.

Mini-pickups can tow a lightweight trailer with relative ease—something on the order of a folding tent trailer or perhaps a lightweight boat. A word of caution, though: Gas mileage goes down when towing a trailer, usually a lot. Trailers also mean that additional spare tires and other equipment will be needed.

The major problem that small-vehicle operators should look out for is overloading the vehicle, particularly a small car. Overloading is almost certainly the biggest single cause of flat tires and broken suspension systems along the Alaska Highway. It is easily avoided.

Molded into the rubber on the sidewall of your car's tires is the load capacity of the tire. Assuming you have the same tires on all four wheels, the load that can be safely carried by your car is four times the load capacity listed on one of the tires. This is the total weight of the car and its contents (the latter includes the people riding in the car). If your loaded car is going to exceed that capacity, replace your tires with tires designed to carry a greater load. Any competent tire dealer should be able to assist in selecting tires of greater load capacity for your vehicle. Make sure the spare tire is exactly like the four on the ground. The small "do-nut" spares, popular in recent years as a means of reducing weight in small cars, are utterly worthless on the Alaska Highway. You need a full-size spare tire.

If the car sags significantly when loaded, add heavy-duty shocks or air shocks, even heavier springs if necessary. These are fairly routine things that shouldn't take a mechanic more than a couple of hours. The relatively few hours and the minimal funds spent on getting just the right tires and reinforcing your suspension system are solid insurance against flat tires and broken suspension systems.

Gas costs for a small car going from Dawson Creek to Fairbanks, roughly 1,500 miles, should be less than $100 (U.S.). That's figuring 30 miles per gallon and an average price of $1.75 (U.S.) per gallon of fuel.

Five nights in a motel for two people plus three restaurant meals a day will total about $600, one way from Dawson Creek to Fairbanks. Five nights in a campground will run about $50, possibly less, plus $150 or so for groceries along the way. Tent campers should throw in a couple of extra bucks for a shower now and then.

Recommendations: **Mini-pickup**—Nissan King Cab, four-cylinder engine, five-speed manual transmission, with or without four-wheel drive. Relatively indestructible. Will deliver about 22 to 24 miles per gallon with four-wheel drive, a couple extra miles per gallon for two-wheel-drive models.

Small car—Subaru stationwagon, manual transmission, four doors. Lots of value and reliable performance for the money. About 30 miles per gallon.

PICKUP TRUCKS

Far and away the favorite vehicles of northern residents living outside the major cities are pickup trucks of any size or brand—usually four-wheel-drive pickup trucks. The reason for this is quite simple: In a rugged environment, a stoutly built pickup offers multiple uses and requires no more care than a car.

Northerners haul firewood, moose meat, friends, snow machines and all-terrain vehicles in the back of pickups. They drive them to work, they drive them to fishing holes, they pull trailers with pickups. Everything a car could do for them, a pickup can usually do better. Many veteran travelers on the Alaska Highway would make the same argument.

We're talking now about the mid- or full-size pickups, pickups designed to haul or pull heavy loads, pickups that can be purchased with extended cabs to haul big loads and lots of people at the same time.

These days, when it comes to selecting a pickup—a pretty straightforward operation just a few years ago—things can get pretty confusing. American manufacturers offer three basic sizes: mini, mid-size and full-size. Japanese manufacturers, on the other hand, may offer only one basic size in terms of outside dimensions, but the way a particular mini is built might upgrade its capabilities so they're similar to larger-size pickups. Nissan's "Hard Body" line is probably the most obvious example. Essentially, this is the same pickup recommended as a mini-pickup elsewhere in this chapter, but the "Hard Body" designation means a V-6 engine, heavier construction and a greater load-carrying capacity.

If the various sizes alone aren't enough to confuse potential buyers, the variety of engine, transmission and axle ratios available ought to be enough to drive anyone to the local tavern for some attitude adjustment. Pickups identical in appearance can vary in gas mileage from 10 or less to as much as 20 miles per gallon, depending on engine and axle-ratio combinations.

When looking for a full-size pickup inside the dealer's showroom, you'll find that three options are immediately apparent: half-ton, three-quarter-ton and one-ton models. Supposedly these descriptions are based on load capacities. Things get goofy when the dealer tells you about heavy-duty three-quarter tons that can carry a ton and a half or more, or one-tonners that can carry two-ton loads, and so on.

How do you sort this all out? First, be certain in your mind ahead of time what you want a pickup to do. If you're not going to carry a big cab-over camper and not pull a heavy trailer, smaller engines in half-ton trucks will do the job nicely, particularly if coupled to a four-speed manual transmission. Gas mileage in these rigs is usually pretty good as well, almost certainly 16 miles per gallon or better.

On the other end of the scale are the heavy haulers, the heavy-duty, three-quarter-ton and larger rigs, pickups with load range E tires, reinforced suspensions and big engines. Gas mileage on these rigs can be much less than 10 miles per gallon up to around 15 miles per gallon, depending on the engine and axle ratio you select and the load you are going to carry or pull. These rigs will carry anything you're likely to put in them and pull trailers weighing 6,000 pounds or more.

The easiest way to sort out the axle-ratio problem is to remember that the smaller the number, the better the gas mileage. Take Chevrolet, for example. A three-quarter-ton Chevy pickup with a 350-cubic-inch engine is commonly available with three axle ratios: 3.43, 3.73 and 4.10. One of these numbers will be printed on the factory invoice provided with the truck. Given otherwise similar equipment, the 3.43 axle provides better mileage than the 3.73, the 3.73 better mileage than the 4.10. However, the 4.10 axle handles the bigger loads with much less effort. If you're going to haul a big camper or pull a big trailer, the 4.10 axle is probably the better choice; otherwise you will find yourself operating in lower gears whenever there are hills to climb, the kind of driving that burns a lot of gas in just a few miles. Again, it all boils down to the question of what you want out of your truck. Be sure of what you want before you wind up in a dealer's showroom talking to a salesman—and don't let the salesman talk you into more truck than you need.

Unless you already own one, purchasing one of the heavier-duty pickups is pretty much a waste of money if you just want it to drive north in and haul a couple of suitcases. In that situation, you're better off with a mini-pickup or even a passenger car.

If, however, you plan some serious backcountry exploring, pulling a trailer, hauling a camper or moose hunting, then a big truck is for you. Any of those items requires the power and the capacity that only a full-size, three-quarter-ton or larger pickup can offer.

Do you need four-wheel drive? Probably not, unless your trip extends into the winter months or you plan to do a lot of off-road driving. Given a choice, most Alaskans buying a pickup will opt for four-wheel drive if they have sufficient money—it does add about $2,500 to the cost of a full-size pickup. But these are people who spend 6 months or more driving on snow and ice where four-wheel drive makes a lot of difference in the daily commute.

Then, too, there are those who live to see how far off the road they can get in their trucks. Four-wheel drive, big tires and just about any other option imaginable are for them. They have a lot of fun and get to a lot of places in summer. The big tires, though, are lousy on ice. It's hard to stop a truck wearing that kind of rubber when the roads are icy. Narrow tires are much better on ice, providing the most pounds-per-square-inch on the road, which translates to better stopping power. Wide tires also tend to "float" quite a bit on gravel roads at speeds above 40 miles per hour, which tends to make the truck weave from side to side. Unless you're a serious summer mud-bogger, stay away from the after-market wide tires.

Commonly, pickup trucks seen along the Alaska Highway, both two-wheel and four-wheel drive, carry campers of various shapes and sizes. The most basic camper is little more than a shell rigged over the truck bed in which the owner has built a simple cot and perhaps a couple of other conveniences. Top-of-the-line cab-over models may extend 3 feet past the rear bumper with a 7-foot or longer extension over the cab of the truck. These latter campers can be purchased with almost every convenience imaginable, including generators for 110-volt power, air conditioners, microwave ovens and full-fledged showers with hot and cold water. (Who needs 110-volt power, you say—just ask any teenager who has just stepped out of the shower with wet hair.)

While the camper shells will fit on trucks of any load capacity, it takes absolutely the biggest three-quarter-ton or one-ton models to safely haul the big cab-overs—that means Ford, Chevy or Dodge. Each of these manufacturers will have options like a camper-special package, reinforced springs, air-bag shock absorbers, transmission coolers, spare batteries with isolators, and so on. If you're planning to haul a big camper (or tow a heavy trailer), get them all—literally anything that says heavy duty. Getting them furnished with the pickup saves having to put them on later, and with some 3,000 pounds of camper, you'll want all these things sooner or later.

Installing a camper will require some minor modifications to your pickup truck; any competent camper dealer can make these easily. If you buy a used camper to install on your truck, you're probably money ahead engaging a camper dealer to make the modifications to your truck and to get everything in working order. As a minimum, you will need extended rear-view mirrors, a wiring harness for the camper, braces to hold the camper to the truck, probably hydraulic shocks for the cab-over portion, some sort of trailer hitch system outside the bumper hitch on your pickup and folding steps for entering the camper. Doing all this and doing it right is quite a chore for the first-time camper owner.

Gas costs for a full-size pickup going from Dawson Creek to Fairbanks (about 1,500 miles) should be about $175—with no trailer or camper. With either a camper or trailer, gas costs will increase to about $250 or slightly more.

Recommendations: **Full-size pickup**—Chevrolet heavy-duty, three-quarter-ton pickup with a 350-cubic-inch V-8 engine. For camper shell and modest loads, 3.73 axle. For hauling big campers or other heavy loads, including heavy trailers, 4.10 axle with automatic transmission and cruise control. Chevrolet pickups are generally cheaper than comparably equipped Fords. Both Ford and Chevy are quite common in remote areas, so finding spare parts should pose few difficulties. Dodge does offer pickups comparable in every respect to the Fords and Chevys, but there are fewer Dodge dealers in the North.

Pickup campers—Lance Campers in Los Angeles, a brand available only in western states, builds probably the best line of pickup campers on the market today. Tightly built campers to fit pickups of all sizes are available. Prices may be slightly higher than the nationally available brands like Coachman and Jayco, but Lance campers are definitely worth the extra money. The camper shown frequently in this book is a Lance 900, 11.3 feet long, with the extended cab-over compartment. For brochures and a list of dealers, write to: Lance, The Family Camper, 10234 Glenoaks Blvd., Pacoima, CA 91331-1689.

RECREATIONAL VEHICLES

This category can encompass just about anything. For the purposes of this book, though, we'll stick with travel trailers (including fifth-wheelers) and motorhomes. Campers were dealt with in the pickup truck section.

Far and away, sleep-aboard RVs are the most popular vehicles on the Alaska Highway. Some would argue that in the past 20 years the Alaska Highway has been redesigned and rebuilt for RVs. Though that may be stretching things a bit, it's not hard to see that campgrounds and side roads have been fixed up to allow for easier passage of these long, wide rigs.

Travel trailers come in two basic models—a standard trailer with a square front that can be pulled by any vehicle, car or truck, with a suitable hitch and sufficient power and weight. The other kind would be the fifth-wheel trailer, increasingly seen following pickups to Alaska and across the lower 48 as well. The hitch for a fifth-wheel trailer sits in the middle of a pickup-truck bed, and part of the living space inside the trailer, usually a bedroom, is accessed by stairs leading to a compartment above the trailer hitch.

Trailers range from the most basic—with a couple of beds, a stove and a hand-pump water system—to the ultimate in luxury—fully carpeted, with bathtubs, central heating, air conditioning and all the conveniences attainable. You'll see both the basic and the luxurious—and everything in between—on any given day along the Alaska Highway. And, very quickly, you'll realize the half truth behind a favorite highway joke—the bigger the travel trailer, the fewer people sleeping in it. Retired couples who spend much of their lives on the road generally have the biggest and most luxuriously appointed trailers. Younger couples with children, and probably limited disposable income, cram everybody inside a tiny trailer. Both groups have lots of fun on the Alaska Highway.

A key thing to look for in a trailer are tandem (two or even three) axles, which are a safety requirement. Travel trailers can be somewhat top-heavy, and a sudden flat tire on a single-axle trailer may flip it over. And make sure that all piping (water, propane and sewer) is tucked out of the way.

Recommendations: **Camping trailers**—A 20- to 26-foot fifth-wheel or standard trailer made by one of the larger manufacturers—Coachman, Wilderness, Jayco or others. Stay away from the lesser-known brands whose warranties may not be accepted in the North's rural areas. The trailer should hold plenty of fresh water (25 gallons or more) and have holding-tank capacity for all the water on board. Dump stations are infrequent along the highway. If you have the option, choose vinyl floors rather than carpeting—mud and dirt are much easier to clean off of vinyl.

Tow vehicles—Any full-size pickup will suffice as a tow vehicle. Other capable tow vehicles include Chevrolet Suburbans and full-size Chevrolet Blazers, Ford Broncos and Dodge Ramchargers. Full-size automobiles with big engines will also work quite well, though these are increasingly rare. For smaller trailers, mid-size pickups and the scaled-down versions of the Bronco, Blazer and Ramcharger are adequate, as are the relatively new down-sized vans. Rear-wheel drive is much better for trailer towing than front-wheel drive.

There are two basic configurations of motorhomes: Class C (mini) and Class A. Class A motorhomes are the mostly flat-fronted rigs that closely resemble buses. Class C motorhomes have a Ford or Chevy van front end with a cab-over compartment like a pickup camper. From behind the cab to the rear they are as wide, tall and boxy-looking as Class A motorhomes.

Class C motorhomes are available in lengths to 26 feet (commonly) or 28 feet (rarely), the shortest being 19 or 20 feet long. Class A motorhomes start at about 20 feet and go up from there all the way to Greyhound bus size. Rigs in the 26-foot to 36-foot length are the most common Class A motorhomes seen on the Alaska Highway. Class C motorhomes of 24 or 26 feet are the most frequently seen in this model.

The most limiting factor on motorhomes is the amount of overhang behind the rear wheels. The greater the overhang, the fewer places a rig can go—it will drag going through shallow ditches on campground turnoffs or swing out on a turn, possibly snagging on rocks or brush alongside narrow campground roads. Generally speaking, the longer the motorhome, the greater the overhang.

Gas mileage on these rigs is—you guessed it—lousy. About 7 miles per gallon. The reasons are quite simple: big engines and lots of weight. However, there's really a lot of truth to a bumper sticker seen in recent years along the Alaska Highway: "Sure it gets lousy gas mileage for a car, but it gets great mileage for a house."

At 7 miles per gallon, it will cost about $350 just for the gas to drive from Dawson Creek to Fairbanks. But there are no hotel fees. Throw in $150 for food and $50 for campgrounds in the same period, and you can actually drive a motorhome from Dawson Creek to Fairbanks for less money than folks in a small car who are staying in motels and eating in restaurants. Sounds ridiculous, but it's the truth.

The problem is the cost of the vehicle to start with. Well-equipped small cars can be purchased for $8,000 to $10,000. Well-equipped motorhomes start at more than $30,000 and go up from there.

Before starting north in a motorhome, hang mud flaps behind the rear wheels. Gravel kicked up by these wheels will quickly make the rear quarter panels look like the victims of several shotgun blasts if mud flaps are not used.

Recommendation: A 26-foot Class C motorhome from one of the major manufacturers. This size rig should offer most of the comfort that motorhomes are prized for, yet it does so in a small enough package that you won't be overly limited in where you can and can't go. Get the biggest engine available (usually a 460-cubic-inch engine on Ford chassis and a 454 on Chevy chassis), an automatic transmission and cruise control. You'll quickly find these are easy rigs to drive.

WHICH OPTION IS BEST?

Besides the pickups, small cars and recreational vehicles described in this chapter, there are a multitude of other options available for those driving to Alaska. Broncos and Blazers, mentioned briefly, are quite popular. So are Jeep Wagoneers, Dodge Ramchargers and a host of other vehicles, both foreign and domestic. As long as you stay away from the exotic, any vehicle made these days should handle the trip safely.

However, after 17 years of driving the highway and using every one of these kinds of vehicles at least once (Nissan pickup, Jeep Wagoneer, Dodge Ramcharger, Winnebago Class A motorhome, Georgie Boy Class C motorhome, Ford F250 pickup and Dodge half-ton pickup), my preference is a heavy-duty, three-quarter-ton pickup truck and a large cab-over camper. This rig provides most of the comfort of a motorhome, though in somewhat more crowded conditions, and it offers almost unlimited flexibility. There is almost no place this rig won't go, gas mileage is generally better than with motorhomes, and, properly rigged, it handles exceptionally well.

Finally, camping—whether in a motorhome, trailer, pickup camper or tent—goes a long way toward making an Alaska Highway trip a meaningful experience. Over the years, we've pulled over for the evening in old gravel pits at roadside just because a good-looking fishing stream flowed nearby, and we've stopped in campgrounds in stunningly picturesque places dozens of miles from the nearest motel or lodge. Campers can stop at their leisure, whenever they find something more to explore or just some scenery they want to savor. For most Alaska Highway adventurers, the extra effort required by camping is more than compensated for by the additional opportunities it provides.

The Cheapest Way: Tent camping from a small car. Round trip from Seattle to Fairbanks can be done for about $750 worth of gas, food and campground fees.

The Most Expensive Way: Driving a big, gas-guzzling rig, staying in motels/hotels/lodges and dining in restaurants. Round trip from Seattle to Fairbanks would cost a minimum of $1,500, probably closer to $2,000.

5

PREPARING YOUR VEHICLE

Though it's probably been done before with little planning and even less preparation, and likely will be again, a safe, comfortable drive to and from Alaska requires work ahead of time. One should not suddenly decide to go, throw a change of clothes in a bag, back the car down the driveway and head north. More than anything else, your car, truck or RV, the chariot that will carry you on this northern adventure, needs some attention before you start. Nothing major, mind you, just some fairly routine tasks that can all but ensure a safe and breakdown-free trip.

A quick check of a map of North America will give you some idea of why you want to put some time and perhaps a few dollars into your vehicle before starting out. A round trip to Alaska from Seattle will easily put 5,000 miles on your vehicle. If you're starting in Florida, double that. And your car, truck or RV gets to do all the work as well. At least, you *hope* it gets to do all the work. Because if it breaks down and doesn't do the work you planned for it, you are going to be doing a lot of work in potentially unpleasant environments—like lying in the mud under your car on a rainy day. That's no way to spend even a small part of your vacation.

RUNNING GEAR

Tires—The best tires that you can afford will do more for your car on the Alaska Highway than anything else. Good tires can absorb some of the strain imposed by errant driving or less-than-efficient road crews. But, most of all, good tires will provide you with considerable peace of mind in a land where the few tires you might find to buy in an emergency could be frightfully expensive.

Steel-belted radials, ideally with an all-season tread instead of a straight summer tread, are the best way to go in the warm-weather months. The all-season tread might generate slightly more road noise on pavement but provides surer traction when gravel roads are wet. Full-fledged snow tires and studded tires are not needed during summer months; in fact, studded tires are illegal in most areas between May and September. Winter drivers, however, will want studded snow tires and should carry tire chains as well.

Be sure your spare tire is the equal of the four tires on the ground. There are a couple of reasons for this. If you should tear up one of your tires, you have an equivalent tire available as a replacement. The tire you first find to replace the destroyed one may have to be a compromise of sorts; few places along the highway have complete tire shops with all the various sizes available. The other reason for having a high-quality spare is that you might have to drive a good number of miles after a flat before you can find a place to get a tire fixed or replaced.

A note about spare tires: Two or more spares are probably not necessary. Many travelers on the Alaska Highway go to great lengths to carry extra spare tires, tying them to the roof or whatever. In fourteen trips on the Alaska Highway, I can remember only one instance when a traveler needed more than a single spare—my father-in-law's trip north in 1989. That year he had two flats in quick succession on his trailer in an area of road construction.

The last thing to remember about tires has already been said but bears repeating. Make sure the load capacity of your tires is equal to or greater than the actual weight of the loaded vehicle plus its occupants. To do otherwise is to risk catastrophic failure of one or more of your tires at highway speeds.

Brakes—Equally important are your brakes. If you have the slightest doubt about the stopping ability of your car, have a mechanic adjust or repair the brakes. Troublesome things to check for are a brake pedal that fades—that is, it tends to take more and more pressure to maintain a given level of stopping power—and a grinding noise whenever you apply pressure to your brakes. If either of these conditions exists, get the brakes checked out.

U-joints—In the linkage that connects your transmission to the rear axle (assuming you have a rear-wheel-drive car) are two U-joints. These are at the ends of the drive shaft, the long steel shaft running down the center of the underside of your vehicle. If you hear or feel a distinct "clank" or "clunk" when you put the vehicle in gear, your U-joints are probably worn. Replacing them is a simple matter for any competent mechanic.

You can also check the U-joints by firmly grabbing the drive shaft and trying to twist it back and forth. A slight bit of play is normal, but if you have too much play, you'll again hear the clank or clunk sounds.

Leaks—While you're under the car, look for signs of fluid leaks in three key areas: the rear differential (the bulge in the middle of the rear axle on rear-wheel-drive cars), around the transmission and under the engine. If you find any evidence of fluid leakage at all, check it out before you leave.

You might also check around the inside of each wheel for evidence of leaking brake fluid.

Bolts—Take a selection of wrenches underneath the car with you. Place a wrench on every nut and bolt you can reach to ensure that it is tight. In this case, a few minutes' prevention is worth many hours of cure if it keeps bolts from wiggling loose as you jounce along gravel roads or roads roughened by frost heaves. Things like this are much easier to fix in your driveway ahead of time than they are somewhere at roadside in northwestern Canada or Alaska.

Suspension system—Well before your trip, test the loading of your vehicle. Place inside the vehicle all of the gear, clothing and other items you plan to take north, along with all the people who will ride along. If the rear end sags significantly under the load, your suspension system will need upgrading. There are several options, including reinforced springs, heavy-duty shocks and adjustable air shocks. A mechanic can recommend which combination is best for your vehicle. A suspension system inadequate for the load will either fail itself or cause the failure of your tires, even if the tires are adequate for the loaded weight of the vehicle.

Weight—When you load your vehicle to test the suspension, take a few minutes to drive it to a truck scale near your home. Weighing a vehicle takes only a moment, and this is the best way to find out if the load-bearing capacity of your tires is equal to the load you plan to carry. Most states maintain weigh stations at regular intervals along major highways. A quick phone call to the state highway department should suffice to gain you permission to have a vehicle weighed. Major trucking companies also have scales to check their vehicles before sending them out on a run. There may be a slight charge for this service, but it's well worth it.

ENGINE

Tuneup—Have a complete tuneup done by a competent mechanic before you set out for Alaska. As a minimum this should consist of a compression check, timing check, spark-plug check/replacement, low- and high-speed idle adjustments, choke adjustment, cap and rotor check/replacement, fan belt check and a check of all radiator and heater hoses.

If you are driving north in the winter months, take advantage of this opportunity to have the mechanic install a **circulating heater** in the heater-hose system. This allows you to plug the car in at night to keep the engine moderately warm for easier starting in the morning. In the Far North you'll soon notice that most parking lots have electric boxes by each stall to allow people to plug in their cars.

Winter drivers should also have the **antifreeze** in the radiator adjusted so that it's adequate for temperatures of 40 degrees below zero (F) or colder.

Oil, filter, lube—As part of the tuneup, have the oil and oil filter changed and ask for a complete lube job. Almost certainly you'll need another oil change somewhere in the course of your trip, but the lube job should hold you for the whole distance. In summer, most vehicles use 10W-30W or 10W-40W oil; in winter, 5W-30W or 5W-20W. Check the owner's manual for your vehicle to make certain these oils are suitable for your engine.

Along the highway, you may want to change oil more often than your owner's manual recommends. Lots of dust and the heavy loads common to vehicles driving the Alaska Highway are hard on engines. Thus, if the owner's manual recommends changes every 5,000 miles, you should probably change oil every 3,000 miles or so. Fresh oil is cheap insurance for your engine.

Spare parts—Once your mechanic has done all these things and totted up the bill, you need to add a few spare parts to the invoice before you pay him. Carry spare fan belts (most cars these days have two or more) and make sure you have one of each kind. Also buy a couple of cans of oil, a spare oil filter, air filter, radiator hoses and heater hoses. You probably won't need any of these (except perhaps the oil filter), but if you do, there's a lot of security in having them at hand instead of hoping the next gas station along the highway might have the right size. The $30 to $40 these extra parts will cost are well worth it. And if you don't need them at roadside, you've got them available for the next time you tune up your car.

GENERAL ITEMS

Flying gravel kicked up by cars in front of you or by oncoming cars is tough on **headlights**. Carry at least one spare. Vehicles that have a four-headlight system will need two spares; the low-beam and high-beam lamps are different.

For just a few bucks you can purchase clear plastic headlight covers that can be installed in just a couple of minutes. If these are not available in your home town, you can have them installed in Dawson Creek before you start on the Alaska Highway.

Flying gravel also chips **windshields**. Options here are few. Most insurance companies, however, don't hold you to your deductible for replacing a chipped windshield. If yours does, ask for a slightly higher premium to cover broken glass for the duration of your trip.

Over the years, many ingenious devices have been rigged up to keep rocks from striking the windshield. Usually these take the form of a heavy wire screen, held in place by a framework of aluminum or wood. Cumbersome in appearance, these do offer some protection, though probably the time and effort required to build them is worth more than the damage they might prevent.

Those driving pickups with campers or Class C motorhomes should fasten some sort of plastic or cardboard over the forward-facing window in the cab-over compartment. The glass in these windows is not the same strength as your windshield and can shatter easily. Duct tape will usually handle the installation with ease.

Flying gravel can also puncture your **radiator**, though this is fairly unlikely. If you're worried about this, fasten a heavy piece of window screening (not the new nylon material, but metal) over the outside of your grill. You can tie this in place with stout string or baling wire.

Underneath your vehicle, a few things may or may not need doing for an easier trip. If your **gas tank** sits aft of the rear wheels, rig some sort of cover over the bottom of it for protection. The easiest way is to loosen the metal straps that hold the tank in place and slide a rubber or flexible-plastic mat between the straps and the tank. Retightening the straps will firmly lock the rubber mat in place. If there are no straps around your **fuel tank,** clean it off thoroughly and glue a mat over the bottom of the tank. Hardware stores carry a variety of suitable adhesives.

Also underneath your vehicle, look to see if there are any **fuel filters in glass housings.** Though not found much anymore, these used to be fairly common on motorhomes. Needless to say, gravel kicked up by tires will make short work of any glass container on the underside of a vehicle.

Whether or not you pull a trailer or another vehicle, **mud flaps** are a good idea. Without them, gravel kicked up by your rear tires will quickly blast the paint off the rear quarter panels. Also, mud flaps reduce the amount of gravel you'll throw behind you into the path of following cars. If you tow a trailer or other vehicle, mud flaps are a must.

If your vehicle does not have **outside rear-view mirrors** on both sides, install them. These can be rented from a place like U-Haul if you just want them for this trip and not as a permanent fixture on your car. Safety is the prime concern here; mirrors on both sides give you additional rearward visibility. This is particularly important if you load a car so full that you can't see completely through the rear window.

Finally, check your **windshield wipers.** If the rubber blades have a season or two of use on them, it's best to replace them. These will get a workout on a trip to and from Alaska.

TOOLS

Even if you don't have the faintest idea of how to use tools, carry a basic set sufficient for minor repairs at roadside. If you don't know how to use tools to work on a car, almost certainly someone who stops to lend assistance will.

Here's a short list suitable for most eventualities, along with some odds and ends that belong in a tool box. If you're so unfamiliar with tools that you don't know what these things are, carry this list to a hardware store and ask a clerk for assistance.

- Claw hammer
- 10-inch crescent wrench
- 8-inch crescent wrench
- Three-eighths-inch drive socket set with ratchet (get metric sockets for foreign-built vehicles)

- Set of box/open-end wrenches (again, metric wrenches for foreign-built vehicles)
- No. 1 and No. 2 common screwdrivers
- No. 1 and No. 2 Phillips screwdrivers
- Standard pliers
- Long-nose pliers
- Channel locks (big, adjustable pliers)
- Vise-grips
- Wire-splicing tool
- Assorted wire connectors and terminals (these can usually be purchased in kit form with the wire-splicing tool listed above)
- Roll of electrical tape
- Flat file for metal
- Three-quarter ax
- Folding shovel
- Plastic bucket
- Roll of duct tape
- Tube of Super Glue
- Pair of coveralls
- Flashlight and batteries
- Battery jumper cables
- Roll of baling wire or stout string (60-pound-test or stouter monofilament fishing line is great)
- Pocket knife

Except for the jumper cables, coveralls, ax, shovel and bucket, these items should fit easily into a fairly small tool box that you can tuck behind or under your seat. Be sure and keep your tools where you can get to them easily.

Additionally there are a couple of things provided with your vehicle, notably a **jack**, jack handle and **lug wrench** for changing tires. If you pull a trailer, make certain your jack will fit the trailer and that you have a lug wrench available for the trailer wheels. It almost never fails that the lug nuts on trailers are of different size than the lug nuts on the tow vehicle.

Motorhome drivers whose rigs are equipped with generators for 110-volt power will find that an **electric drill** and a set of drill bits come in handy. Seems strange, but those who carry power drills almost always have cause to use them, whether for their own needs or while lending assistance at roadside.

A few extra items that you might want to carry along include:

- Can of brake fluid
- Bottle of windshield washer fluid
- Rivet gun and assortment of rivets (you will need either a hand drill or power drill to use these)

- Can of WD-40 lubricant or equivalent
- Vehicle tow strap
- Tarp or heavy plastic
- Assortment of sheet-metal screws, nuts and bolts
- 50 feet of quarter-inch nylon rope
- Window cleaner and roll of paper towels

Ideally, you'll never need to use any of these tools or spare parts on your trip. Tens of thousands of people drive to Alaska and back each year and have little if any need of making repairs en route. However, there are so many unpredictables involved with a trip of this nature that it's best to be prepared. Being prepared, as well, contributes much to your confidence and helps solve quickly any problems that might develop.

6

WHAT TO BRING

This is a chapter of lists—clothing and equipment lists that I've developed over two decades of northern travel. While nothing here qualifies as an earth-shattering revelation, these lists do provide for almost any eventuality, and, if followed, will yield all you will need for a safe, comfortable driving trip to Alaska.

WHAT TO KEEP ON THE SEAT BESIDE YOU

This sometimes seems so obvious it's often overlooked. Then there's much grinding of teeth and swearing the first time a moose or a bear steps out alongside the road and you realize your camera or binoculars are buried somewhere in the trunk. Animals are not likely to wait patiently at roadside while you scramble around searching for things, especially if you have to get out of your car to do it.

- This book. Use it as necessary to keep up to date with the kinds of terrain you're traveling through and distances yet to cover.
- Map
- Binoculars
- Camera and extra film
- Notebook and pencil. You never know when you might want to jot down the address of someone you meet—or even make a note of an error in this book so you can later send a testy letter to the author. Notebooks are good, too, for keeping track of where you take various pictures. Also, you may want to keep running totals of your expenses.

CAMPING GEAR

Tent Campers—(*Much of this list will also apply to motorhome/camper/travel trailer campers, though kitchen utensils here are held to minimal levels; motorhomes and their like have more room for that kind of gear.*)

Tent campers should pay particular attention to packing their camping gear. Most of it should go in last, so it's immediately available when you stop to set up camp for the night.

Tent—
Allow sufficient space inside the tent for each person and some gear storage for that person—about 20 square feet or so per camper. If in doubt about tent space for the number of people in your party, take along another tent. When selecting a tent, pick one with stand-up headroom if you can. Lying in a pup tent while trying to wiggle into and out of your clothes gets old in a hurry.

Do not, under any circumstances, bring an orange tent to the Far North in the summer months. In a land that never darkens, trying to sleep inside an orange tent is like trying to sleep under a searchlight. Stick with darker greens, browns and blues. You'll sleep a lot better.

Tents should be lightweight but strong. And each tent should have a separate, detachable rain fly, a sewn-in floor and mosquito netting. Big canvas wall tents, long a favorite in northern hunting camps, are unwieldy and far from insect-proof. Used in semipermanent hunting camps in the fall, for which they were designed, they're fine—usually there are few bugs around then and you don't have to move the thing every day. A tent good for Alaska Highway travel must be light, strong, weatherproof and easy to set up and take down.

Practice setting up and taking down your tent several times before you head north. This will pay big dividends if you're in a hurry (maybe it's raining) the first time you try to set it up.

Small flashlight—
There's nothing worse than stumbling around inside a dark-colored tent looking for a tiny piece of gear. A small flashlight, one that can be rolled up inside the tent when you break camp so it's always there when you set the tent up, will be appreciated almost every day of your trip. Don't forget to include spare batteries and a spare bulb with your outfit.

Sleeping bags. One per person—
Choices here are many and varied. Those who plan to be on the road only during June, July and August need bags adequate to temperatures down to about 30 degrees (F). Those who will be on the road in May and September should have bags adequate for about 15-degree temperatures. Tent campers in other months of the year should have sleeping bags rated to -30 degrees or colder.

Bags filled with goose down are great—lightweight and compressible—as long as they are dry. Down offers absolutely no insulation when wet. On the other hand, new bags lined with synthetic fibers such as Dupont's Hollofil are great insulators wet or dry and they're also relatively light. But synthetic-filled bags are not readily compressible, and they occupy more space when packed away for traveling.

Bulkier and heavier cloth bags are fine, too, for car camping—again, as long as they are dry. But don't expect these to be serviceable when wet or in temperatures much below freezing.

Pad or air mattress. One per person—
A quality air mattress offers the best sleeping support possible for ground beds. But air mattresses are prone to develop leaks. If you choose to go with air mattresses, carry a repair kit and know how to use it. Also, air mattresses require a certain amount of effort each evening to inflate. If uncertain about your lung power, carry a small hand or foot pump to accomplish this task.

Pads come in a variety of materials. Probably the best pads available are part foam, part air mattress. Available in most outdoor stores, these roll up tightly. In camp, you unroll them and open the air valve; the mattress partially inflates as the foam expands. After that, a couple of breaths by the user fills them firmly.

Other pads might include simply a piece of foam encased in a ripstop nylon shell, a dense urethane foam mattress that is very thin and light but offers surprising comfort or even a 6-foot-by-2-foot piece of bubble wrap that will suffice for a couple of nights. Whichever way you choose to go, be sure to get full-length pads. Half- or three-quarter-length pads are available for backpackers, but these leave your feet and knees on the cold, hard ground.

A quick word about folding camp cots: these are generally more trouble than they're worth. They take up considerable space in the car, and sleeping on one is not nearly as warm as sleeping on the ground. If you do choose to use cots, carry a large supply of old newspapers. On cold nights, put several layers of newspapers over the cot before you put your sleeping bag on it; this will keep you surprisingly warm.

For those who want to know how it's done by oldtimers in the North, a tanned caribou hide is the answer. Dense, hollow hairs over pliable leather make sleeping in a snowbank a warm experience. Lay the hide out just as any other ground cloth, hair side up. You'll be thoroughly insulated from the ground and increase the comfort rating of your sleeping bag by a factor of 10 degrees or more.

Last, as far as sleeping comfort is concerned, consider taking a pillow along for each person. These can be used by passengers in your vehicle for additional comfort while motoring down the road.

Lightweight canvas dining fly—
This should be packed last so it's the first thing out of your vehicle in camp. Prop it up over a campground picnic table with a couple of old tent poles or a pole dragged out of the woods, and tie it to trees and bushes with stout cord. You should be able to walk under it from any direction without stooping. Be sure to slope the sides away from the center so rain will run off.

The idea of setting up a dining fly has been with us for decades—it's been in the Boy Scout Handbook for 50 years or more—and probably qualifies as one of the best camping techniques around. Yet few people use it. A rain fly over your picnic table provides a dry place for cooking and eating, a place to stand out of the weather without crawling into your tent and a dry spot for packing and unpacking your gear. It should be the first thing you put up in camp and the last thing you take down. Tarps sized 12 feet by 16 feet are about right, with stout grommets sewn in at regular intervals around the outside edge. In a pinch, you can make a dining fly out of several yards of plastic sheeting that is at least 4 mils thick.

Gas lantern and carrying case—
Buy a lantern that uses the same fuel as your camp stove, either propane or white gas. That saves having to carry around two different kinds of fuel supplies.

During the summer, a lantern has little use as a light source in Alaskan camps—it never really gets dark. However, you'll have some camping in darkness in more southern climes as you head north or return home, so a lantern is a valid investment.

In camp in Alaska, there's an often overlooked function for lanterns—they are perfect devices for drying wet clothing or sleeping bags. Light the lantern, set it on the picnic table (which is under the rain fly) and rig a rack over the lantern to keep objects from actually touching it. The heat given off by the lantern will quickly dry damp clothes and sleeping bags placed on the rack above it.

Carry several extra mantles for your lantern and know how to install them. Any outdoor equipment store should be able to assist you in selecting the proper mantles for your lantern. Also pick up a small funnel for filling the lantern if you have a model that uses a liquid fuel.

Camp stove—two or three burners—
Though there's a lot of romance in the idea of cooking over an open fire in the north woods, in practice such an activity is a real pain. Smoke-blackened pots have to be scrubbed and scrubbed to get them clean, and few people have the skills necessary to properly regulate the heat from a fire, which leads to either burned or raw food.

By all means have a campfire if you're able; it's the center of social activity in camp and a means of warmth. But do the bulk of your cooking on a camp stove; it's faster, cleaner and simpler.

Kitchen utensils—
This is a pretty basic list, but it covers most cooking situations likely to occur in camp:
- Two frying pans (with antistick coating)
- Three pots of varying sizes

- Plastic or nylon spatula
- Wooden spoon
- Table knives—one per person with one spare
- Forks—one per person with one spare
- Teaspoons—one per person with two spares
- Dinner plates—one per person with two spares (for serving plates). Use paper plates whenever possible for ease of cleanup.
- Bowls—one per person with two spares. Again, paper products will make cleanup easier.
- Cups—one per person with one spare. (Tupperware offers a fine set of cups for campers and a very good set of bowls with lids that double as small plates.)
- Can opener
- Two plastic tubs about 18 inches square and 8 inches deep for doing dishes. These tubs are also great containers for your kitchen utensils.
- Assorted kitchen knives
- Tongs for handling hot food
- Large fork and large spoon for cooking
- Aluminum coffee pot. Even if you don't drink coffee or use instant coffee while camping, this is great for heating water for any hot drink.
- Containers for spices—salt, pepper and whatever else you like. Tupperware makes sets of these that are very convenient, indestructible and have lids designed to keep out moisture.
- Hot pads for handling pans
- Wash rag for dishes

Kitchen extras, if you want to get fancy:
- Dutch oven for baking. Takes a certain amount of practice to get things right with coals from your fire, but once you've figured it out you can produce hot rolls, biscuits, pies and any number of other goodies.
- Fireplace popcorn popper
- Cork screw—for those romantics who want to share a bottle of wine around the fire
- Portable charcoal broiler (with charcoal and charcoal lighter) for barbecues. Several models are available that fold into small packages for traveling.
- Colander—makes draining pasta easier
- Large griddle that fits over two burners on camp stove. Great for hotcakes.

Kitchen consumables:
- Paper towels

- Aluminum foil
- Wooden matches
- Hand soap
- Dish soap
- SOS/Brillo pads or other pot scrubbers
- Garbage bags

Author's note: The secret to camp cooking is to keep things simple and use as few dishes and utensils as possible. For example, if your menu calls for hot dogs, don't boil them in a pan of water. Cut a couple of green sticks, scrape the bark off one end and have a wiener roast over the campfire. Other tips include things like the pan used just for boiling water—it doesn't need to be washed. Or don't set out a full service of silverware for each meal; set out just those utensils needed or use plastic, disposable flatware. When you take time to think about it, you'll find that you can prepare wholesome meals using very few dishes and utensils, all of which saves considerable time at cleanup.

Motorhomes/Campers/Travel Trailers—Obviously tents, dining flies, sleeping pads, lanterns and the like are not needed here. And, depending on the rig, it's possible to leave sleeping bags behind as well and go with regular bedding. Other than those items, the above lists are valid for RVs as well as for tents. However, the extra space and creature comforts available in these rigs offer added possibilities. Here are just a few items in that category:

- Electrical appliances. If your rig has a generator or if you expect to spend most nights in private campgrounds with electrical hookups, many of the devices in your kitchen at home will serve you well on a trip to Alaska. The biggest problem may be storage space; thus you may have to set a few priorities.
- Toaster
- Blender
- Food processor
- Hot-air popcorn popper
- Small microwave oven (more and more rigs are being equipped with these when they are built)
- Coffee maker
- Electric griddle

For the refrigerator/freezer:

- Ice trays
- Tupperware containers for mixed juices and other liquids

Extra utensils:
- Ice cream scoop
- Grater for cheese and vegetables
- Mounted paper-towel rack
- Assorted baking pans
- Roasting pan
- Additional pots and pans of your choice

Author's note: Over the years we've found that a camp stove is a valued addition to our motorhome supplies. There are times when the weather is just great outdoors and you don't want to be cooped up inside to cook. And when we fry outdoors the fish we catch, the odor doesn't permeate our bedding.

GENERAL CAMPING GEAR FOR ALL SITUATIONS:
- Three-quarter ax
- Folding shovel
- Plastic bucket
- Firewood saw
- Pocketknife for each member of the party old enough to use it safely. Avoid big sheath knives—a big knife on your belt signals greenhorn status. These knives have no real function other than decoration.
- Folding camp chairs (optional)
- Insect repellent
- Potable water

CLOTHING

Personal clothing—the jeans, socks, shirts, underwear and whatever else you wear from day to day—won't be subject to a list. Usually, sufficient changes of clothes good for from 5 to 7 days will suffice. About once a week, plan on devoting half a day or so to doing laundry. Most private campgrounds offer laundry facilities, and all of the larger towns in the North have laundromats.

Shirts should be a mix of long- and short-sleeved. Shorts, in lieu of long pants, are optional, though be certain your week's worth of clothing does include several pairs of long pants.

For women, dresses or skirts are strictly optional in the North. You might want to include one for a fancier evening on the town in Anchorage, but otherwise pants are acceptable in virtually every situation you're likely to encounter in northwestern Canada and Alaska.

For traveling in the colder months, wool is still the preferred material for pants and shirts, though some of the new synthetics are making inroads here. Long underwear is a must as well. Old hands in the North universally agree that you should dress in layers for dealing with the cold.

Besides routine personal clothing, here's a list of the other things you'll probably need:

- **Rain gear**—This can take two forms: either a full suit of rain gear, pants and hooded jacket, or a hooded rain parka that hangs almost to the ground. A trip to Alaska is an outdoor vacation, and rain gear allows you to move around in the weather in relative comfort. Purchase rain gear one size larger than you normally buy so you can wear it over a warm jacket. Temperatures are usually pretty cool when it rains in the North. Gore-tex rainwear is increasingly popular in the North. It's generally much more comfortable to wear than the heavier oilcloth or rubberized materials.

- **Gloves/mittens**—Summer travelers will appreciate a lightweight pair of gloves. Winter travelers should carry heavily insulated mittens, even gauntlets.

- **Warm vest or jacket**—Each traveler will need one or both of these. Summer temperatures in Alaska can range from just above freezing to 90 degrees (F) or more. A jacket is a must. Winter travelers should have parkas.

- **Cap**—A baseball-type cap will usually suffice in the summer months. For spring, fall and winter travel, stocking caps are best. Many travelers appreciate the stocking caps during cool, rainy summer days, too.

- **Footwear**—Gym shoes or other comfortable shoes are adequate for most day-to-day use in camp and on the road. Those planning to do more extensive day hikes or even add some backpacking to their trips will appreciate a hardier pair of hiking boots. Smooth-bottomed leather shoes are relatively functionless along the Alaska Highway. As a minimum, shoes should have dense foam rubber soles, molded rubber soles with some sort of tread pattern or, for hiking boots, lug soles made of Vibram or similar material. Footgear very popular in coastal Alaska are knee-high rubber boots. These are also called "southeast sneakers" by some Alaskans, a reference to the wet climate in the rain forest belt along the southeastern coast. When selecting footwear, start with the realization that sometime on your trip you're going to get your feet wet and probably muddy. Waterproof and/or washable are the two key words to remember.

- **Socks**—In addition to the socks you wear from day to day, pack a pair or two of heavy wool socks for each member of the party. Few things are more uncomfortable than cold feet, and wool socks will keep feet reasonably warm even when wet.

FISHING GEAR

A wide variety of fishing opportunities exist for fishermen along the Alaska Highway and within Alaska. Along the highway, the primary species available are lake trout (to 30 pounds or more), northern pike (to 25 pounds), Dolly Varden (to about 4 pounds) and arctic grayling (to about 4 pounds).

In Alaska, these four species are also available along with five species of Pacific salmon—pinks (humpies), 3 to 10 pounds; sockeye (reds), 5 to 15 pounds; silvers (cohos), 8 to 20 pounds; chums (dog salmon), 10 to 25 pounds; and kings (chinooks), 15 to 90 pounds—plus rainbow trout (a few ounces to 25 pounds or more), Pacific halibut (10 to 400 pounds) and other saltwater fish, primarily different species of rockfish.

Trying to carry enough gear to cover all these situations is mind-boggling. However, you can narrow it down and still be prepared for most eventualities. (Don't bother bringing your own gear for halibut. Most visitors take charter boats after halibut, and the operators provide tackle sufficient for the largest catch. If you go for halibut on your own, tackle rentals can be arranged.)

Spin- or Bait-cast Fishing:
- A medium-weight rod with reel capable of holding 150 yards or more of 15- to 20-pound test line. This rig will handle most situations for salmon, northern pike and lake trout.
- A lightweight rod with reel holding up to 100 yards of 4- or 6-pound test line. This rod is for grayling, rainbows and Dolly Varden.
- Lures. Popular lures for northern fishing include:
  Pixies—Pounded silver spoons with a colorful plastic insert. Preferred insert colors are green and pink. **Mepps spinners**—The "0" size, plain silver Mepps is probably the greatest grayling lure ever devised. Other Mepps spinners up to the very largest will take every fish available in Alaska or northern Canada. **Assorted spoons of varying sizes**—Red-and-white and black-and-white seem to be preferred color combinations. Large spoons are particularly effective for northern pike but will also work for salmon and lake trout. Rainbows and grayling will hit small spoons. **Vibrax spinners**—Similar to Mepps spinners, but lure body makes a buzzing sound when dragged through the water. This lure was extremely hot in the late 1980s. Various sizes will catch all fish listed. Preferred colors seem to be plain silver or a silver blade with a fluorescent green body. **Rapalla jigs**—Great for lake trout. Large sizes will take halibut.
- Baits. In Alaska more fish fall to bait than lures. These are readily available; no need to carry your own. **Whole or cut-plug herring**—Available at most tackle stores in coastal areas. Troll for salmon and lake trout. Jig for halibut. **Salmon roe—**

Commercial roe available. Fresh roe from a salmon caught yourself is better. Usually big globs of it rigged on a treble hook bounced along the bottom will produce salmon in streams or big Dolly Varden. **Single salmon eggs**—Commercially available in jars from most tackle stores. Best for rainbows in lakes. Patske's Balls o' Fire are most popular.

- Assortment of lead weights up to and including large 2-ounce weights for trolling.
- Spare fishing line
- Varying sizes of swivels
- Long-nosed pliers
- Landing net (particularly needed if fishing from a boat)
- Club for subduing large fish
- Filet knife
- Flashers for trolling
- Folding gaff (needed for large salmon and lake trout caught from a boat)
- Steel leaders for northern pike
- Hip boots or chest waders
- Tackle box or other equipment container

Fly Fishing:
Other than rods, lures, flashers, lead weights and steel leaders, most of the other tackle listed under spin- and bait-casting will be needed here. Fly fishermen should also remember that big fish are caught primarily near stream bottoms. Except for grayling, fish deep for best success.

- Rod designed for #8 or #9 line. Should have plenty of backbone. Reel should carry fly line with a 10-foot, fast-sinking tip and 50 yards or more of 20-pound test or heavier backing. Salmon, northern pike and big rainbows.
- Rod designed for #5 or #6 line. Use floating line. Backing optional. For grayling and most trout fishing.
- Flies: **Grayling**—This fish is a fly fisherman's dream come true. Grayling will hit almost any fly tied on a #10 hook or smaller, fished wet or dry. Most popular flies are winged black gnats and mosquitoes. Use a short leader, 3 to 4 feet long. **Rainbows**—Muddlers and woolly worms. Also an egg-sucking leech and various egg patterns, the latter usually pink with a red eye. **Northern pike**—Big, bright streamers. Red-and-yellow or red-and-white. Rig 12-inch shock tip of 40-pound leader material at end of 8- to 10-foot, 12-pound-test leader before tying on fly. A pike's teeth will make short work of light line. **Salmon**—Big and bright, usually streamers fished just off the bottom. Also popular is a fly called the Alaska MaryAnn. You'll have to inquire locally in Alaska to find these. Try McAfees Fly Shop, 750 W.

Dimond, in Anchorage (907) 344-1617, for MaryAnns and almost any other fly used in Alaska.

For Boat Fishermen:
- Life jackets. One per person. Wear at all times on the water. The water in most northern lakes and all Alaskan coastal regions is very cold. If you fall in, you likely will quickly become incapacitated and unable to swim.
- Depth finder (also called fish finders). Depending on the weather, fish will hold at different depths. These sonar devices will allow you to find them much faster.
- Down riggers. Particularly effective fishing in salt water for salmon or in deep lakes for lake trout.
- Motor suitable for extended slow trolling. Troll backwards in calm water conditions if your motor won't run slow enough to troll effectively.
- Large cooler. Many Alaskans strap a large plastic garbage can in place near the transom to hold the fish they expect to catch. Fill half full with crushed ice before starting out.

CAMERA EQUIPMENT

The most sophisticated camera equipment in the world produces few pictures if not used. If you're uncomfortable with single-lens-reflex cameras and the assortment of interchangeable lenses available, stick with the smaller cameras you normally use.

For those who prefer the high-tech world available to camera buffs, here are my recommendations:
- **Film**—Color slide films usually provide the sharpest, most-colorful pictures, though they require extra processing if you want prints. For best results, use Kodachrome (either ASA 25 or 64) or Fujichrome (either ASA 50 or 100). Faster films offer additional opportunities in low-light situations, but the trade-off is usually grainier pictures with less color saturation. Carry several dozen rolls of film. Although film is available most places in the North, it will likely be fairly expensive. It's better and cheaper to bring your own.
- **Camera**—One or two camera bodies of your favorite type. If you carry two, they should have the same lens mounts so you don't have to carry two sets of lenses.
- **Lenses—20mm wide-angle lens**—Great for working close up, such as when out fishing in a small boat. **50mm "normal" lens**— Should be fairly fast lens, f1.2 or f1.4, to provide more options when the light is weak. **35-105mm or 35-135mm zoom lens**— If you detest zooms, a series of lenses covering these ranges should be carried. The new generation of zoom lenses, however,

pretty much mutes the old arguments about zooms not being sharp enough. **Telephotos of 200mm or larger**—(optional). These are primarily for those interested in photographing wildlife. They will require a tripod for use, and these lenses tend to get fairly heavy if you have to carry them any distance.

- **Tripod**—Use whenever possible. A tripod all but eliminates camera shake and almost always yields better pictures.
- **Electronic flash**
- **Spare batteries for camera and flash**
- **UV or skylight filter on all lenses**
- **Polarizing filter**
- **Yellow, orange and red filters** for black-and-white photography. Use to enhance skies and clouds.
- **Lens tissue**
- **Carrying bag for equipment**

Author's note: As a magazine editor, I made part of my living taking photographs, often on very short notice. My ready bag contains only what I consider essential equipment—I really don't like lugging around a lot of gear. It contains a Nikon FE2 camera body, a 20mm lens, a 50mm lens and a 35-135mm zoom along with an electronic flash. That plus 20 rolls of film and the filters listed above keeps me instantly ready for almost any situation I might have to face. Altogether, the bag weighs about 12 pounds. On extended trips, I add a second Nikon camera body equipped with a 35-105mm zoom lens and additional film. This equipment, plus a pocket-size Rollei 35 that I carry everywhere, has never failed me. In the few instances when a longer telephoto lens would have been handy, I've simply used my feet to get closer. All of the photographs in this book were taken with just the equipment in my ready bag.

MISCELLANEOUS

The following items of equipment don't necessarily fit in any category already discussed, but they represent several other necessities and good ideas.

- Day pack. Bring along a small one that can be wadded up and stuck in an odd corner. It's really handy for carrying a lunch if you're exploring a trail or walking down the shore of a lake.
- First aid kit. An absolute necessity. It's often a long way between medical facilities in the North.
- Sewing kit
- Toiletries. Everybody has favorites in this department, so a list is not needed. It's a good idea to carry more than one towel per person, as these have many uses. Electrical devices like hair dryers, curling irons and electric shavers will work in Canada.

Electric power in Canada is delivered at 110 volts, just as in the United States.

- Entertainment. A few odds and ends to support various hobbies or favorite leisure activities are nice to have along—to kill time on rainy days or for plain relaxation. Here are a few ideas:
    Cribbage board
    Deck(s) of playing cards
    Sewing, knitting or crochet projects
    A few favorite books
    Travel games like checkers or backgammon

PACKING

I have already mentioned where to pack and carry certain items. In general, remember that the first thing you need should be the last thing packed; thus the last thing you need should be the first thing packed.

It's also a good idea to use duffel bags instead of suitcases. Soft-sided containers are easier to put away in most cases. And if you want to take advantage of some fly-in fishing trips while traveling, most pilots will insist on duffel bags for your gear. A wide variety of sizes are available, some that open only at the narrow end, others that offer full-length zippers. Place a piece of adhesive tape on each bag and write on the tape the contents of that bag, to save opening several bags searching for just one item.

When loading your vehicle, it's usually a good idea to put heavy items as far forward and as low as possible, particularly if you're driving a passenger car. This tends to shift more weight to the front wheels and results in a more stable ride. Also, pay attention to the weight you load to the far right or left sides of a vehicle. Putting all the heavy items on one side may make your car or truck lean uncomfortably.

Eighty percent of the Alaska Highway is in Canada.
Canada operates under the metric system.
Distances are in kilometers.
Speed limits are in kilometers per hour (kph).

The following conversions are accurate to within 1 mph:

10 kph = 6 mph	65 kph = 39 mph
20 kph = 12 mph	70 kph = 42 mph
25 kph = 15 mph	75 kph = 45 mph
30 kph = 18 mph	80 kph = 48 mph
35 kph = 21 mph	85 kph = 51 mph
40 kph = 24 mph	90 kph = 54 mph
45 kph = 27 mph	95 kph = 57 mph
50 kph = 30 mph	100 kph = 60 mph
55 kph = 33 mph	105 kph = 63 mph
60 kph = 36 mph	110 kph = 66 mph

The most frequent speed-limit sign on two-lane rural roads is 90 kph, roughly equivalent to the 55 mph speed limits in the United States.

Distances convert on a similar pattern:

1 kilometer = 0.6 miles
100 kilometers = 60 miles
150 kilometers = 90 miles
200 kilometers = 120 miles
300 kilometers = 180 miles

If in doubt about converting any distance or speed, here's a simple solution: Multiply any figure given in kilometers by six, then drop the last digit of your answer. Examples:

243 km x 6 = 1,458
Drop the 8 and you have approximately 145 miles.

622 km x 6 = 3,732
Drop the 2 and you have approximately 373 miles.

92 kph x 6 = 552
Drop the 2 and you have 55 mph.

7

DRIVING TIPS

Driving to Alaska means driving in Canada, a foreign country with a similar language but different customs, traditions and laws. Of particular note for drivers is the metric system. Speed limits and distances throughout Canada are given in kilometers per hour (kph) and kilometers (km), respectively. Until conditioned to using kilometers for measuring distance and speed, U.S. drivers will enjoy a moment's worth of mental math recalculating each speed and distance sign they see.

Insider's Tip: Most vehicles of recent vintage offer a kilometers-per-hour scale on the speedometers. Use it to judge speeds in Canada whenever possible. On dial-and-needle speedometers, kph measurements are usually printed in small numbers underneath the miles-per-hour equivalents. On most cars with digital displays of speed, there is a kph setting that can be engaged.

The road system in Canada differs in one major respect as well: There is no network of interstate highways lacing the country together. Multilane, limited-access highways do exist, mostly near major cities, but these are relatively few.

The plus side, however, is that most of the Canadian roads leading to the start of the Alaska Highway are among the best-engineered and best-maintained roads in North America. Because of this, driving in Canada is an absolute delight. Only when you enter remote areas in northwestern Canada are roads less than excellent, and this is not for any lack of trying on the part of the Canadians. It's just that wilderness roads are frightfully expensive to build and maintain. Even these, however, are being continually upgraded.

Maintenance and road-repair crews will be highly visible almost everywhere in Canada during the summer months. Because Canada is a northern country with severe winters, extensive road maintenance and construction can be performed only in the warmer months. There will be delays for lengthy sections undergoing repair or rebuilding during the summer. Expect and plan for the delays; figure one or two delays of up to 30 minutes for each driving day.

Insider's Tip: When lengthy traffic delays occur, take advantage of the time to step out of your car and walk around. Talk to fellow travelers in the cars near yours, pick a wildflower from a roadside ditch to press in your scrapbook or get out the camera for a picture, particularly if you're in scenic areas like the Canadian Rockies.

In reality, getting to the start of the Alaska Highway is little different from driving on roads around your home town. Once past Dawson Creek or entering the Cassiar Cutoff northbound at New Hazelton, British Columbia, things require a little more attention.

On the Alaska Highway, the first 300 miles or so from Dawson Creek to Fort Nelson are pretty much like the rest of Canada's major highways. Over the years, as more and more people have moved to this area, it has gradually been built up. The road is a high grade of asphalt.

Past Fort Nelson and on the Cassiar Cutoff, the road becomes a little more remote, hence a little more exciting. Those stretches from here north that are paved won't necessarily be of the same quality of paved stretches already traveled. Often the pavement is made of crushed rock and oil compressed into a pavement-like surface by the vehicles driving over it (not laid down by paving machines). While this certainly makes for a solid, dependable road, it does present some problems.

Crushed-rock-and-oil pavement can be extremely slippery when wet. Slow down in the rain. Curves are not as likely to be banked adequately, and lower speed limits are posted for winding stretches. Heed these. Road shoulders are likely to be narrow or almost nonexistent and probably fairly soft when wet. Avoid slipping over to the road shoulders at highway speeds. Conversely, if forced to stop, pull as far to the side as possible. Try to avoid stopping in areas where cars coming from either direction cannot see you in plenty of time to either slow down or drive around you.

On gravel, high speeds get you into trouble, whether the road is wet or dry. Gravel roads create more friction; thus you increase fuel consumption when trying to maintain highway speeds. Loose gravel acts almost like ball bearings under your tires as well. It's much easier to get into a skid on gravel roads.

Insider's Tip: Absolutely the worst tires available for high-speed driving on gravel roads are the oversize, wider-than-normal, high-flotation tires favored by off-road enthusiasts. These tires tend to float on gravel and can make vehicle control marginal at speeds of 50 mph (80 kph) or faster. Use the narrowest tires that offer adequate strength for your loaded vehicle.

When wet, northern gravel roads act as if they have been greased. In Canada, a wetting agent is applied to most gravel roads to hold down the dust during warm, dry periods. This increases the slickness of the road during periods of rain. Slow down, way down.

Wet gravel roads also mean mud, lots of it. Avoid tailgating—the car in front of you will quickly cover you with mud. Watch out for oncoming vehicles, big trucks in particular. These can instantly throw enough water and mud on your vehicle to temporarily blind you. Keep your windshield wipers going constantly and make certain you have an adequate supply of fluid in your windshield washing system.

Dust, even though it is partially controlled by wetting agents, can be unbelievable during dry periods. Again, avoid tailgating and watch carefully for dust clouds thrown up by oncoming vehicles. Under certain conditions, it's wise to slow almost to a stop and pull as far to the right as possible when a dust cloud threatens to engulf you. Losing all visibility for a few seconds, as often happens, can be extremely hazardous when you're traveling 50 mph (80 kph).

Watch your rear-view mirror carefully at all times. Many long stretches of the Alaska Highway and side roads offer limited opportunities for passing. If traffic starts stacking up behind you, find a place to pull over so these vehicles can get around. In Alaska it is against the law not to pull over when traffic piles up behind you.

Plan for frequent stops. Driving on narrow, winding roads in heavy dust or on rain-slick highways takes a lot of concentration. You'll be much safer if you take time to relax and refresh yourself at frequent intervals.

Once on the Alaska Highway system, don't be overly ambitious in your daily driving goals. About 300 miles (500 km) a day allows plenty of time to stop and check out the scenery or wildlife and does not commit you to a frantic "I-have-to-get-there" pace. The traveling chapters in this book are broken down into segments of about 300 miles per day for this very reason. A safe, rewarding trip to and from Alaska is best achieved if you heed three simple words: TAKE YOUR TIME.

When planning your trip, allow plenty of flexibility in your schedule. It would be a shame, for example, to allow just a lunch stop near a lake and then find out that the lake trout were really biting. Be able to take a day out of your schedule now and then to sample the fishing or hike a trail you didn't expect to find. Your trip will be much more meaningful.

When on the Alaska Highway and its side roads or on alternate routes, drive with your headlights on at all times. It's the law on Canadian portions of the road, and it makes sense.

Insider's Tip: When you stop for gas and to clean your windshield, take a moment to wipe off your headlights and taillights as well. These can be covered with mud just as easily as any other part of your vehicle.

In Alaska and toward the northwestern part of the Alaska Highway in Canada, for many folks there is an unexpected hazard—permafrost. Permafrost is permanently frozen ground underlying the surface of the land. It is constantly shifting, wreaking havoc with things like highways. Often you can find ice (frozen ground) by digging a shallow hole, even in July or August. In places, that frozen ground is hundreds, even thousands of feet thick.

Permafrost usually shows up in unexpected dips or bulges in the surface of paved roads. Hitting these at high speed can sometimes tear the suspension right out of a vehicle. Even the best-engineered and newest roads in Alaska can develop permafrost heaves within a few weeks. Road maintenance crews try their hardest to post signs warning of the worst of these, but there are so many in some years that it's hard for them to keep up.

Insider's Tip: When driving almost any road in Alaska or near the end of the Canadian portion of the road, watch for the solid white line marking the road shoulder to your right. If it appears to squiggle up ahead, you are approaching an area of active permafrost heaving. Slow down.

Broken down into basics, these five simple rules will go far to making your trip safe and comfortable.
- Slow down, particularly on gravel roads.
- Allow plenty of time.
- Drive with headlights on at all times.
- Plan a flexible travel schedule.
- Be a courteous driver.

In reality, nothing on this short list is more than plain common sense. Most people driving to and from Alaska ultimately recognize these simple truisms. You'll be ahead of the game if you start out with them in mind.

· ——— 8 ——— ·

CHOOSING A ROUTE

Just getting to the start of the Alaska Highway will be an adventure in itself for most people. There are literally dozens of possibilities. In the pages that follow, suggested routings and alternate routings are presented for people starting from anywhere in the United States or Canada. All lead to a single town in northern British Columbia, Dawson Creek, Mile 0 of the Alaska Highway.

In this chapter, the United States and Canada are broken down into four distinct regions: the West Coast (California, Oregon, Washington and British Columbia); the Rocky Mountain states together with the Western Plains (the latter including Texas, Oklahoma, Kansas, Nebraska, South Dakota, North Dakota, Alberta and Saskatchewan); the Midwest (essentially the Mississippi Valley states, Manitoba and western Ontario); and the East (everything from Florida to Quebec and including Canada's maritime provinces).

Sample routing is provided from a major U.S. city in each of these regions as well as an alternate route for those desiring some options. Primary routes were chosen by the simple expedient of selecting the shortest driving distance from the sample city to Dawson Creek. To vary your trip, consider using one route northbound and the other for your return.

Mileages are rounded to the nearest 50. Trips to and from Dawson Creek are figured at about 450 miles a day, which should prove a comfortable figure on the better roads stretching across the built-up parts of North America.

Those who don't live exactly in the cities featured will have to adjust their own travel times and distances based on their individual situations. For example, the West Coast trip as defined here starts in San Francisco. If you live in Los Angeles, add an extra day and 450 miles (one way) to the figures presented as part of the sample trip.

51

For ease in finding a suggested route most appropriate to your home, this chapter is broken into four sections based on the regions described above. Page numbers for those sections are as follows:

Please remember that the routes described here are only suggestions. Spend some time with maps plotting your trip, and you'll quickly see the possibilities are virtually uncountable for people starting a trip to Alaska from almost any point in Canada or the contiguous 48 states. Ultimately, it all boils down to how much time you have and the things you and your companions most want to experience while traveling.

===========   Section 1   ===========

West Coast

Sample Itinerary

San Francisco, California, to Dawson Creek, British Columbia

Primary Route

TIME REQUIRED: 4 days (no side trips)

MILEAGE: 1,650 miles (2,750 kilometers)

OVERNIGHT STOPS:
Grants Pass, Oregon
Seattle, Washington
100 Mile House, British Columbia
Dawson Creek, British Columbia

POSSIBLE SIDE TRIPS EN ROUTE
(and minimum additional time required):
Crater Lake National Park, Oregon (1 day)
Mount Rainier National Park, Washington (1 day)
Vancouver Island, British Columbia (2 days)

ROUTING:
San Francisco to Grants Pass:
I-80, San Francisco to Sacramento
I-5, Sacramento to Grants Pass

Grants Pass to Seattle: I-5
Seattle to 100 Mile House:
    I-5 to Canada 1 (at or near Vancouver)
    Canada 1 to Cache Creek, British Columbia
    B.C. 97, Cache Creek to 100 Mile House
100 Mile House to Dawson Creek: B.C. 97

Alternate Route

TIME REQUIRED: 4 days (no side trips)

MILEAGE: 1,800 miles (3,000 kilometers)

OVERNIGHT STOPS:
    Bend, Oregon
    Oroville, Washington
    Tête Jaune Cache, British Columbia
    Dawson Creek, British Columbia

POSSIBLE SIDE TRIPS EN ROUTE
    (and minimum additional time required):
    Lava Beds National Monument, California (1 day)
    Crater Lake National Park, Oregon (1 day)
    North Cascades National Park, Washington (1 day)
    Banff National Park, Alberta (1 day)
    Jasper National Park, Alberta (1 day)

ROUTING:
    San Francisco to Bend:
        I-80, San Francisco to Sacramento
        I-5, Sacramento to Weed, California
        U.S. 97, Weed to Bend
    Bend to Oroville: U.S. 97
    Oroville to Tête Jaune Cache:
        U.S. 97 to Canadian Border
        B.C. 97 to Kamloops, British Columbia
        B.C. 5, Kamloops to Tête Jaune Cache
    Tête Jaune Cache to Dawson Creek:
        B.C. 16 to Prince George, British Columbia
    Prince George to Dawson Creek: B.C. 97

West Coast—Primary Routing

Travelers heading north from the Far West have available the most obvious routing to Dawson Creek, British Columbia. Just head north until you get there.

But what you have along the way is nothing short of spectacular. Using the primary routing north from San Francisco, start by heading east on Interstate 80 to **Sacramento**, California, where you intersect the major north-south route in the West Coast states—Interstate 5. Moving north on I-5, travelers enter the Cascade Mountains, Mount Shasta being the most obvious peak in north-central California. Northbound from Sacramento, the major California cities encountered are Redding, Weed and Yreka. Weed is where the primary and alternate routes recommended here diverge.

Mostly the terrain is mountainous; as you approach the Oregon border, the Cascades are to the right and the Siskiyou Mountains are to the left. Once in Oregon, the major cities prior to Grants Pass are Ashland and Medford. Ashland is the home of the University of Southern Oregon, a small liberal arts school of excellent reputation.

Insider's Tip: Ashland hosts a thriving Shakespearean theater in the summer months. The outdoor theater (just as in Shakespeare's time) sits on a bluff above Lithia Park, a small jewel of a park laced with pleasant pathways. If you have the time, a night of Shakespeare followed by a lingering walk in Lithia Park combine for an unforgettable evening.

Travelers desiring to add Crater Lake National Park to their itineraries turn east on Oregon 62 in Medford. It takes about 2 1/2 hours to drive to the park from Medford.

Moving on to Grants Pass, you'll find a modest-sized city on the banks of Oregon's Rogue River and surrounded by forested mountains. Full facilities are available for travelers, and the pace in Grants Pass is pretty laid back, allowing for plenty of relaxation if you select this as an overnight stop.

Leaving Grants Pass, it's a comfortable 1-day drive to Seattle, all of it on I-5. From Grants Pass to Roseburg, the mountainous terrain continues. Leaving Roseburg you drop into Oregon's Willamette Valley. This long, broad valley hosts Oregon's finest farms. The climate is relatively mild all year long, and rainfall is more than adequate for almost any crop.

Major cities in the Willamette Valley include Eugene and Salem (Oregon's capital). Neither is particularly large; both offer full facilities for travelers at very reasonable prices.

Leaving Oregon's breadbasket, you approach Portland and the surrounding towns that have pretty much been absorbed as bedroom communities for the city. An obviously western city, Portland and its suburbs sprawl across miles of low, rolling hills. Sixty or so miles to the east, Mount Hood, Oregon's highest peak, rises above the city.

Interstate-5 continues through Portland, across the Columbia River. The city continues north of the river, but here it is known as Vancouver, Washington. If at all possible, avoid workday rush hours when traveling through the Portland-Vancouver area. Freeways are jammed during those times.

Insider's Tip: The easiest route past Portland is to take the Interstate 205 exit near Tualatin and drive around the east side of the city. I-205 intercepts I-5 again just north of Vancouver. The traffic is much lighter on I-205 than it is on I-5 in downtown Portland.

North of Vancouver, Mount St. Helens, the volcano that erupted in 1980, is to your right (east). The mountain is not nearly as tall now as before the eruption, and the jagged edge of its crater is clearly visible from the highway. Even today, Mount St. Helens occasionally spews small amounts of steam and ash into the air, so there exists the possibility of witnessing a minor eruption as you drive past.

Heading for Seattle, you'll pass first through Olympia, Washington's capital, located near the southern edge of Puget Sound. I-5 meanders through several tricky curves passing through Olympia, so be on the alert.

Approaching Olympia, Mount Rainier is to the right. Several options for driving to Mount Rainier National Park are available prior to reaching Olympia or between Olympia and Seattle. Allow a minimum of a full day if you wish to add this side trip to your journey north.

One could argue that Seattle actually starts when you enter the city limits of Tacoma, Washington's second-largest city, officially about 20 miles south of Seattle. Over the years the two cities have grown to the point that they form a long, slender metropolitan area strung out along the eastern shore of Puget Sound. All told, you'll have about 50 miles of city freeway driving from the southern edge of Tacoma to the northern parts of Seattle. It, too, can be extremely crowded during workday rush hours. Interstate 405 offers an alternative route around the east side of Seattle if you wish to avoid Seattle's downtown areas.

In the 1980s, Seattle and the surrounding area experienced a phenomenal growth of business and industry. To a large extent the highway system has been unable to keep pace, and prices for almost any service and for land have soared. Those who wish to remain overnight in the Seattle area might want to look at smaller communities just north of the city for more reasonably-priced accommodations, among them Edmonds and Everett.

Leaving Seattle, northbound to Alaska, the excitement begins to mount. This is the day you cross over into Canada and begin edging away from the more crowded parts of the North American continent. Ahead are the Canadian Rockies of British Columbia. As you travel farther and farther north, the cities and towns become smaller and farther apart.

Interstate 5 continues to the Canadian border, then becomes B.C. 99 from the border into Vancouver. Should you not wish to enter Vancouver itself, take advantage of the first available access route to Canada 1. Turn east on Canada 1.

Insider's Tip: You can shave about 50 miles off your trip north if you turn east on Washington 542 in Bellingham, then follow it to Washington 9, which leads north to Sumas. Cross the border at Sumas and intercept Canada 1 just north of town.

The last city of significant size prior to reaching Canada is Bellingham, Washington. Bellingham is the southern terminus of the Alaska Marine Highway, a system of ferries with stateroom accommodations for passengers and space for vehicles. Many travelers opt to drive their vehicles on the ferry either coming or going to Alaska. The northern terminus of the ferry system is Haines, Alaska, about 150 miles from the Alaska Highway, altogether about 600 miles from Fairbanks. Chapter 13 of this book provides a much more detailed look at the ferry system and provides information on reservations.

Canada 1, an east-west route just north of the U.S.–Canada border, is also referred to as the Trans-Canada Highway. More than 3,000 miles long, it is the major artery connecting eastern Canada to western Canada. When you intercept this highway east of Vancouver, it actually leads you north to the town of Cache Creek. At Cache Creek, Canada 1 turns eastward and Alaska-bound travelers continue north on B.C. 97.

However, before intercepting B.C. 97, the 120 miles of Canada 1 from Hope to Cache Creek provide some of the most spectacular scenery of the entire trip—the Fraser River canyon.

Leaving Hope, the river is to the east. Thirty-three miles farther, the road crosses the river and clings to the east side of the canyon. Appropriately, the river crossing is made near Hell's Gate, at least partially descriptive of this raging, frothing river roaring out of the mountains. The road follows the canyon for nearly 75 miles. The vistas are awe-inspiring. Numerous tunnels lace the route. The road is first-rate, and almost all uphill sections provide broad passing lanes.

Pulling out of the canyon, Canada 1 follows the Thompson River into Cache Creek. Fisherman can find all sorts of excuses for spending time in or around the Thompson River, among them: steelhead to 30 pounds in the spring, king and silver salmon in the summer and fall and rainbow trout and Dolly Varden almost any time of the year.

In and around Cache Creek (population about 1,300), there are public and private campgrounds, fishing opportunities and open country. If you need groceries for an RV or other odds and ends, Cache Creek is a fairly good place to shop for them.

From Cache Creek, it's about 70 miles to 100 Mile House, a slightly larger town of about 1,900 folks. For those ready to stop for the night, there are plenty of campgrounds, restaurants, motels and other travelers' services. There is good fishing in the immediate area as well if you feel the need to wet a line.

The history of 100 Mile House is colored with fur trappers and later with teamsters who hauled the freight necessary to build Canada's frontier; it was a stop on the old Caribou Wagon Road. Visitor information is available at the kiosk next to the bird sanctuary in the center of town.

Leaving 100 Mile House, the road heads almost straight north until jogging eastward for the final 75 miles or so into Dawson Creek. Major towns along this stretch are Quesnel, Prince George and Chetwynd. But, it's the names of the smaller towns along the way that begin to hint at the rich, relatively recent history of the Canadian wilderness. Driving north, you'll pass through Lac la Hache, Bear Lake, Fort McLeod and McLeod Lake. At McLeod Lake, a turnoff leads a short distance to Mackenzie on the shores of Williston Lake, the largest manmade reservoir on the North American continent. Williston Lake is a hefty body of water, close to 100 miles long north and south, with a 75-mile spur snaking east from the northern part of the lake. Plenty of fish here as well, including rainbows, Dolly Varden, Arctic char and grayling.

Moving north to Chetwynd, Alaska-bound travelers have an option. If you don't wish to visit Dawson Creek, you can turn left in Chetwynd on B.C. 29 to Fort St. John on the Alaska Highway. This will cut about 50 miles from your trip, but you do miss Dawson Creek and the opportunity to compare notes with numerous other northbound travelers. Dawson Creek is a natural gathering point for those heading to Alaska and for those just returned. The campgrounds and hotels will be full of trail talk from the Alaska Highway on almost any summer evening.

Dawson Creek's best campgrounds are in the last half-mile or so before the junction on the edge of town where you turn left for Alaska or right for the city center. All Dawson Creek–area campgrounds tend to fill up early during the summer. If campgrounds close to town are full, continue toward Alaska; several more are within a few miles on the Alaska Highway itself.

Also, take a few moments to investigate the visitors center in Dawson Creek. Turn right toward the city center at the junction. The visitors center is just a short distance down the street on your left. It has plenty of parking for even the largest RVs.

West Coast—Alternate Routing

Sometimes the most obvious isn't necessarily the best. This alternate routing from San Francisco to Dawson Creek could make a strong argument to that effect.

This route offers much less freeway driving and adds about 150 miles to the trip, but there are some major "finds" along the way, the kinds of things most people who stick to the obvious will miss.

Using San Francisco as a starting point, the route is the same to Weed, California, north of Sacramento on I-5. At Weed, turn off on U.S. 97, the road you will follow all the way to the Canadian border. Prior to the completion of I-5 in the early 1960s, U.S. 97 was a major north-south route through Oregon. Now most of the heavy traffic sticks to I-5, particularly the truckers.

After getting on U.S. 97, the first town of any size is Klamath Falls, Oregon, about 75 miles away and less than 20 miles north of the California-Oregon border. Just prior to entering Oregon, California 161 leads to the east through marshes heavily used by waterfowl. Lots of bald eagles and other birds of prey can often be seen as well. This road provides access to Lava Beds National Monument after it connects to California 139. Allow an extra day if you want to make this side trip.

Northbound from Klamath Falls (locally called K-Falls) the road parallels Upper Klamath Lake for miles. Just past the lake, about 22 miles from town, is a turnoff on Oregon 62, which leads to Crater Lake National Park. This would be another 1-day side trip well worth taking; Crater Lake is little more than an hour's drive from Klamath Falls.

Insider's Tip: If you visit Crater Lake, be sure to take the 2-hour boat trip around the inside of the caldera. This is literally a ride through the inside of an ancient volcano, and it is thrilling. Getting to the boats requires a 1.1-mile hike down the inside wall of the caldera at Cleetwood Cove. The hike out is rather heavy exercise, but most who dare find the experience worth the effort.

Back on U.S. 97, you travel through the east (dry) side of the Cascade Mountains. Approaching Bend, the Three Sisters are to your left and Mount Jefferson is somewhat farther north. The forests along the road are semi-arid stands of ponderosa and lodgepole pines and other conifers. Open areas are mostly sagebrush.

North of Bend, the road runs through mostly open country with cattle ranches and sagebrush being the predominant features. Little more than halfway between Bend and the Columbia River is Shaniko, more or less a ghost town these days and worth an hour or two of exploration. Talk to the few people who remain to gain a sense of the history behind the abandoned or little-used buildings. If it's open, sit down for a family-style meal in the hotel.

U.S. 97 crosses the Columbia River into Washington at Biggs, then runs north for about 60 miles to Toppenish. From just beyond Toppenish to a few miles past Ellensburg, U.S. 97 combines with I-82, a pleasant drive past Yakima and through the Yakima River Valley. Past Ellensburg, I-82 becomes I-90, the major route leading west to Seattle from central Washington. Just after the starting on I-90, U.S. 97 turns off northbound, winding into the

Wenatchee National Forest. After several hundred miles of driving in the high deserts of eastern Oregon and Washington, it's nice to see trees again.

About 55 miles after you turn off of I-90, U.S. 97 combines with U.S. 2 and jogs southeast to Wenatchee. The routes separate in Wenatchee, with U.S. 97 following the Columbia River. Little less than 40 miles north of Wenatchee is the community of Chelan at the southern edge of Lake Chelan, a long, narrow reservoir leading northwest toward the Lake Chelan National Recreation Area, which adjoins North Cascades National Park.

Insider's Tip: A ferry runs the length of Lake Chelan to the tiny community of Stehekin on the north end of the reservoir. Visiting Stehekin is a real treat; there are very few communities left in the contiguous 48 states that are unreachable by road. The ferry ride itself, through the narrow gorge filled by the lake, is inspiring as well.

From Chelan, U.S. 97 continues to the Canadian border just north of Oroville, Washington. En route to the border, at Okanogan, Washington 20 leads west to North Cascades National Park. Allow an extra day if you want to take time to drive through this park.

After entering Canada, B.C. 97 swings through the Okanogan Valley. This valley is Canada's fruit basket, and travelers in late July and August will find dozens of roadside stands offering the freshest of the year's crop. Besides the fruit, there are vegetables, but it's the fruit that commands the greatest attention.

This is a very scenic stretch of road, winding for miles along the shores of Okanogan Lake, even crossing the lake at one point. There are occasional stretches of four-lane highway as well.

Insider's Tip: Travelers considering a routing through the Okanogan Valley should schedule their trips for July and August when the year's crop of fruit is most abundant. It would almost be a shame to travel this stretch in June before the fruit ripens for harvest.

North of Vernon on the eastern side of the lake, drivers have two options—continuing on B.C. 97, which turns west for Kamloops, or first driving north to Salmon Arm, then turning west on Canada 1, which also leads to Kamloops. Both routes offer similar scenery and they join together just a few miles before entering Kamloops.

At Kamloops, turn north on B.C. 5. It's about a 5-hour drive to Tête Jaune Cache. The closer you get to Tête Jaune Cache, the better the scenery. The mountains of, first, Banff, then Jasper national parks lie to the east and every mile brings you closer to these magnificent wilderness parks.

Those wishing to visit either park will have to turn east at Tête Jaune Cache on B.C. 16, also known as the Yellowhead Highway. An optional route would be to start on Canada 1 at Salmon Arm and drive east to Banff National Park. In the park, turn north on Alberta 93 and follow it to Jasper, where it intercepts Alberta 16. Turn left to Tête Jaune Cache. Canada lists all of the above-described roads in and around these parks as "Scenic Routes." There's plenty of justification for these designations.

From Tête Jaune Cache, follow the Yellowhead Highway (B.C. 16) to Prince George, where it intersects B.C. 97, which leads north to Dawson Creek. Prince George is a fairly large town, timber being a primary industry. From here north, the alternate route joins the final leg of the primary route recommended for travelers from the West Coast. Dawson Creek is about 250 miles north of Prince George.

Section 2

Rocky Mountains/Western Plains

Sample Itinerary

Denver, Colorado, to Dawson Creek, British Columbia

Primary Route

TIME REQUIRED: 4 days (no side trips)

MILEAGE: 1,800 miles (3,000 kilometers)

OVERNIGHT STOPS:
    Spearfish, South Dakota
    Regina, Saskatchewan
    Edmonton, Alberta
    Dawson Creek, British Columbia

POSSIBLE SIDE TRIPS EN ROUTE
    (and minimum additional time required):
    Badlands National Park, South Dakota (1 day)
    Mt. Rushmore National Memorial, South Dakota (1 day)
    Jasper National Park, Alberta (1 day)
    Banff National Park, Alberta (1 day)

ROUTING:
  Denver to Spearfish:
      I-25, Denver to Cheyenne, Wyoming
      U.S. 85, Cheyenne to Spearfish
  Spearfish to Regina:
      U.S. 85, Spearfish to U.S.–Canada border
      Saskatchewan 35, border to Weyburn, Saskatchewan
      Saskatchewan 39, Weyburn to Corinne
      Saskatchewan 6, Corinne to Regina
  Regina to Edmonton:
      Saskatchewan 11, Regina to Saskatoon, Saskatchewan
      Saskatchewan 16, Saskatoon to Edmonton
  Edmonton to Dawson Creek:
      Alberta 16, Edmonton to Wabamun, Alberta
      Alberta 43, Wabamun to Valleyview, Alberta
      Alberta 34, Valleyview to Grande Prairie, Alberta
      Alberta/B.C. 2, Grande Prairie to Dawson Creek

Alternate Route

TIME REQUIRED: 5 days (no side trips)

MILEAGE: 1,850 miles (3,100 kilometers)

OVERNIGHT STOPS:
  Buffalo, Wyoming
  Great Falls, Montana
  Calgary, Alberta
  Prince George, British Columbia
  Dawson Creek, British Columbia

POSSIBLE SIDE TRIPS EN ROUTE
      (and minimal additional time required):
  Yellowstone/Grand Teton national parks (2 days)
  Custer Battlefields (1 day)
  Glacier National Park (1 day)
  Calgary Stampede (1 day; allow 1–10 days in mid-July)

ROUTING:
  Denver to Buffalo: I-25
  Buffalo to Great Falls:
      I-90, Buffalo to Billings, Montana
      U.S. 87, Billings to Great Falls
  Great Falls to Calgary:
      I-15, Great Falls to U.S.–Canada border
      Alberta 4, border to Lethbridge, Alberta
      Alberta 3, Lethbridge to Fort Macleod, Alberta
      Alberta 2, Fort Macleod to Calgary
  Calgary to Prince George:
      Canada 1, Calgary to Lake Louise, Alberta
      Alberta 93, Lake Louise to Jasper, Alberta
      Alberta/B.C. 16, Jasper to Prince George
  Prince George to Dawson Creek: B.C. 97

Rocky Mountains/Western Plains
—Primary Routing

This route parallels the Rocky Mountains to the west until reaching Cheyenne, Wyoming. Heading more or less straight north from Cheyenne, the mountains recede to westward and travelers cross the western edge of the great plains. To some, driving the plains is boring; to others, however, it inspires awe. The endless horizons seem to extend forever.

Leaving Denver on I-25, the trip is routine freeway driving. Maneuvering around Cheyenne is not at all tricky; it seems almost too simple if you're used to the maze of on- and off-ramps that characterize freeway driving in and around large cities. Cheyenne, even though it's Wyoming's largest city, just isn't all that large—about 50,000 people live there.

North of Cheyenne, on U.S. 85, the road wends its way through mostly open country. As you approach the South Dakota border—the road actually parallels it for about 90 miles before crossing—the Black Hills are to the east. The most famous attraction within these hills is Mount Rushmore, where likenesses of four U.S. presidents have been carved out of a rocky hillside. Travelers desiring to visit Mount Rushmore should turn east on U.S. 16 before crossing the South Dakota border.

Insider's Tip: Combining Mount Rushmore and Badlands National Park makes for a superb 2-day excursion in southwestern South Dakota. Lush forests and dense crowds greet visitors to Rushmore in summer. Sixty miles to the east, a desolate, lunar-like landscape and relatively few people await visitors to the Badlands. The contrast is compelling.

Those who choose not to visit the Badlands or Rushmore will continue north on U.S. 85 to Spearfish, if they wish to keep to this proposed itinerary. Spearfish is fairly small and facilities are available, though limited. Should all options be closed for overnighting, continue north for another 10 miles to Belle Fourche. Away from the freeway (U.S. 85 crosses I-90 at Spearfish) there should be less demand for available accommodations.

Continuing north, U.S. 85 passes some of the last expanses of natural grasslands left on the great plains. Shortly after crossing into North Dakota, the Little Missouri National Grasslands are on the west side of the road for 100 miles or more.

The only North Dakota town of any size encountered on U.S. 85 is Williston, about 70 miles south of the Canadian border. Williston rests on the northwest corner of Lake Sakajawea, a monstrous reservoir created by damming the Missouri River at Pick City, more than 110 miles to the southeast.

From Williston, the road runs straight north almost 60 miles, with hardly a curve to be found. Then there's a slight westward jog to tiny Fortuna, then north again for 5 miles or so to the U.S.–Canada border. In Canada, the road becomes Saskatchewan 35.

Saskatchewan is Canada's premier prairie province—miles and miles of endless horizons and seemingly boundless wheat fields stretching as far as the eye can see. Roads, too, stretch straight into the horizon and beyond—not much need for curves in this part of the world.

Jog northwest for 45 miles at Weyburn on Saskatchewan 39, then due north again on Saskatchewan 6 for 24 miles into Regina, Saskatchewan's capital and largest city. Travelers' services are plentiful here, and you should have little trouble finding a place to overnight.

Head northwest from Regina on Saskatchewan 11, a multilane highway for the entire 152 miles to Saskatoon. At Saskatoon turn west on Saskatchewan 16 (also known as the Yellowhead Highway). Saskatchewan 16 leads generally northwest to North Battleford and Lloydminster, the latter where you cross Saskatchewan's western boundary into Alberta. Change your watches from Central time to Mountain time at Saskatoon.

From Lloydminster it's about 150 miles into Edmonton, Alberta's capital. Full facilities are available for travelers.

Insider's Tip: Edmonton is home to the largest shopping mall in the world. Dedicated shoppers will find hundreds of stores, restaurants and theaters all under a single roof.

From Edmonton, continue west on Alberta 16 for 31 miles to Wabamun. At Wabamun turn north on Alberta 43, a road stretching along about 185 miles of pretty lonely country to Valleyview. Be on the lookout for waterfowl in the ponds, creeks and rivers at roadside. Alberta's waterways are the breeding ground for great numbers of waterfowl each summer. Drought conditions in the late 1980s have lessened their numbers, but travelers can still spot thousands upon thousands of ducks if they take the time to look.

At Valleyview, really just a road junction, turn left on Alberta 34 to Grande Prairie. As the name implies, this is flat, or at best slightly rolling country with vast fields under cultivation. Alberta 34 intersects Alberta 2 four miles north of Grande Prairie. Alberta 2, later B.C. 2, will take you the rest of the way into Dawson Creek, the start of the Alaska Highway.

Rocky Mountains/Western Plains
—Alternate Routing

In the opinion of many, this routing offers perhaps the grandest scenery of any route leading to Dawson Creek, British Columbia. Travelers follow the Rocky Mountains from Denver deep into Canada. Many of the western hemisphere's premier national parks are either right on the road or just a short side trip away from the route.

From Denver, head north on I-25. In Cheyenne, stay on I-25 through Casper and on to Buffalo, Wyoming. For those wanting to take a side trip to Yellowstone and Grand Teton national parks, access routes lead west from Casper (U.S. 26), Buffalo (U.S. 16) and from just north of Sheridan (U.S. 14). The latter offers probably the most spectacular scenery.

In Buffalo, I-25 ends and travelers take I-90 north out of town. I-90, as a limited-access freeway, ends north of Sheridan. From there it is still called I-90, even though it doesn't become a multilane road again for nearly 60 miles. I-90 crosses the Wyoming-Montana border about 15 miles after the four-lane highway ends.

About the time I-90 becomes a freeway again, the Custer battlefields are just east of the highway. A lot of research has been done in recent years on these battlefields, and the Park Service historians on duty are able to tell a fascinating story about what actually happened to Custer and his men at the battle of the Little Bighorn. It's well worth a stop.

Also, once in Montana, the lands on both sides of the road are part of the Crow Indian Reservation. Indian reservations are private property. Make certain you have permission before you go exploring the lands at roadside.

Stay on I-90 to Billings, Montana. There, turn north on U.S. 87, which gradually makes its way northwest to Great Falls. This is part of Montana's fabled "Big Sky Country." Vast horizons seemingly go on forever in all directions. Early mornings, before the heat-induced haze of afternoon sets in, are the best times to appreciate this incredible landscape.

At Great Falls, it's back on the interstate again, I-15 this time. I-15 ends at the Canadian border, little more than 100 miles from Great Falls.

In Canada, the road becomes Alberta 4. Stay on it to Lethbridge. From there, Alberta 3 leads west to Fort Macleod. There, turn north on Alberta 2 to Calgary.

Insider's Tip: For 10 days in mid-July, Calgary stages the Calgary Stampede, probably North America's finest rodeo/western party. It's well worth a few days to take part in the fun.

And, if you thought the mountain scenery so far was something special, wait until you depart Calgary on Canada 1, then turn north on Alberta 93. This road follows the Continental Divide north through first Banff and then Jasper national parks. It is a stunning drive to Jasper, then west across the Continental Divide to Tête Jaune Cache on B.C. 16, thence to Prince George, British Columbia. This spectacular scenery defies description.

At Prince George, turn north on British Columbia 97 and follow this road to Dawson Creek, as described in Section 1 of this chapter.

<hr>

Section 3

Midwest

Sample Itinerary

Chicago, Illinois, to
Dawson Creek, British Columbia

Primary Route
TIME REQUIRED: 5 days (no side trips)

MILEAGE: 2,050 miles (3,400 kilometers)

OVERNIGHT STOPS:
Minneapolis, Minnesota
Winnipeg, Manitoba
Saskatoon, Saskatchewan
Edmonton, Alberta
Dawson Creek, British Columbia

POSSIBLE SIDE TRIPS EN ROUTE
(and minimum additional time required):
Voyagers National Park, Minnesota (2-3 days)
Banff, Jasper national parks, Alberta (2 days)

ROUTING:
Chicago to Minneapolis:
I-90, Chicago to Tomah, Wisconsin
I-94, Tomah to Minneapolis
Minneapolis to Winnipeg:
I-94, Minneapolis to Fargo, North Dakota
I-29, Fargo to U.S.–Canada border
Manitoba 75, border to Winnipeg
Winnipeg to Saskatoon:
Canada 1, Winnipeg to Regina, Saskatchewan

Saskatchewan 11, Regina to Saskatoon
Saskatoon to Edmonton: Saskatchewan/Alberta 16
Edmonton to Dawson Creek:
    Alberta 16, Edmonton to Wabamun, Alberta
    Alberta 43, Wabamun to Valleyview, Alberta
    Alberta 34, Valleyview to Grande Prairie, Alberta
    Alberta/B.C. 2, Grande Prairie to Dawson Creek

Alternate Route

TIME REQUIRED: 6 days (no side trips)

MILEAGE: 2,600 miles (4,350 kilometers)

OVERNIGHT STOPS:
    Sioux Falls, South Dakota
    Buffalo, Wyoming
    Great Falls, Montana
    Calgary, Alberta
    Prince George, British Columbia
    Dawson Creek, British Columbia

POSSIBLE SIDE TRIPS EN ROUTE
    (and minimum additional time required):
    Badlands National Park, South Dakota (1 day)
    Mount Rushmore National Memorial, South Dakota (1 day)
    Yellowstone National Park, Wyoming (1 day)
    Glacier National Park, Montana (1 day)

ROUTING:
    Chicago to Sioux Falls: I-90
    Sioux Falls to Buffalo: I-90
    Buffalo to Great Falls:
        I-90, Buffalo to Billings, Montana
        U.S. 87, Billings to Great Falls
    Great Falls to Calgary:
        I-15, Great Falls to U.S.–Canada border
        Alberta 4, border to Lethbridge, Alberta
        Alberta 3, Lethbridge to Fort Macleod, Alberta
        Alberta 2, Fort Macleod to Calgary
    Calgary to Prince George:
        Canada 1, Calgary to Banff, Alberta
        Alberta 93, Banff to Jasper, Alberta
        Alberta/B.C. 16, Jasper to Prince George
    Prince George to Dawson Creek: B.C. 97

Midwest—Primary Routing

Probably no greater contrast exists for scenery on any route leading to Dawson Creek than starting in the corn and soy bean fields near Chicago and winding up in the north woods in Canada.

Leaving Chicago on I-90, drivers pass through low, rolling terrain—mostly farmers' fields interspersed with wooded creek bottoms—in northern Illinois, Wisconsin and on into Minnesota. This is good, easy driving, all on interstate highways. Stay on I-90 to Tomah, Wisconsin, then change to I-94 for Minneapolis.

As you approach Minneapolis, and later drive through Minnesota, cultivated fields give way more and more to forests, though small rural towns continue to dot the landscape. Travelers wishing to add Voyagers National Park to their itineraries will turn off I-94 in Minneapolis and head north on I-35. Voyagers, a relatively new national park, celebrates the legacy of the Canadian *voyageurs* who first explored south-central Canada and the north-central states more than 200 years ago.

Insider's Tip: Voyagers National Park is primarily water, a chain of lakes on the U.S.–Canada border in northern Minnesota. Absolutely the best way to experience it is to rent a houseboat from one of the concessionaires near the park and spend several days lazily motoring from one anchorage to another. The fishing's good, and the scenery wonderful, especially in the fall when the leaves turn.

For those not visiting Voyagers National Park, continue out of Minneapolis on I-94 to Fargo, North Dakota. At Fargo, turn north on I-29. I-29 follows the eastern edge of North Dakota to the U.S.–Canada border. From the border, Manitoba 75 leads north to Winnipeg, the capital and largest city in the province. North of Winnipeg are some of the largest freshwater lakes in North America: Lake Winnipeg, more than 250 miles long; Lake Manitoba, 120 miles long; and Lake Winnipegosis, about 150 miles long. Beaches and boat-launching facilities are available, particularly on Lake Winnipeg about 35 miles north of the city.

From Winnipeg, head west on Canada 1 to Regina, Saskatchewan. Much of this route is multilane highway, and it's a comfortable drive. Saskatchewan is considered one of Canada's prairie provinces, and as you head westward, more and more wheat fields decorate the landscape.

At Regina, turn northwest on Saskatchewan 11, another multilane highway leading to Saskatoon. In Saskatoon, those who wish to detour through Banff and Jasper national parks should turn west on Saskatchewan 7, which becomes Alberta 9 at the Saskatchewan-Alberta border.

Alberta 9 continues to Calgary; from there follow Canada 1, then Alberta 93 to Banff and Jasper national parks. Routing through the parks and on into Dawson Creek is described in Section 2 of this chapter.

From Saskatoon, Saskatchewan/Alberta 16 leads on to Edmonton, Alberta. Routing from Edmonton to Dawson Creek has already been described in Section 2 of this chapter.

Midwest—Alternate Routing

Two obvious choices confront travelers going west from Chicago before heading north: Interstate 80 and Interstate 90. I-90 is actually a little shorter and offers a few extras along the way.

As before, leave Chicago on I-90. Instead of turning off on I-94 at Tomah, Wisconsin, continue west on I-90 to Sioux Falls, South Dakota's largest city. Plenty of travelers' services are available here.

Interstate-90 continues almost straight across South Dakota to the Wyoming border. However, before entering Wyoming, both Badlands National Park and Mount Rushmore National Memorial are just to the south of the freeway. Spending the night in or near Badlands allows travelers to drive through the park, then through Rushmore, all in a single day. Both sites are worth the time to visit.

Insider's Tip: Badlands National Park is essentially a desert. It can be exceedingly hot, with little shade to provide relief from the sun. Carry plenty of water.

From the region around Badlands and Rushmore, continue west to Buffalo, Wyoming. From here the route north to Dawson Creek is the same as that given for the alternate routing under the Rocky Mountains/Western Plains section.

======= Section 4 =======

East Coast

Sample Itinerary

New York City, New York, to Dawson Creek, British Columbia

Primary Route

TIME REQUIRED: 7 days (no side trips)

MILEAGE: 2,900 miles (4,850 kilometers)

OVERNIGHT STOPS:
  Ottawa, Ontario
  Sault Ste. Marie, Ontario
  Thunder Bay, Ontario
  Winnipeg, Manitoba
  Saskatoon, Saskatchewan
  Edmonton, Alberta
  Dawson Creek, British Columbia

POSSIBLE SIDE TRIPS EN ROUTE
  (and minimum additional time required):
  Michigan's Upper Peninsula (2 days)
  Isle Royale National Park, Lake Superior (1 day)
  Banff, Jasper national parks, Alberta (2 days)

ROUTING:
  New York City to Ottawa:
    I-87, New York City to U.S.–Canada border
    I-15 (Canada), border to Montreal
    I-40 (Canada), Montreal to Ottawa
  Ottawa to Sault Ste. Marie: Quebec 17 (Canada 1)
  Sault Ste. Marie to Thunder Bay: Quebec 17
  Thunder Bay to Winnipeg:
    Quebec 17, Thunder Bay to Manitoba border
    Canada 1, border to Winnipeg
  Winnipeg to Saskatoon:
    Canada 1, Winnipeg to Regina, Saskatchewan
    Saskatchewan 11, Regina to Saskatoon
  Saskatoon to Edmonton: Saskatchewan/Alberta 16
  Edmonton to Dawson Creek:
    Alberta 16, Edmonton to Wabamun, Alberta
    Alberta 43, Wabamun to Valleyview, Alberta
    Alberta 34, Valleyview to Grande Prairie, Alberta
    Alberta/B.C. 2, Grande Prairie to Dawson Creek

Alternate Route

TIME REQUIRED: 8 days (no side trips)

MILEAGE: 3,400 miles (5,650 kilometers)

OVERNIGHT STOPS:
Akron, Ohio
Chicago, Illinois
Sioux Falls, South Dakota
Buffalo, Wyoming
Great Falls, Montana
Calgary, Alberta
Prince George, British Columbia
Dawson Creek, British Columbia

POSSIBLE SIDE TRIPS EN ROUTE
(with minimum additional time required):
Badlands National Park, South Dakota (1 day)
Mount Rushmore National Memorial, South Dakota (1 day)
Yellowstone National Park, Wyoming (1 day)
Glacier National Park, Montana (1 day)

ROUTING:
New York City to Akron: I-80
Akron to Chicago: I-80
Chicago to Sioux Falls: I-90
Sioux Falls to Buffalo: I-90
Buffalo to Great Falls:
I-90, Buffalo to Billings, Montana
U.S. 87, Billings to Great Falls
Great Falls to Calgary:
I-15, Great Falls to U.S.–Canada border
Alberta 4, border to Lethbridge, Alberta
Alberta 3, Lethbridge to Fort Macleod, Alberta
Alberta 2, Fort Macleod to Calgary
Calgary to Prince George:
Canada 1, Calgary to Banff, Alberta
Alberta 93, Banff to Jasper, Alberta
Alberta/B.C. 16, Jasper to Prince George
Prince George to Dawson Creek: B.C. 97

East Coast—Primary Routing

Obviously, when starting from the East Coast, travelers have a lengthy trek just getting to the start of the Alaska Highway at Dawson Creek. But, by using this primary route, there's a much greater opportunity to sample Canada's generous hospitality.

Northbound from New York City, I-87 gets you on your way in a hurry. Within a few hours you'll be driving past the Adirondacks, with Lake

Champlain to your right. The biggest plus, as you get farther north in New York, is that you'll leave behind the congestion and big-city hustle and bustle. For the next several weeks on your way to and from Alaska, the driving should be much more relaxed, with a couple of obvious exceptions, like driving through Montreal.

Crossing into Canada just north of Champlain, New York, I-87 becomes Canada's I-15, which takes you on into Montreal. In Montreal you'll have to do some big-city freeway maneuvering until you exit the west side of town on I-40. Stay on I-40 through Ottawa until it ends in about 15 miles. From there take Ontario 17 westward to Sault Ste. Marie, which sits just across a narrow neck of water from Sault Ste. Marie, Michigan. This waterway, with locks for Great Lakes shipping, joins Lake Superior to Lake Huron. Those wishing to spend a few hours or a few days exploring Michigan's remote Upper Peninsula would cross back into the United States on the bridge at Sault Ste. Marie.

Continuing on Ontario 17, the road skirts the north shore of Lake Superior for several hundred miles to Thunder Bay. At Thunder Bay, you can arrange a visit to Isle Royale National Park by detouring south on Ontario 61 to Grand Portage, Minnesota. Boat service to Isle Royale is available from Grand Portage.

Insider's Tip: Isle Royale offers the first real taste of northern wilderness for those who want to devote a day or two to exploring. More or less in its natural state, Isle Royale has offered a relatively undisturbed laboratory for biologists to study the interaction between wolves and moose. It was here that L. David Mech developed much of his information leading to the balance of nature theory back in the late 1950s and early 1960s.

Leaving Thunder Bay, continue westbound on Ontario 17. At Kenora, about 20 miles from the Manitoba border, the road crosses a narrow arm of Lake of the Woods, a large lake partly in Ontario and partly in Minnesota. Fishermen won't have to try real hard to find excuses to hang around this lake for a few days.

Once in Manitoba, Ontario 17 officially becomes Canada 1, the trans-Canada Highway. Though it might not be flagged as Canada 1 east of Manitoba, Ontario 17 is actually the eastern extension of the highway.

From the Manitoba border, it's about 60 miles to Winnipeg. From Winnipeg, continue west and north as outlined in Section 3 of this chapter.

East Coast—Alternate Routing

This routing offers travelers the option of taking part of the most-traveled east-west route in the United States, Interstate 80, which stretches from New York City to San Francisco.

Basically, all you do is drive west out of New York City on I-80, and stay on that highway until you reach Chicago, some 800 miles away. Assuming you actually start in the city, you'll cross northern New Jersey, central Pennsylvania, northern Ohio and northern Indiana. When you leave Indiana, you enter Chicago.

Most of I-80 is a toll road in Ohio and Indiana. Also, the same road is both I-80 and I-90 in those two states. After coming together in Cleveland, the two interstates don't divide again until Chicago.

Cities along the route include Cleveland, Toledo, South Bend and Gary. All figure prominently in industry around the Great Lakes. With the exception of South Bend, all these inland cities have ports for ocean-going ships, which reach the Great Lakes via the St. Lawrence Seaway.

In Chicago, you have the option of taking either of the routes described in Section 3 of this chapter. The primary (shortest) route described in Section 3 was used to compute the mileage listed for this alternate routing from New York City to Dawson Creek.

Mile post "0" of the Alaska Highway, downtown Dawson Creek, British Columbia.

NORTH TO ALASKA

Getting to Dawson Creek, British Columbia is, of itself, more adventure than many drivers experience in a lifetime. However, driving north to Alaska on the Alaska Highway, which begins in Dawson Creek, is the expedition that lures people this far in the first place. Here begins the last great driving adventure remaining in North America.

This chapter is laid out in five sections, each section representing a comfortable day's drive of about 300 miles. All told, it's slightly more than 1,500 miles from Dawson Creek to Fairbanks, Alaska. Each section will open with pertinent driving information, condensed for ready reference. On each of these information pages is a blank for you to write in your starting mileage—to aid you in keeping track of distances driven and distances remaining to go. Distances given for services are in miles (with kilometers in parentheses) from the departure point for that section of the trip.

Along the route, kilometer posts are placed at 5-kilometer intervals. The zero point for the kilometer posts is downtown Dawson Creek. These continue all the way to the Alaska-Yukon border. Some of these get knocked down every year, so don't be distressed if some seem to be missing.

Campground note: Public campgrounds are run by government agencies and have few amenities available beyond gravel parking sites and (sometimes) grassy spots for tents along with picnic tables and outhouses. Private campgrounds usually offer some hookups for RVs as well as dump stations, showers and laundromats. Public campgrounds will cost about $6 to $8 per night; private, from $10 to $20. Public campgrounds are usually in more scenic/wilderness locations. In these listings, state, national, provincial park or territorial campgrounds denote public campgrounds managed by government agencies. All others are privately owned campgrounds.

Dawson Creek, B.C., to Fort Nelson, B.C.

STARTING MILEAGE:_____

MILEAGE: 283 miles (472 km)

DRIVING TIME: About 6 hours

TOWNS EN ROUTE (all offering most travelers' services): **Taylor**, 35 miles (56 km); **Fort St. John**, 47 miles (76 km); **Charlie Lake**, 51 miles (81 km); **Wonowon**, 101 miles (162 km); **Pink Mountain**, 141 miles (226 km); **Sikanni Chief**, 159 miles (257 km); **Prophet River**, 227 miles (366 km); **Muskwa Heights**, 278 miles (451 km); **Fort Nelson**, 283 miles (472 km)

GAS AVAILABLE (besides towns listed above): **Highway 29 Junction**, 54 miles (86 km); **Shepherd's Inn**, 72 miles (115 km); **Danny's Sportsman Inn**, 143 miles (238 km)

CAMPGROUNDS (provincial parks are public campgrounds; most towns listed above have private campgrounds as well): **Kiskatinaw Provincial Park**, 17 miles (28 km); **Alaska Highway Campgrounds and RV Park**, 17 miles (28 km); **Taylor Landing Provincial Park**, 34 miles (55 km); **Beatton Provincial Park**, 50 miles (80 km); **Ron's Tent and Trailer Park**, 51 miles (82 km); **Shepherd's Inn**, 72 miles (115 km); **Pine Hill Motels**, 102 miles (163 km); **Danny's Sportsman Inn**, 143 miles (238 km); **Buckinghorse River Provincial Park**, 173 miles (279 km); **Prophet River Provincial Park**, 266 miles (431 km); **Andy Bailey Lake Provincial Park**, 266 miles (431 km)

LODGING (besides these, all towns listed above, except Muskwa Heights, offer overnight lodging): **Shepherd's Inn**, 72 miles (115 km); **Pine Hill Motels**, 102 miles (163 km); **Danny's Sportsman Inn**, 143 miles (238 km)

MAJOR TERRAIN FEATURES: Mostly low, rolling hills along this stretch; farmland gradually gives way to forests; major rivers crossed: Peace and Sikanni

WILDLIFE: Black bears, white-tailed deer, moose, raptors

FISHING: Northern pike, whitefish, walleye, grayling, perch, occasionally rainbow trout

================= Section 1 =================

Dawson Creek, B.C., to
Fort Nelson, B.C.

With about 65,000 people in the immediate area, Dawson Creek is the last town of this size until you reach Fairbanks, which has a similar areawide population. The Fort St. John area, less than 50 miles away on the Alaska Highway, is about 80 percent the size of Dawson Creek and its environs, but after that, only Whitehorse, Yukon, offers an area population of any size—about 18,000 people. In other words, you'll pass the homes of more people in the first 50 miles of the Alaska Highway than you will on the entire 1,475 miles from Fort St. John to Fairbanks.

During the summer, Dawson Creek just hums with activity. Obviously, it's the gathering point for the 100,000 or more vehicles headed to Alaska each year. Also, there is considerable farming, oil and natural gas production and lumbering in the immediate area.

Insider's Tip: Those driving live-aboard RVs should fill their propane tanks in Dawson Creek. Sitting on top of some of the largest natural gas fields in North America, Dawson Creek's propane is unbelievably cheap, just a few cents per liter.

Approaching Dawson Creek from the south on British Columbia 97 as most travelers do, all you need do is turn left at the stop sign. You cannot continue straight ahead except into a gas station. Turning right will lead to the downtown area and the monument marking Mile 0 of the Alaska Highway. The Alaska Highway is actually British Columbia 97 all the way to Watson Lake, Yukon, where it becomes Yukon 1. Numeric signs for 97 and printed signs for the Alaska Highway—both mean the same thing—will guide you north throughout the rest of British Columbia.

Those desiring to spend the night in Dawson Creek should plan to arrive fairly early in the day. Campgrounds and hotels both fill quickly within or near the city. An average of 1,000 vehicles daily pass through Dawson Creek en route to Alaska or other destinations along the Alaska Highway during the summer months. Just as many pass through on return trips. Things will tend to spread out a bit as you get farther down the road, but at Dawson Creek, everybody tends to gather at least once.

Look closely at the other northbound vehicles in the campgrounds in Dawson Creek or at the hotels. Odds are quite good that you'll see these people again and again on your way north. A pleasant afternoon and evening in Dawson Creek is a good time to make acquaintances that can often turn into long-lasting friendships. The very fact that most visitors in Dawson Creek have the same goal strongly suggests shared interests. Many travelers, in fact, team up with new-found friends to make the drive north together.

Heading northwest out of town, things at first don't seem much different from the several hundred miles of Canada you drove through prior to reaching Dawson Creek. If anything, it might seem slightly more crowded. That's because the part of British Columbia between Dawson Creek and Fort St. John is the population center in the northern part of the province. Traffic will be relatively heavy except late at night or very early in the morning.

Traveling either very late or very early is not without advantages. This far north, days are very long. Sunsets are late—10 P.M. or later—during the summer, and sunrise is early—like 3:30 A.M., so available daylight is rarely a factor. And you'll markedly increase your odds of seeing wildlife if you drive the roads at these times. The major liability would be for those traveling late at night; you may have to hunt for a campground or hotel with lodging space. Those traveling early in the day can stop in midafternoon when space is available almost everywhere.

The major terrain feature in the first hour's driving out of Dawson Creek is the Peace River, one of the largest and most impressive waterways in the Canadian North. The wild country of British Columbia and Alberta drained by this stream is often known as the Peace River Country. You'll cross the river about 35 miles out of Dawson Creek. The river offers clear water with plentiful populations of northern pike, rainbows and grayling. Campers who want to sample the fishing should stop at Taylor Landing Provincial Park, right on the banks of the river. A boat-launching ramp is available.

Insider's Tip: Boaters on the Peace River should use caution. Water-level fluctuations are common as dams upstream of the park are used to adjust water flow on an almost-daily basis.

About 12 miles beyond the Peace River Bridge is Fort St. John, the last town of significant size prior to reaching Fort Nelson, 235 miles farther on. Fort St. John also offers reasonable prices for motor fuel and for propane, though both will be priced slightly higher here than in Dawson Creek. A wide range of hotels/motels, campgrounds and restaurants are available in Fort St. John.

Insider's Tip: If at all possible, plan your refueling stops for the larger towns along the Alaska Highway. Almost without exception, gasoline will be cheaper in the larger communities than at small roadside businesses well away from populated areas.

These days, probably the real adventure of the Alaska Highway begins after you pass Fort St. John. Up to Fort St. John, facilities have kept pace with growing populations over the last several decades. Travelers don't really begin to touch the Alaska Highway wilderness until they pass Fort St. John. To many longtime Alaska Highway travelers, the real wilderness adventure doesn't even start until you're past Fort Nelson, the second day of this suggested itinerary. However, there are many unspoiled vistas and beautiful spots between Fort St. John and Fort Nelson.

In and around Dawson Creek and the first 50 miles or so of the Alaska Highway, visitors in late July will see expansive acreages of brilliant yellow flowers in cultivated fields. This is canola, also known as rape seed, used in the production of a vegetable oil. The other common crop is hay.

Besides the visual impact of farmers' fields, the odor of natural gas will often be present in the early miles of the Alaska Highway. This doesn't mean you have a leak in your propane system. Several natural gas refining plants are scattered along the road system, and the smell can carry quite a distance. Fort St. John, for instance, almost owes its existence to the large number of natural gas facilities in or near the town.

By the time you've gone a hundred miles or so, the farms pretty much give way to forests, mostly small spruce and birch. No really big trees are evident from the road, but the forests of small trees can be quite dense. This pattern will repeat itself often as you go north. Larger trees are generally found only in coastal parts of Alaska and British Columbia or deep in protected stream valleys.

Insider's Tip: When making a fire in camp, take a moment and try to count the growth rings in a small log cut up for your campfire. Though these trees are very small in diameter, they are often very, very old. Rings will be so closely spaced in some trees that they are often impossible to count without a magnifying glass. Growing seasons are short in the North Country, thus each annual ring is very thin. The farther north you go, the thinner the growth rings on trees.

Unless you're up very early in the morning when deer might be moving about, the wildlife you're most likely to see in the farming areas are raptors (birds of prey), including eagles, hawks and, with luck, a falcon or two.

Once you move into forested areas, black bears are much more numerous, though generally shy and retiring. Often the best place to see a bear is at the local landfill. Campgrounds may have bears about as well, particularly bears with a taste for raiding garbage cans. Away from refuse disposal sites, peer intently from your vehicle into the underbrush along creek bottoms; you might be rewarded with a glimpse of a black bear. Don't expect these bears to deliberately make themselves visible in open areas. Tracks in the soft mud of stream banks are often the only visible sign that black bears are in the area.

Your chances of seeing moose will increase after you leave the farming areas behind. Very early or very late in the day are the best times to see moose. Look closely in areas with good browse—low-growing alders and other bushes. Moose tend to stay close to areas offering plenty of food.

Insider's Tip: Lines of stopped cars at roadside are often a good indication that there is wildlife around. In the North these are variously known as bear jams or moose jams, depending on the animal being observed.

Northbound from Fort St. John, history buffs will want to watch for the Sikanni River about 110 miles farther on. One of the few original bridges from the Alaska Highway still stands across this river, although it is no longer in use. It can be seen to your left as you cross the river on the current bridge. Just across the bridge you can stop at Sikanni Chief and ask permission to walk down to their riverfront property for a better look at the bridge. This is private property, so be certain to obtain permission from the people in the store before driving or walking down to the riverbank.

If you don't have enough gas to go the remaining 130 miles to Fort Nelson, fill up at Sikanni Chief. Their prices are fair, considering how far away the gas comes from. The same can't be said for the only other gas station between Sikanni Chief and Fort Nelson.

That other gas station is 65 miles farther on at Prophet River. In 1989, gas there was priced at 69.9 cents per liter (about $2.20 U.S. currency for a U.S. gallon), absolutely the highest price I paid for gas in 6,000 miles of North Country driving while preparing this book. Certainly this operator has a right to charge whatever he likes for fuel, but he seems to be taking advantage of his location as the only gas station between Sikanni Chief and Fort Nelson.

If you must stop at Prophet River for gas, buy just enough to get your vehicle to Fort Nelson, where gas costs about 12 cents less per liter. It's about 60 miles from Prophet River to the next gas station on the outskirts of Fort Nelson.

A pleasant part of Prophet River is the provincial park of the same name. Follow the signs and turn left off the highway, then drive about half a mile on a gravel road. This access road crosses the original Alaska Highway (no longer in use, but still visible) and an airstrip. There's an excellent chance of seeing black bears in or near this campground.

Approaching Fort Nelson, you roll across the Muskwa River bridge on the edge of town. The Muskwa River at this point represents the lowest elevation above sea level on the entire Alaska Highway, about 1,000 feet. An impressive span, the bridge was built in 1970 to replace the old one, which was in danger of washing out during breakup every year. The Muskwa River can rapidly rise 20 feet or more during periods of heavy rain or snow melt.

Two major private campgrounds are within the city limits of Fort Nelson, one on the eastern edge of town and another on the western. Both are full-service and include laundromats, showers and a car-washing station.

Original Alaska Highway bridge over the Sikanni River. (Burned in 1992.)

Fort Nelson, B.C., to Watson Lake, Yukon

STARTING MILEAGE:_____

MILEAGE: 330 miles (550 km)

DRIVING TIME: 8 to 10 hours

TOWNS EN ROUTE (all offering most travelers' services): **Summit Lake,** 89 miles (148 km); **Muncho Lake,** 152 miles (253 km); **Liard River,** 193 miles (321 km); **Watson Lake,** 330 miles (550 km)

GAS AVAILABLE (besides towns listed above): **Steamboat,** 49 miles (82 km); **Tetsa River Services,** 74 miles (123 km); **Rocky Mountain Lodge,** 95 miles (158 km); **MacDonald River Services,** 107 miles (178 km); **Toad River Lodge,** 121 miles (202 km); **Double "G" Service,** 153 miles (255 km); **Highland Glen Lodge,** 159 miles (265 km); **Muncho Lake Lodge,** 161 miles (268 km); **Coal River Lodge,** 230 miles (383 km); **Fireside,** 240 miles (400 km); **Contact Creek Lodge,** 286 miles (477 km)

CAMPGROUNDS (provincial parks are public campgrounds; most towns listed above have private campgrounds as well): **Tetsa River Provincial Park,** 63 miles (105 km); **Tetsa River Services,** 74 miles (123 km); **Summit Lake Provincial Park,** 90 miles (150 km); **Rocky Mountain Lodge,** 95 miles (158 km); **115 Creek Provincial Park,** 100 miles (167 km); **The Poplars Campground,** 124 miles (207 km); **Double "G" Service,** 153 miles (255 km); **Strawberry Flats, Muncho Lake Provincial Park,** 154 miles (257 km); **Highland Glen Lodge,** 159 miles (265 km); **MacDonald Campground, Muncho Lake Provincial Park,** 159 miles (257 km); **Muncho Lake Lodge,** 161 miles (268 km); **Lower Liard River Lodge,** 193 miles (322 km); **Liard River Hotsprings Provincial Park,** 194 miles (324 km); **Coal River Lodge,** 230 miles (383 km); **Contact Creek Lodge,** 286 miles (477 km)

LODGING (besides these, all towns listed above have overnight lodging available): **Steamboat,** 49 miles (82 km); **Rocky Mountain Lodge,** 95 miles (158 km); **Toad River Lodge,** 121 miles (202 km); **Double "G" Service,** 153 miles (255 km); **Highland Glen Lodge,** 159 miles (265 km); **Muncho Lake Lodge,** 161 miles (268 km); **Lower Liard River Lodge,** 193 miles (322 km); **Coal River Lodge,** 230 miles (383 km)

MAJOR TERRAIN FEATURES: The Rocky Mountains; mountainous, mostly forested; steep grades, hairpin curves; major rivers crossed: Liard and Coal

WILDLIFE: Moose, black bears, Stone sheep, white-tailed deer, caribou (in the spring), grizzlies (rarely)

FISHING: Lake trout, grayling, northern pike, whitefish, Dolly Varden

Section 2

Fort Nelson, B.C., to Watson Lake, Yukon

Though the Muskwa River bridge on the southeastern edge of Fort Nelson is the lowest elevation above sea level on the Alaska Highway, within 100 miles of leaving Fort Nelson, travelers will cross the highest point above sea level along the route. Fort Nelson lies on the eastern edge of the Rocky Mountains.

About 3,500 people live in town, with a total of perhaps 5,500 living in the town and its immediate area. Within a very few years, Fort Nelson will celebrate its 200th anniversary, marking it as one of the oldest settlements along the Alaska Highway. The site of the present city is the fifth site of the actual town, as it has been moved several times in its history to avoid flooding and other calamities.

In its early days, Fort Nelson existed primarily to service the fur trade. It was named for Lord Nelson, the British admiral who was victorious at Trafalgar. As recently as 35 years ago, Fort Nelson was still a frontier town without electrical power, telephones or running water. Today the city is fully modernized. Its primary industry is forestry. The railroad reached Fort Nelson in 1971. This is the last community along the Alaska Highway to have railroad service that connects to the major lines serving North America. Fairbanks, it's true, is served by the Alaska Railroad, but that line runs only south, to Anchorage and Seward. The Alaska Railroad does not connect to the continent-wide network of railroads that have grown up since the 19th century. Fort Nelson is literally the end of the line insofar as railroads are concerned.

Leaving Fort Nelson, northwest bound, travelers embark on the most beautiful stretch of the Alaska Highway, and the stretch that normally offers the most bountiful opportunities to observe wildlife. In fact, it's almost possible to guarantee wildlife on this stretch of the road, unlike all of the other segments described in this chapter.

The Rockies are nothing if not rugged. Very quickly travelers will begin twisting their way up the mountains, through thickly forested areas with glimpses of ragged, granite peaks often available. This is not a stretch of road to plan on driving fast. Grades approach 10 percent in some areas, and hairpin curves, both climbing into and descending from the mountains, are numerous.

Insider's Tip: Leave Fort Nelson very early in the morning if at all possible. This will greatly increase your chances of spotting wildlife at roadside, particularly black bears and white-tailed deer.

Services are much fewer and much farther apart along this stretch of road. Though there are a good many lodges and gas stations, these tend to be concentrated in and around Muncho Lake, about halfway between Fort Nelson and Watson Lake. However, the provincial parks (public camp-grounds) that sit alongside the road are a real plus factor. Some of these are in absolutely stunning locations.

This stretch of road is a good one to break down into 2 days instead of 1. If you do so, you should plan to stop near either Summit Lake or Muncho Lake.

Signs along the road will suggest various turnouts for stopping to view such things as the Muskwa River Valley and Indian Head Mountain. The latter is an outcropping of rock eroded into what appears to be the profile of a face. It's a good place to take a break, too, coming more or less at the halfway point in the intense driving required to negotiate the curves and grades leading to the summit of the Rockies. The turnout for Indian Head Mountain is about 59 miles from Fort Nelson. Glimpses of the face in the rock can be had from the road, if you're quick.

Fishermen will want to stop and sample the Tetsa River along this part of the road. Good Dolly Varden and grayling fishing is available, and the fish are pretty good size. Try small flies (black gnats probably being tops for grayling) or small silver spinners. Salmon eggs will also entice fish. A good place to try is Tetsa River Provincial Park, about 63 miles from Fort Nelson. Campsites in this park are right on the river and offer great access for fishermen. Be sure you have a current British Columbia fishing license.

Insider's Tip: Big fish almost always hold near the bottom in northern streams, the one notable exception being grayling. Fly fishermen will almost always catch larger fish by fishing wet flies instead of dry, particularly for trout and Dolly Varden.

About 88 miles from Fort Nelson, the Alaska Highway enters Stone Mountain Provincial Park. It winds through the park for about 10 miles, past the settlement of Summit and over the crest of the Rockies. Starting here and for the next 50 miles or so comes the almost-certain guarantee of seeing wildlife.

Stone sheep, which inhabit the peaks of the northern Rockies, come down to lick minerals from the surface of the road. For most of the summer, mostly ewes and lambs—called nursery bands—are visible at roadside. Travelers in spring, right after breakup, have a much better chance of seeing the big full-curl rams at roadside. The rams quickly head for the high country once summer begins in earnest.

Be prepared to stop. These Stone sheep aren't likely to be too excited by the presence of your vehicle. Often, you will be able to drive to within a few feet of these animals to snap a picture or two right out of the car window. The best places to be alert for sheep are where steep, jagged rock outcroppings—which mean safety for the sheep—come very close to the road. Most often these are cuts made in rocky areas to make room for the road. If you spook the sheep for any reason, they almost always run into the rocks, where very few people or predators can follow. And, drive carefully in sheep country. There are numerous blind corners and small rises that can have sheep on the other side.

While you're in the sheep country, several of the prettiest campgrounds in British Columbia are at roadside. Summit Lake Provincial Park and the two campgrounds within Muncho Lake Provincial Park are unsurpassed for scenery. And there are fishing opportunities for lake trout at both, though some sort of boat is probably necessary.

Insider's Tip: Boaters in these northern waters should always take care to wear life jackets. Water temperatures are extremely low—just above freezing—and boaters dumped overboard in accidents will quickly become unable to function properly. A life jacket lengthens the amount of time rescuers have to reach you. Unless you are right next to shore when an accident happens, you will almost certainly require assistance.

Because this area is mountainous, watch the weather carefully. Sudden winds and squalls can arise, becoming almost instantly dangerous. Always leave yourself an option in case of sudden changes in the weather. Also, please note that snow is possible during any month of the year in the Rockies. Though infrequent in the summer, it still can fall in June, July and August.

Beyond Summit Lake, down the west side of the Rockies, lies Muncho Lake, called by many the prettiest lake along the Alaska Highway. The blue color of this lake in deep areas and the green in shallow almost seems unreal.

The enhanced color, though, is easily explained. There's considerable copper in the mountains surrounding Muncho Lake. Leached into the lake, it forms a copper oxide that suspends in the water. Though the amount of copper oxide is small compared to the volume of the lake, there's enough of it to show up as enhanced pigment. Take plenty of pictures of Muncho Lake—few of your friends will believe your explanation of the color.

Die-hard fishermen have been known to salivate at the thought of Muncho Lake. Lake trout to 50 pounds or more swim in its deep-blue depths. These are natural fish, no stocking programs here. June and July are usually the most popular months for lake trout fishing, and you'll probably need a boat and heavy-duty equipment for trolling. Boats can be rented from lodges near the highway.

Insider's Tip: For very short periods twice a year, lake trout are available to shore-bound anglers on almost any large northern lake. In late May, as the ice starts to go out, try casting in the limited open water close to shore, particularly near the inlets of small streams. After a long winter under the ice, lakers are hungry and can often be taken near the surface at the edge of the ice with light tackle. In late September, just before freeze-up, lakers can again be found close to shore.

Muncho Lake is best viewed in the early morning calm of a sunny summer day. By most afternoons, a breeze ruffles the surface, and the reflections of the surrounding mountains are washed away. The road winds along the shore of Muncho Lake for several miles, offering numerous vantage points.

Thirty miles or so past Muncho Lake is the most popular public campground on the Alaska Highway, Liard (locally pronounced *leerd*) River Hotsprings Provincial Park. The government of British Columbia has provided bath houses and walkways at two pools a short distance from the campsites. Floating around in these pools at the end of a day's driving on the Alaska Highway is an experience not soon forgotten.

Usually the lower pool is fairly crowded. The upper pool, however, a quarter-mile or so farther on, is often less crowded, particularly late in the evening. Though skinny-dipping is officially prohibited, those heading for

Liard River Hot Springs is among the most popular stops along the Alaska Highway in Canada. It's well worth the visit.

the upper pool late in the evening should give warning of their presence to avoid possible embarrassment.

This campground fills up very early on most days. So if you want a campsite, plan for an early afternoon arrival. Late arrivals in self-contained RVs can park in the parking lot near the trailhead to the hot springs pools. The fee is the same in the parking lot or in a campsite if you spend the night.

Liard Hotsprings also offers a great chance for seeing moose. Usually there are a couple hanging around near the boardwalk that crosses the warm-water swamp en route to the lower pool. Late in the evening or early in the morning are the best times to see these big ungulates.

If the park is full, there is a small private campground less than a half-mile south of the park entrance. Lower Liard River Lodge, as it's called, also has overnight lodging available. The lodge overlooks the Liard River bridge, the only suspension bridge along the Alaska Highway.

There are two fairly dangerous sections of highway prior to reaching Watson Lake. The first of these is a 4.5-mile stretch about 50 miles past Liard River. The second is of lesser length about 10 miles farther on. Both are well marked.

About 28 miles prior to reaching Watson Lake, the road crosses the Hyland River. Good fishing here for rainbows, Dolly Varden and grayling.

Insider's Tip: When stream fishing along the Alaska Highway, don't expect to catch a lot right next to the road or under a bridge. Everybody who drives north fishes in those spots. Instead, walk a short distance up- or downstream from the road, and you'll likely be in waters hardly ever fished. A good way to measure is to walk until there are no more footprints on the bank. Usually a half-mile or so (6 or 7 minutes of walking) is plenty.

Approaching Watson Lake, Yukon, drivers will actually zigzag back and forth across the British Columbia–Yukon border three times after passing through Fireside, though the border may not be marked at every crossing. Between these crossings, once again in British Columbia, is a settlement called Lower Post. No travelers' services are available here. A short gravel road leads to the site, originally a Hudson's Bay Company trading post. Now there's a B.C. Forest Service field office installed in Lower Post, but little else.

Once you enter Yukon Territory, the actual road itself becomes much improved. Other than annual short stretches repaired each season, this good road continues for more than 400 miles, until well past Whitehorse.

Entering Watson Lake, the best campgrounds are the private facilities on the south side of town. Although there are campgrounds on the far side of town, those on the south side seem to be the most popular.

Watson Lake, Yukon, to Whitehorse, Yukon

STARTING MILEAGE:_____

MILEAGE : 271 miles (452 km)

DRIVING TIME: 7 to 8 hours

TOWNS EN ROUTE: **Teslin,** 163 miles (272 km); **Whitehorse,** 271 miles (452 km)

GAS AVAILABLE (besides in Teslin, above): **Cassiar Highway Junction,** 13 miles (22 km); **Rancheria,** 74 miles (123 km); **Rainbow's Inn,** 85 miles (142 km); **Swift River,** 97 miles (162 km); **Morley River Lodge,** 140 miles (233 km); **Teri-Tori Campsite,** 157 miles (262 km); **Halstead's,** 166 miles (277 km); **Johnson's Crossing,** 196 miles (327 km); **Jake's Corner,** 224 miles (373 km); **Klondike Highway 2 Junction,** 261 miles (435 km)

CAMPGROUNDS (territorial campgrounds are public campgrounds): **Green Valley Trailer Park,** 7 miles (12 km); **Cassiar Highway Junction,** 13 miles (22 km); **Rancheria** (RV park), 74 miles (123 km); **Rancheria Territorial Campground,** 74 miles (123 km); **Rainbow's Inn,** 85 miles (142 km); **Morley River Lodge,** 140 miles (233 km); **Teri-Tori Campsite,** 157 miles (262 km); **Halstead's,** 166 miles (277 km); **Mukluk Annie's,** 171 miles (285 km); **Teslin Lake Territorial Campground,** 172 miles (287 km); **Johnson's Crossing,** 196 miles (327 km); **Squanga Lake Territorial Campground,** 208 miles (347 km); **Marsh Lake Territorial Campground,** 247 miles (412 km); **Sourdough Country Campsite,** 261 miles (435 km); **Wolf Creek Territorial Campground,** 264 miles (440 km); **Pioneer Trailer Park,** 268 miles (447 km)

LODGING (besides those available in Teslin): **Cassiar Highway Junction,** 13 miles (22 km); **Rancheria Hotel-Motel,** 74 miles (123 km); **Rainbow's Inn,** 85 miles (142 km); **Swift River,** 97 miles (162 km); **Morley River Lodge,** 140 miles (233 km); **Halstead's,** 166 miles (277 km); **Mukluk Annie's** (cabins), 171 miles (285 km); **Lakeview Resort and Marina,** 237 miles (395 km)

MAJOR TERRAIN FEATURES: Mostly low, rolling hills; alternating partly open and forest lands; major rivers crossed: Upper Liard, Teslin, Yukon

WILDLIFE: Black bears, moose, caribou (occasionally), grizzlies (rarely)

FISHING: Lake trout, northern pike, grayling

========= Section 3 =========

Watson Lake, Yukon, to Whitehorse, Yukon

If you're headed up the Alaska Highway and staying close to this book as you go, you've probably raised your eyebrows a time or two. Various longtime businesses along the Alaska Highway list their locations as mileages from Dawson Creek—but those mileages don't coincide with anything given here, or at least don't come within 20 miles or so of what's given here.

Well, both this book and those businesses are right. When the older businesses were built, the Alaska Highway was a longer road. Thus, a gas station put up at, say, mile 550 some 25 years ago might actually be at mile 535 today. Ever since the Alaska Highway was built, but especially in the past 20 years, engineers and road crews have been hard at work straightening the twisting path selected by the first surveyors. So, every year the Alaska Highway gets a little shorter.

Take Whitehorse as an actual example. Officially, Whitehorse has been at Mile 918 (from Dawson Creek) ever since the road was built. However, in the almost half-century since, the road has been rerouted to bypass Whitehorse, and, as already noted, has been considerably shortened. The turnoff for downtown Whitehorse is now just 884 miles from Dawson Creek. That's a difference of 34 miles.

At Watson Lake, the difference between the official mileage and the reality is 22 miles. Watson Lake these days is actually 613 miles from Dawson Creek, but it's still listed as being at mile 635.

Locating a business or a home by its mileage from a known point is fairly common throughout the North. And, because there are relatively few roads outside the towns, it's a convenient practice. As you drive along rural roads, you'll regularly see mailboxes listing mileages as an address, or signs on lodges and gas stations listing a mileage. That the mileages are actually shorter than the official address is simply a sign of progress.

Don't let these distances confuse you. Just remember that the actual distance these days is almost always less than the mileage a longtime highway business gives in its name or even in its official address.

To get an even better idea of how tortuous and twisted the original route was, visit the Alaska Highway Interpretive Center before leaving Watson Lake. It's right alongside the highway with the sign forest, the latter all but impossible to miss as you drive past. In the center, a 40-minute movie details the building of the road, and various displays highlight different aspects of the construction.

After you've seen the movie, walk outside into the sign forest, the

Alaska Highway's oldest—and perhaps only—tradition. Back in 1942, a homesick soldier stationed in Watson Lake put up a sign for his hometown. Ever since, travelers to Alaska have been carting along road signs pirated from local highways to hang at the same location. Today, thousands upon thousands of signs from all over the world decorate a "forest" of poles put in place to hold them all. By all means, bring along a sign of your own from your hometown to put up. Just about anything will do—a street sign, a "welcome to . . . " sign, a license plate or a sign for some local attraction. Most popular seem to be signs frequently seen at city limits, that is to say, a sign with the name of a town and a number indicating either elevation or population.

The best part of the sign forest is putting up a sign one year, then returning several years later to try to find it again. As you walk through the sign forest, you'll almost certainly come across people trying to do just that.

Once your visit to the interpretive center and the sign forest is over and you head northwest out of Watson Lake, you'll quickly realize that the wilderness is growing ever closer. Just compare the condensed information page for this section with the same page in previous sections. In this entire day's suggested drive, there's only one other town between Watson Lake and Whitehorse: Teslin. And, when you get to Teslin, you'll quickly see that it's a pretty small town. From here north to Fairbanks, all those spare parts for your vehicle suggested in earlier chapters will hold greater meaning. Though gas stations come along at fairly regular intervals, the odds of these remote businesses having exactly the right size fan belt or other minor item are fairly remote.

Insider's Tip: "Drive on the top half of your gas tank," was some sage advice I received on my first trip up the Alaska Highway two decades ago. It's still good advice. For various reasons, businesses fail every year, and the very gas station you plan to patronize may not be open on the day you choose to arrive. This is no time to cut things close.

Shortly after leaving Watson Lake, you'll come to the junction of the Cassiar Highway. The Cassiar is a north-south road that connects British Columbia's Yellowhead Highway 16 with the Alaska Highway. It's an alternate route for either northbound or southbound travelers. It is covered in more detail in Chapter 11 of this book.

Except for a couple of lodges and a territorial campground or two, the Alaska Highway is pretty much unpopulated for most of the 160 miles to Teslin. The terrain is mostly boreal forest with small creeks and rivers crossing the route or running alongside the road. Most of the clear streams will offer opportunities for grayling fishing.

The scenery along this stretch of road is far from boring; however, it does strike some travelers as repetitive. More than one first-timer on the Alaska Highway has been heard to remark, "Don't you ever run out of mountains?" or words to that effect.

Indeed, there are a lot of mountains. Though still more or less a part of the Rockies, most of the groups of mountains in this area have additional names, like the Cassiar Mountains to the left and the Pelly Mountains to the right as you're northbound. You actually leave the Rockies as you approach Teslin. From Teslin on, the mountains to your left are extensions of the Coast Range, the ragged spine that marks the boundary between southeastern Alaska and Canada. Were you to carry things to extremes, it could be argued that the Coast Range is the extension of the Cascade Mountains of Washington and Oregon.

Teslin Lake, with the community of Teslin about midway along its eastern shore, is the first of three major lakes along this portion of the Alaska Highway. All three lakes are partly in Yukon and partly in British Columbia. If you choose to fish Teslin, Atlin or Tagish lakes, be certain you have the appropriate fishing license for the part of the lake you wish to use. All three lakes are roughly 100 miles long and 2 to 5 miles wide. All offer excellent lake trout, northern pike and grayling fishing, though it helps to have a guide the first time you go looking for fish in these massive bodies of water. Guides are available in and around Teslin if you want to try out this first of the three big lakes.

Insider's Tip: A great place to stop on Teslin Lake is Halstead's, about 3 miles beyond the town. A campground, lodge, restaurant and gas station are all in one place. The home-baked goodies in the store are more than worth the stop (try the Yukon rhubarb pie!), and so are the friendly folks who make up the family that operates this business. Boat rentals and fishing guides are available here.

Coming into Teslin, drivers cross the Nisutlin Bay bridge, the longest over-water span on the Alaska Highway, which crosses an arm of Teslin Lake. Teslin itself is home to about 350 people. Some 2,200 feet above sea level and this far north, Teslin offers a pretty cool climate, even in summer. The average date for the last spring frost is in mid-June. Fall frosts start the latter half of August, so Teslin averages little more than 60 consecutive frost-free days each summer. All travelers' services are available in or near Teslin, but choices are fairly limited.

Leaving Teslin, the road follows the lake shore to Johnson's Crossing at the north end of the lake. A bridge crosses the Teslin River, which flows out of the lake. It's 32 miles from Teslin to Johnson's Crossing, which gives you some idea of just how big this lake really is.

After Johnson's Crossing, it's 28 more miles to Jake's Corner, a road junction offering a couple of options for travelers. Jake's Corner is not an official name. The name of the gas station and cafe at the junction is "Jake's Crystal Palace," according to the sign. However, the spot has locally been known as Jake's Corner for decades.

The Alaska Highway continues straight ahead to Whitehorse from Jake's. If you turn left on the Atlin Road, there's another junction just a short distance away. The Atlin road continues to the left at this junction, the road straight ahead leads to Tagish and Carcross. Page 91 details the Atlin Road trip.

The road leading to Tagish and Carcross offers an alternative route to Whitehorse from Jake's Corner. It leads first to Tagish, little more than a campground and a collection of summer homes at the bridge over the Tagish River. The Tagish River is a short, wide stream joining Tagish Lake to the south with Marsh Lake to the north. A territorial campground sits next to the road on the east side of the bridge.

Fishermen should be aware that this bridge produces some of the finest catches of lake trout in Yukon Territory in late June and July. Fish from 5 to 20 pounds are regularly taken by locals and vacationers fishing with bait from the fishwalk thoughtfully built onto the north side of the bridge. For bait, use fresh-frozen herring, available at the small marina near the bridge, or jig for the cisco visible in the river and use one of them for bait. Those with a boat will find excellent trolling for lakers in both Marsh and Tagish lakes, as well as pockets of northern pike and grayling. If you like to fish, this is a great place to spend a couple of days.

The Atlin Road.

Back in 1978, my son, Eric, caught his first fish from the Tagish River bridge . . . sort of. He was 5 at the time, and Dad had paid about $7 for one of those cheap rod, reel and line starter kits. The whole family, including grandparents, hiked out on the bridge, baited up and dropped their lines into the water. Sure enough, the first fish to bite took Eric's bait. Eyes wide with excitement, he reeled forwards and backwards, shouting all the while. Then the fish flopped on the water's surface just below his feet. He took one look at that 7-pound lake trout, screamed, threw his rod into the air and lit out for camp at a dead run. Grandma went after the boy; Mom caught the fishing rod and finished reeling in the fish. Dad's still laughing.

The Atlin Road:
A Great Side Trip for Alaska Highway Travelers

From Jake's Corner, a narrow gravel road leads 58 miles south to Atlin, British Columbia, a town often called Canada's Little Switzerland. This is, without exception, the most beautiful setting anywhere in northwestern Canada.

The drive takes less than 2 hours if you elect to do it nonstop. However, there are a couple of places worth visiting along the way.

The first of these is Snafu Lake Territorial Campground, about 16 miles south of the Alaska Highway. Canoeists will thoroughly enjoy this chain of small lakes connected by narrow sloughs. Fishermen will find hungry pike at almost every turn, and wildlife enthusiasts will have a chance to see grizzly bears and moose along the shores of the various lakes. Some years back my family experienced the thrill of watching a grizzly chase a moose through shallow water and along the lake shore. When last seen going over a hill, the moose was winning.

Two miles beyond the Snafu Lake turnoff, there's an old abandoned trapper's cabin at the right side of the road. This is great for investigating how trappers built small log cabins to house themselves over long winters. It's small by almost any standard, with low ceilings. Walk inside and try to imagine spending several months alone in this tiny shelter.

From just beyond the cabin, the road follows the shore of Atlin Lake all the way to Atlin. Snow-capped mountains are visible in almost any direction from Atlin, the lake is a sparkling blue jewel, and the setting is all but unbelievable. The town itself looks like something out of the Old West.

From Atlin, drivers can venture east through active gold-mining country for about 12 miles to Surprise Lake. The more adventurous can continue into the hills above Surprise Lake, though this road isn't recommended for large motorhomes or trailers.

Pine Creek, Surprise Lake's outlet stream, is crossed twice, the last time within sight of the lake. There is excellent fishing for grayling right at this second bridge.

Also from Atlin, drivers can venture south for an additional 16 miles on Warm Bay Road. There are several fairly primitive campgrounds along this road, which parallels the lake shore.

Though this side trip can be done in a day, you'll feel cheated if you do. Better to allow 2 days and plan to overnight in one of the campgrounds or the hotel in Atlin.

For more information on overnight accommodations and visitors' attractions, contact the Atlin Inn: (604) 651-7546.

Skagway, Alaska:
A Step Back into Alaska's Past

Klondike Highway 2 runs 99 miles from the Alaska Highway junction to Skagway, Alaska, part of the route paralleling the narrow-gauge White Pass and Yukon Railway.

The railroad has been mostly closed for the past several years, though in 1988 it opened again for day trips from Skagway to Lake Bennett and back. Plans are afoot to open the railroad during the summer for transportation between Skagway and Whitehorse. If these plans come to reality, leaving your vehicle in Whitehorse and taking the train will be a much-sought-after excursion.

Klondike 2 runs due south, passing at least one very unique terrain feature before reaching Carcross—a small desert of sand dunes about 32 miles south of the junction.

Just past the dunes is the town of Carcross, with limited visitor services.

From Carcross the road proceeds 66 miles south, across White Pass in the Coast Range to Skagway. The scenery is spectacular. Windy Arm of Tagish Lake, then Tutshi Lake are to the left; craggy peaks fill the skyline in all directions. Watch closely for Rocky Mountain goats on the most rugged, inaccessible ridges.

At the summit of White Pass, you enter Alaska. The road descends quickly into Skagway with steep grades and hairpin curves. Watch for U.S. customs on your right, just a few miles before reaching Skagway. All vehicles entering from Canada must stop. Canadian customs is open from 9 A.M. to 9 P.M., and U.S. customs from 8 A.M. to 8 P.M. These take into account the time zone change at the border. When it's 8 A.M. in Skagway, it's 9 A.M. just across the border in Canada.

Much of Skagway is now a National Historic Park, as is the Chilkoot Trail, which begins a few miles out of town near the abandoned site of Dyea. False-front wooden buildings, some dating back to the gold rush, still characterize the town. By all means, drive out to Dyea and hike at least a few hundred yards on the Chilkoot Trail. You'll almost certainly meet some hiking groups who are planning to hike the trail to Lake Bennett, a rather arduous climb.

In Skagway, the best time to visit is on the 4th of July. The party lasts all day and includes events for young and old alike. The parade, back and forth along Broadway, is large by the standards of the size of the town.

Additional information for Skagway can be had from the Skagway Convention and Visitors Bureau, Box 415, Skagway, AK 99840.

If you elect to continue on the Alaska Highway from Jake's Corner, it's about 48 more miles to the turnoff for downtown Whitehorse. En route, you will drive along the north shore of Marsh Lake and cross the headwaters of the Yukon River as it flows out of Marsh Lake. This, the most famous of the North's great rivers, flows almost 2,000 miles through Yukon Territory and Alaska to its outlet in the Bering Sea on Alaska's west coast. The Yukon was the great transportation artery that served the Klondike gold rush at the end of the 19th century and other gold rushes in the early 20th century in Alaska. Several of the sternwheelers that carried people and supplies have been restored over the years and can be seen in Whitehorse, Dawson and Fairbanks.

Prior to reaching the turnoff for downtown Whitehorse, the road intersects Klondike Highway 2, which leads south to Carcross and Skagway, Alaska. This is another great side trip and should be considered by anyone interested in the gold-rush history of the North. Skagway was the starting point for argonauts rushing to the Klondike gold fields near Dawson. Would-be miners sailed to Skagway, hiked over the treacherous Chilkoot Trail to Lake Bennett and built boats to float through Bennett, Tagish and Marsh lakes into the Yukon River.

Insider's Tip: Campers planning to overnight near Whitehorse and then make the side trip to Skagway should consider staying at the Sourdough Country Campsite just a few hundred yards from the junction with Klondike 2. The private campground offers full hookups for RVs, grassy sites for tents and has excellent laundry and shower facilities. It's a great place to unwind and divest yourself of some trail dust.

From the junction with Klondike 2, it's about 11 miles to the turnoff for downtown Whitehorse. This road actually makes sort of a loop through the city and rejoins the Alaska Highway on the other side of town. Those who elect not to visit downtown Whitehorse will have about 3 miles on the Alaska Highway to where the other end of the loop turns off for downtown. Mileage measurements for the next section of this chapter will be made from this second access road (westernmost) to Whitehorse.

Whitehorse, Yukon, to Beaver Creek, Yukon

STARTING MILEAGE:_____

MILEAGE: 282 miles (470 km)

DRIVING TIME: 7 to 8 hours

TOWNS EN ROUTE: **Haines Junction**, 98 miles (163 km); **Destruction Bay**, 165 miles (275 km); **Beaver Creek**, 282 miles (470 km)

GAS AVAILABLE (besides towns listed above): **Mackintosh Lodge**, 105 miles (175 km); **Bayshore Motel**, 145 miles (242 km); **Burwash Landing**, 175 miles (292 km); **Kluane Village**, 198 miles (330 km); **Pine Valley**, 227 miles (378 km); **Bear Flats Lodge**, 247 miles (412 km); **White River Lodge**, 248 miles (414 km)

CAMPGROUNDS (territorial campgrounds are public campgrounds; towns listed above have private campgrounds as well): **Kusawa Lake Territorial Campground**, 40 miles (67 km); **Pine Lake Territorial Campground**, 94 miles (157 km); **Mackintosh Lodge**, 105 miles (175 km); **Bayshore Motel**, 145 miles (242 km); **Cottonwood Park**, 148 miles (247 km); **Congdon Creek Territorial Campground**, 153 miles (255 km); **Burwash Landing**, 175 miles (292 km); **Kluane Village**, 198 miles (330 km); **Pine Valley**, 227 miles (378 km); **Lake Creek Territorial Campground**, 232 miles (387 km); **Bear Flats Lodge**, 247 miles (412 km); **White River Lodge**, 248 miles (414 km); **Snag Junction Territorial Campground**, 268 miles (447 km)

LODGING (besides these, all towns listed above have overnight lodging available): **Mackintosh Lodge**, 105 miles (175 km); **Bayshore Motel**, 145 miles (242 km); **Burwash Landing**, 175 miles (292 km); **Kluane Village**, 198 miles (330 km); **Pine Valley Motel**, 227 miles (378 km); **Bear Flats Lodge**, 247 miles (412 km); **White River Lodge**, 248 miles (414 km)

MAJOR TERRAIN FEATURES: Mostly open, lightly forested country to Haines Junction; Wrangell–St. Elias Mountains to left, Haines Junction to Burwash Landing; low, rolling hills with muskeg, Burwash Landing to Alaska border; major rivers crossed: Takhini, Donjek, Koidern, White

WILDLIFE: Moose, black bears, eagles, caribou (occasionally), Dall sheep and grizzlies (rarely).

FISHING: Lake trout, northern pike and grayling

========= Section 4 =========

Whitehorse, Yukon, to Beaver Creek, Yukon

Whitehorse is a town that bears investigating. First and foremost are the restaurants—some great ones, offering various European cuisines. There is also, to the horror of some parents, a McDonald's, that ubiquitous sign of contemporary civilization. If the kids insist, buy them their favorite gut bomb at McDonald's, then make them wait patiently while you sample the much better fare available in dining rooms in downtown hotels.

The centerpiece of Whitehorse is a riverfront park holding the rebuilt sternwheeler SS *Klondike II* and a barge similar to the type the river steamer used to push back and forth between Whitehorse and Dawson. Parks Canada completely refurbished the *Klondike II* in the late 1970s and early 1980s. As much as is possible, the ship today looks just as it did on its maiden voyage nearly 60 years ago. Tours are conducted through the boat at half-hour intervals, 7 days a week. Each tour lasts about an hour and takes visitors through the entire boat from the engine room to the bridge. The *Klondike II* was last used in active service in the 1950s.

The park holding the boat also hosts Canada's biggest summer event, Canada Day, on July 1. Similar to the U.S. celebration of Independence Day on July 4, Canada Day brings out the finest Whitehorse has to offer. Parades, events and entertainment combine for a day-long festival. The local Royal Canadian Mounted Police even break out their legendary red uniforms for this event.

Insider's Tip: Combining Canada Day in Whitehorse and Independence Day in Skagway makes for a great interlude in early July. In fact, several residents of both Skagway and Whitehorse take in both celebrations every year. Only a hundred miles separate these two towns, so the logistics are pretty simple.

Although Whitehorse offers a great Canada Day celebration, don't forget that Canada Day is a nationwide event. Even the smallest towns throughout northwestern Canada will be hosting some sort of festivity to celebrate July 1. Don't be shy about taking in the action.

Take advantage of your time in Whitehorse to check your vehicle over carefully. You've come several thousand miles by this point, some of it on less-than-perfect roads. It's time to take a good look underneath for loose bolts, to change the oil if appropriate and to closely examine your tires.

There are still quite a few miles to Fairbanks and its full range of car-care services. Some of those miles are pretty lonely ones.

Insider's Tip: Campers who stay in the Whitehorse area for more than a day should investigate Takhini Hot Springs Resort just outside of town. Drive west on the Alaska Highway to where Klondike 2 turns north for Dawson. Follow the signs a few miles north on this road to the turnoff for Takhini. More than 100 campsites, a restaurant and a hot springs pool make this one of the North's more pleasant resorts.

Fill up your gas tank before heading out of Whitehorse. The longest stretch of Alaska Highway without gas available is the 100 miles from Whitehorse to Haines Junction. And Whitehorse offers the last reasonably priced gas until you get almost to Fairbanks.

Gas prices escalate dramatically as you drive from Whitehorse to the Alaska border. If you can manage to do it, avoid filling up in Beaver Creek before crossing into Alaska. Beaver Creek is almost always among the most expensive places to buy gas along the Alaska Highway—it's at the very end of the supply line. If your vehicle can handle it, the best bet is to fill up at Destruction Bay, about 165 miles from Whitehorse and then go all the way to Tok, Alaska, before buying gas again. Tok (rhymes with *coke*) is about 265 miles from Destruction Bay. But again, don't take chances. If in doubt about your vehicle's ability to go 265 miles without a fill-up, purchase extra gas along the way. Although it can be a beautiful place to be stranded in, the wait for help to get gas can be exceedingly long.

Leaving Whitehorse, it's a very comfortable 2-hour drive to Haines Junction, all of it on good wide road. There are no dangerous grades or blind, hairpin curves. The only population concentration of any sort is the Indian village of Champagne, and no services are available there.

Next to the road in Champagne is an Indian cemetery. This is not a tourist attraction, and residents of the community feel very strongly about visitors tramping through their burial sites. Please honor their requests for privacy as posted on signs surrounding the cemetery.

History buffs will again find one of the original highway bridges still standing along this stretch of road. At the Aishihik River, 78 miles from Whitehorse, the original bridge can be seen to the right from the road.

The old bridge, rebuilt in 1942 for the construction of the Alaska Highway, has stood at this site since about 1920. Originally it was used to move freight and passengers across the Aishihik River to Silver City on the shores of Kluane Lake. A turnoff just prior to the bridge in use today leads to the old bridge.

As you approach Haines Junction, the Wrangell–St. Elias Mountains will be straight ahead. This range is on the border of Yukon Territory and Alaska where the Alaska panhandle joins the mainland mass of the state. Mount St. Elias, which peaks 18,008 feet above sea level, straddles the U.S.–Canada border. St. Elias is the second-highest peak in both Canada and Alaska.

At Haines Junction, the Alaska Highway turns off to the right. If you drive straight through town, you will, 150 miles or so later, find yourself in Haines, Alaska. Turn right at the junction if Fairbanks is your goal.

Haines Junction is the headquarters of Canada's Kluane (*kloo-AW-nee*) National Park, which encompasses most of the Canadian portion of the Wrangell–St. Elias Mountains. On the Alaska side, Wrangell–St. Elias National Park, the largest national park in the United States, joins Kluane National Park at the U.S.–Canada border.

At the Kluane National Park and Yukon Government Information Center there are interpretive displays and a slide show. The center is open 7 days a week in the summer from 9 A.M. to 9 P.M. It's well worth the time to stop and have a look.

As you drive out of Haines Junction, Kluane National Park will be continuously on your left until past Kluane Lake at Burwash Landing, some 75 miles farther on. Until you reach the lake, the scenery becomes more impressive with each mile you drive. If the weather is clear, you'll be able to see glaciers on distant mountainsides. Various marked turnouts allow ample opportunity to marvel at the vastness of the Wrangell–St. Elias Mountains.

Approaching the southeastern edge of Kluane Lake, a lengthy bridge leads across one of the rivers feeding the lake. The mountain visible straight ahead as you cross the bridge is Sheep Mountain. Dall sheep, the only pure white mountain sheep in North America, are frequently visible on the slopes of Sheep Mountain. Northbound travelers in May will almost certainly see bands of sheep all over the mountainside. Later in the summer, luck becomes a factor in whether or not you will see Dall sheep from the road.

Across the bridge, at the base of Sheep Mountain, a Parks Canada station provides information on the park. This is primarily a wilderness park; there are no roads into it. If you wish to experience Kluane National Park, you're going to have to get out of your car and do some hiking.

Within a quarter-mile of the Sheep Mountain visitors center is a sign commemorating Soldier's Summit. This is the point where the Alaska Highway was officially opened on November 20, 1942.

Insider's Tip: Hikers in Kluane National Park should stay in groups of two or more. This mountain wilderness is grizzly bear country, as I and one of my cousins can well attest. Talking and laughing during a 1979 hike, we entered an expansive patch of alder on a mountainside. Seconds later a grizzly bear exploded out the far side. Grizzlies are rarely a danger to people traveling in groups; most grizzly attacks are directed at people traveling alone.

After passing the Parks Canada station at the base of Sheep Mountain, the road narrows and twists its way through a series of blind curves along the shore of the lake. This is fairly hazardous driving, so it's best to slow down and take things easy for the 20 miles or so that the road follows the lake shore.

As the road moves away from the lake, travelers pass first through Destruction Bay, then 10 miles farther on, Burwash Landing. At Burwash Landing, the Kluane Museum of Natural History is an excellent stop and a bit of a surprise. Not many travelers expect to find a museum of this quality in such a remote area. It's not large, but very fascinating. There's an admission fee of $1.50 for each adult.

From Burwash Landing to the Alaska border, the road is paved, after a fashion. But, it was a better road when it was gravel. Low-grade pavement is almost impossible to maintain in this region of frost heaves. The next 140 miles offer probably the slowest driving on the entire Alaska Highway because of dips and bulges in the road surface. There's little that can be done other than to slow down and tough it out. Drivers of big motorhomes and vehicles towing large trailers should be particularly careful along this part of the road. Some of these frost heaves can literally tear the suspension out of a vehicle going too fast.

The countryside along here is typical of permafrost regions. The surface is mostly muskeg, sort of half swamp and half ground. Tough to walk across. Trees are mostly stunted spruce. Big trees are a rarity in permafrost areas; tree root systems spread out near the surface instead of penetrating deep into the earth. Because their hold on the ground is tenuous, high winds uproot them easily.

Also, every tree seems to grow at a different angle due to the shifting of the ground. Locally this condition is known as a "drunken forest," a sure indication of permafrost—permanently frozen ground—just a few feet under the surface.

Muskeg areas are also rich in mosquitoes during June and July. Carry plenty of repellent and use it liberally if you get out of your vehicle for any length of time.

By the time you've bounced yourself around on the permafrost heaves from Burwash Landing, Beaver Creek almost seems an oasis, though it's the kind of place not many people would have given a second glance just a few days before. Those desiring hotel accommodations should be early. Bus tours use Beaver Creek as an overnight stop, and many of the rooms available are prebooked. Campers will find a KOA campground in the middle of town. A pleasant site, though not really a great one for tent campers, this campground was designed for RVs. Tent campers should plan to stay at Snag Junction Territorial Campground about 13 miles southeast of town.

Southbound travelers will have to process through Canadian customs at Beaver Creek, usually a fairly simple procedure.

Mount Sanford (Alaska) as seen from the Tok Cutoff.

Beaver Creek, Yukon, to Fairbanks, Alaska

STARTING MILEAGE:_____

MILEAGE: 350 miles (584 km)

DRIVING TIME: About 8 hours

TOWNS EN ROUTE: **Tok**, Alaska, 145 miles (242 km); **Delta Junction**, 253 miles (422 km); **North Pole,** 337 miles (562 km); **Fairbanks,** 350 miles (584 km)

GAS AVAILABLE (besides towns listed above): **First and Last Fuel** (just across Alaska border), 54 miles (90 km); **Wrangell View,** 94 miles (157 km); **40 Mile Roadhouse,** 132 miles (220 km); **Dot Lake,** 192 miles (320 km); **Silver Fox Roadhouse,** 235 miles (392 km); **Richardson Roadhouse,** 281 miles (468 km); **Salcha,** 316 miles (527 km)

CAMPGROUNDS (towns listed above have private campgrounds as well): **Deadman Lake State Campground,** 80 miles (133 km); **Lakeview State Campground,** 88 miles (147 km); **Northway Campground,** 95 miles (158 km); **40 Mile Roadhouse,** 132 miles (220 km); **Tok River State Recreation Site,** 140 miles (233 km); **Moon Lake Wayside,** 163 miles (272 km); **Dot Lake,** 192 miles (320 km); **Cherokee Two Lodge,** 244 miles (407 km); **Delta State Campground,** 254 miles (423 km); **Quartz Lake Recreation Area,** 265 miles (442 km); **Harding Lake State Recreation Area,** 309 miles (515 km); **Chena Lakes Recreation Area,** 334 miles (557 km)

LODGING (besides these, all towns listed above have overnight lodging available): **Wrangell View Motel,** 94 miles (157 km); **40 Mile Roadhouse,** 132 miles (220 km); **Dot Lake Lodge,** 192 miles (320 km); **Silver Fox Roadhouse,** 235 miles (392 km); **Cherokee Two Lodge,** 244 miles (407 km); **Big Delta State Historical Park,** 262 miles (437 km); **Salchaket Homestead,** 309 miles (515 km)

MAJOR TERRAIN FEATURES: Low, rolling hills, mostly forested; mountains to south; major river crossed: Tanana

WILDLIFE: Moose, black bears, eagles, buffalo

FISHING: Grayling, northern pike, rainbows (stocked), salmon

====== Section 5 ======

Beaver Creek, Yukon, to Fairbanks, Alaska

On this leg of the trip you'll quickly note a kind of trade-off. First of all, the road is markedly improved once you enter Alaska, a real treat after the last 150 miles of driving in Yukon Territory.

On the debit side of the ledger, however, the public campgrounds in Alaska are not nearly as well maintained as the territorial campgrounds in Yukon Territory or the provincial parks in British Columbia. With isolated exceptions, this holds true for the entire state. But this distinction is relative. Alaska's public campgrounds are reasonably well maintained; they just don't quite come up to the level that you may have grown accustomed to in Canada.

Distances in Alaska are measured in miles, just as in the rest of the United States. In lieu of kilometer posts at 5-kilometer intervals along the road, as in Canada, there will now be mileposts at 1-mile intervals. Again, some of these get knocked down every year, so don't be distressed if some are missing.

With the exception of gasoline, most travelers' services will be more expensive in Alaska than in Canada. Though the actual dollar figures may seem similar, the U.S. dollar is about 15 percent more valuable than the Canadian dollar. Thus, a $10 camping fee in Alaska would be the equivalent of about $11.50 in Canada.

Road construction projects are treated differently in Alaska, too. Undoubtedly you will have passed considerable road work in the 2,000 or more miles you've already driven in Canada, road work usually done in fairly short stretches with minimal traffic delay problems. In Alaska, however, it's nothing for road crews to completely tear up a 30-to-40-mile section of road and spend 2 years rebuilding it. Thus, traffic delays for road construction in Alaska will likely be longer, and the routes through construction zones more rugged. As in Canada, road crews may be in operation 24 hours a day during the summer months. Construction seasons are pretty short in the Far North.

Leaving Beaver Creek, a narrow, rough, winding road leads about 20 miles to the U.S.–Canada border. This is another stretch where it pays to slow down and take your time. Scenery-wise there isn't much; mostly muskeg and scraggly black spruce line the route.

At the border, a turnout with a large sign is to the left. Most travelers stop here for a short celebration of their trek. If you do stop, take a moment to walk down to the actual border and look north and south. A 20-foot-wide swath cut through the trees marks the border. It stretches beyond the horizon in both directions.

A mile or so past the border, all vehicles and people entering the United States from Canada must pass through U.S. customs. No passport is required for U.S. or Canadian citizens. However, proof of identity and vehicle registration are almost always asked for. Questions pertaining to the value of goods purchased in Canada will likely be asked too. For most travelers, processing at customs takes a few minutes at most.

Insider's Tip: People traveling with pets should carry a health certificate filled out by a veterinarian for each animal. These should be obtained just prior to your departure so they are as current as possible; generally they're valid for 30 days from date of issue. Canadian and U.S. customs officials often ask to see these.

From the border, it's about 125 miles to Tok, the first community of any size right on the highway. En route, however, you will pass a turnoff for Northway, an Indian village about 7 miles south of the road. About 350 people reside in or near Northway, including Chief Walter Northway, who is believed to be more than 100 years old. Even at this age, Chief Northway joined one of the village's annual moose-hunting expeditions in September 1989.

Insider's Tip: Winter travelers should be aware that the region around Northway is often the coldest place in Alaska. In early 1989, temperatures at Northway dipped to nearly 70 degrees below zero.

Northway sits within the 950,000-acre Tetlin National Wildlife Refuge, which was established in 1980. This refuge offers a high density of nesting waterfowl in the summer, along with year-round populations of moose, grizzlies, black bear, wolves, coyotes and red fox. The refuge manager's office in Tok can provide more information about visiting the area. Write to Refuge Manager, Tetlin National Wildlife Refuge, Box 155, Tok, AK 99780, or call (907) 883-5312.

Fishing opportunities are fairly sparse along the first hundred miles or so in Alaska. Deadman Lake State Campground does offer fishermen the chance to catch northern pike averaging a couple of feet long, but these are real skinny fish, locally referred to as snakes.

In Tok there are several opportunities for visitors. First, on the right as you approach town is the Gateway Salmon Bake and Camper Park. Even if you don't plan to camp here, the salmon bake part of the operation offers an excellent meal of fresh Alaska salmon. Salmon bakes began appearing in Alaska in the late 1970s and now are considered some of the best places to eat in the entire state. Generally the salmon is cooked over an open fire and a fixed price allows seconds on the main course and all you can eat of various side dishes.

Tok also bills itself as the "Sled Dog Capital of Alaska." There are daily demonstrations in town for summer visitors, and those who want to obtain a husky or malamute will find plenty of dogs to consider in Tok. Write to Tok Information Center, Box 359, Tok, AK 99780, or call (907) 883-5667 for information on Tok-area activities.

Full repair services for vehicles are available in Tok, along with car washes. Labor rates start at $45 per hour for repairs.

From Tok, it's little more than 100 miles to Delta Junction. About 35 miles prior to reaching Delta, there's a very real possibility of seeing buffalo at roadside. These big animals are the descendants of a transplant of a few buffalo made in the 1920s. The herd now numbers about 350.

One of the attractions for buffalo are farms. In the 1970s, the state of Alaska made an effort to start a large commercial farming operation, primarily barley, near Delta Junction. Commercially, the venture has proved less than successful, though many of the farms on lands leased from the state are still in operation. Mostly these farms are along side roads leading off the highway to the north.

As folks in Delta Junction will quickly tell you, their town is the official end of the Alaska Highway. When the road was built in 1942, a road already existed from Delta Junction to Fairbanks, the final leg of the Richardson Highway from Valdez. In both Delta and Fairbanks are markers commemorating the end of the Alaska Highway. But, since few folks target Delta Junction as the termination of their Alaska Highway experience, this book will use Fairbanks as the ultimate destination for highway travelers.

As its name implies, Delta Junction is a road junction. The Alaska Highway/Richardson Highway continues straight ahead through town; the Richardson Highway leading south to Valdez is to the left.

Just outside of Delta, the trans-Alaska pipeline crosses the Tanana River next to the highway bridge. This is probably the best view of the pipeline anywhere in the state, and there are turnouts on both sides of the bridge for those desiring a longer look. More than a million barrels (44 million gallons) of North Slope oil flow daily through the pipeline to the tanker terminal in Valdez. Taxes on oil provide for more than 80 percent of the state budget. Because of the oil, there is no state income tax or statewide sales tax in Alaska. Any sales taxes charged are local taxes imposed by a city or borough.

The turnout prior to the Tanana River bridge is for Big Delta State Historical Park, featuring a completely rebuilt roadhouse. Rika's Roadhouse, as it is known, was established in 1910 as an overnight stop for travelers on the stage/sled trail from Valdez to Fairbanks. Meals are available to help visitors savor this small part of Alaska's history.

In July, interior fishermen get their first crack at Alaska's legendary king salmon in the Salcha River, about 57 miles from Delta. If the salmon are in, there'll be plenty of cars near the bridge or in the Salcha River Wayside to the right just before crossing the bridge. These fish have migrated half the length of the Yukon River and several hundred miles of the Tanana River before turning into the clear waters of the Salcha. Fishermen pull salmon of 45 to 50 pounds from this stream every year; an average king weighs 20 to 30 pounds. Though this is far from the best salmon stream in Alaska, it's the one most Alaska Highway drivers reach first, and "king-salmon fever" is not easily denied. There are chum salmon mixed in with the kings, though these are not nearly as sought after.

From the Salcha River, it's a pleasant 45-minute drive the rest of the way into Fairbanks.

Insider's Tip: King salmon fishermen should use medium- to heavy-duty spinning or casting rods, with a minimum of 200 yards of 20-pound test line on their reels. Best bait for kings is a glob of salmon roe bounced along the stream bottom. Be sure you have a current Alaska fishing license.

Fairbanks was the site of the second big gold rush after the Klondike Gold Rush of 1898. Between these two events were the discoveries at Nome on Alaska's west coast.

An Italian immigrant prospector, Felix Pedro, discovered gold in a stream about 15 miles north of Fairbanks in 1902. The city was actually established in 1901, when E. T. Barnette was unable to move a sternwheeler loaded with supplies any farther on the Tanana or Chena rivers, which join together just west of town. As Barnette's contract with the boat's skipper spelled out, Barnette, his party and the supplies for a trading post were unceremoniously dumped on the riverbank when it became apparent the boat could proceed no further, due to shallow water. Barnette had hoped to get much farther up the river, to a point near present-day Delta, to take advantage of inside information he had about a trail being built through the region. His seeming misfortune turned into good fortune with Pedro's discovery of gold. The history of early-day Fairbanks revolves around Barnette's wheeling and dealing for gold claims and real estate manipulation.

Thus, Fairbanks was a boom town, but a boom town that survived as a transportation hub for interior Alaska. Its history since the gold rush has been a series of booms and busts, the most recent being the boom that ensued with the building of the trans-Alaska pipeline in the mid-1970s.

In Fairbanks, visitors can relive some of the flavor of past years by riding a modern-day sternwheeler or whooping it up in the Malemute or Palace saloons. The latter is located in Alaskaland, at the edge of downtown Fairbanks. Alaskaland is a theme park dedicated to preserving the gold-rush heritage of Fairbanks.

Campers will find a notable lack of campsites in or close to Fairbanks. A good bet for drivers of self-contained RVs is the Alaskaland parking lot. It is centrally located, offers great access to Alaska's original salmon bake restaurant and, of course, to Alaskaland. The best bet for tent campers is the Chena River Recreation Site near the Chena River bridge on University Avenue, about two miles from Alaskaland.

Fairbanks is a fairly modern city with about 60,000 people residing in the immediate area. Two large military bases, Fort Wainwright and Eielson Air Force Base, are just outside of town.

A must-stop site for travelers is the University of Alaska Museum. Sitting on a hill above the university, the relatively new structure houses a superb collection of Alaskan artifacts and natural history exhibits. Probably the single exhibit most people will remember all their lives is a stuffed Alaska brown bear standing more than 9 feet tall, one of the largest bears ever taken in Alaska.

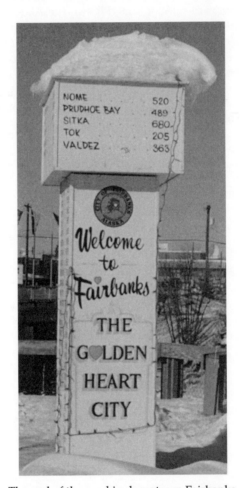

The end of the road in downtown Fairbanks.

$\cdot \longrightarrow 10 \longrightarrow \cdot$

TOURING ALASKA
BY VEHICLE

A few minutes spent with a road map quickly makes it clear that it's impossible to tour *all* of Alaska in a vehicle. Roads just don't exist to the western reaches of the state and throughout most of the Arctic.

However, what roads there are offer scenery the likes of which can be found nowhere else, and these same roads lead to adventures beyond almost anyone's dreams.

This chapter breaks Alaska's road system into three distinct sections. A fourth section on Alaska's roads will start the next chapter, which offers suggested routes for the return trip. As the sections in this chapter are laid out, it would take a minimum of 5 days to cover all the trips listed in the Fairbanks area, 2 or 3 days for the road system between Fairbanks and Anchorage and at least 2 (3 or 4 are better) for the Kenai Peninsula south of Anchorage. These times are minimum figures and leave little additional time for exploring, sampling the fishing or berry picking.

If you have only a week or so to spend in Alaska, it's probably better to select one or, at most, two of these areas and explore them thoroughly. The other parts of the state can wait for a return trip. With rare exceptions, very few visitors are satisfied with a single visit to Alaska.

Fairbanks Area Roads

Chena Hot Springs Road

LENGTH: 57 miles (95 km)

GAS AVAILABLE: **Anders Cache**, 10 miles (17 km)

LODGING: **Chena Hot Springs**, 57 miles (95 km)

CAMPGROUNDS: **Mile 27 State Campground**, 27 miles (45 km); **North Fork Chena River**, 39 miles (65 km); **Chena Hot Springs**, 57 miles (95 km)

WILDLIFE: Moose and black bears

FISHING: Grayling

The Steese Highway

LENGTH: 162 miles (270 km)

GAS AVAILABLE: **Curry's Corner**, 5 miles (8 km); **Miner Ed's Trading Post**, 42 miles (70 km); **Miracle Mile Lodge**, 66 miles (110 km); **Central**, 128 miles (213 km); **Circle**, 162 miles (270 km)

LODGING: **Chatanika Lodge**, 29 miles (48 km); **Miracle Mile Lodge**, 66 miles (110 km); **Central**, 128 miles (213 km)

CAMPGROUNDS: **Chatanika River Wayside**, 39 miles (65 miles); **Cripple Creek**, 60 miles (100 km); **Bedrock Creek**, 119 miles (198 km); **Circle** (on Yukon River banks), 162 miles (270 km)

WILDLIFE: Black bears, moose, caribou (rarely)

FISHING: Grayling

The Elliott Highway

LENGTH: 152 miles (253 km)

GAS AVAILABLE: **Hilltop Cafe**, 5 miles (8 km); **Manley**, 152 miles (253 km)

LODGING: **Manley**, 152 miles (253 km)

CAMPGROUNDS: **Lower Chatanika**, 11 miles (18 km); **Tolvana River** (unimproved), 75 miles (125 km); **Manley**, 152 miles (253 km)

WILDLIFE: Black bears, moose, wolves (rarely)

FISHING: Northern pike and grayling

The Dalton Highway

LENGTH: 414 miles (690 km). Road is open to general traffic only to Disaster Creek, 209 miles (348 km) from the start. Travel beyond Disaster Creek must be authorized in advance by the Alaska Department of Transportation. Permits are not granted to visitors unless valid business requirements necessitate vehicle travel.

GAS AVAILABLE: **Yukon River** bridge, 56 miles (93 km); **Coldfoot Services**, 175 miles (292 km)

LODGING: **Yukon Ventures Alaska**, 56 miles (93 km); **Coldfoot Services**, 175 miles (292 km)

CAMPSITES (no hookups available): **Hess Creek** gravel bar, 24 miles (40 km); **Yukon River** bridge, 56 miles (93 km); **The Arctic Circle**, 115 miles (192 km); **Jim River**, 139 miles (232 km); **Marion Creek**, 180 miles (300 km)

WILDLIFE: Black bears, moose, Dall sheep, grizzly bears

FISHING: Northern pike, burbot, grayling, Dolly Varden

==== Section 1 ====

Fairbanks Area Roads

Unless you're headed south to Anchorage or back down the Alaska Highway toward Canada, all of the driving opportunities in this region start on a single road leading north from town, the Steese Highway. On the Steese, it's 4.6 miles to the turnoff for Chena Hot Springs Road and 11 miles to the Elliott Highway turnoff in Fox. From Fox on the Elliott Highway, it's 73 miles to the start of the Dalton Highway.

All of the mileages given above are for the actual start of the road described. Thus, if you are driving the Dalton Highway, you must first drive 11 miles to Fox, then 73 miles on the Elliott Highway to the start of the road. In this example, you have 84 miles to drive from Fairbanks before you can begin the trip on the Dalton Highway.

All of the Dalton Highway, all but the first 28 miles of the Elliott Highway, and most of the Steese Highway are gravel-surfaced roads. Of these four drives available north of Fairbanks, only Chena Hot Springs Road is completely paved. All suggestions offered in earlier chapters about driving on gravel roads are valid here, with the added provisos that these roads are often less traveled and even more remote, particularly the Dalton Highway. The Dalton was built in the mid-1970s and is locally known as the Pipeline Haul Road or, more simply, the Haul Road.

Chena Hot Springs Road

Winter, summer, spring and fall, this road is Fairbanks' weekend playground. In the summer there are picnicking, camping, hiking, canoeing and fishing for grayling along the banks of the Chena River. In fall, moose and black bear hunters park at roadside and enter likely looking patches of forest. In the winter and spring, cross-country skiers find terrain to test every skill level. Throughout every season of the year, at the end of the road there's an indoor hot springs pool suitable for soaking away your cares. Finally, about 20 miles up the road is one of the Fairbanks area's finest restaurants, Two Rivers Lodge. Try the Cajun barbecued ribs if they're available on the night you visit.

You can drive the road in an hour or so; it's only 57 miles from where it leaves the Steese Highway (4.6 miles from Fairbanks) to the end of the road at Chena Hot Springs Lodge. The first 26 miles wind gently through rolling terrain, the land a mix of occasional fields (mostly hay) and boreal forest. Twenty-six miles into the road, you enter the Chena River Recreation Area for the next 24 miles.

Within the recreation area are several possibilities for canoeists—floats of an hour or more to a couple of days if you want to drift all the way into downtown Fairbanks. Popular day trips for canoeists include floating from Mile 39.5 to Mile 37.9, at most a couple of hours on a lazy afternoon. Longer floats, with the same take-out site at Mile 37.9, begin at Mile 44 and Mile 52.3. The Mile 44 float is about a 7-hour jaunt, the other about 12 to 15 hours if you do it in a single day. The river parallels the road for these trips, though it is often out of sight and earshot of the road.

Besides native fish in the river itself, several small lakes at roadside are stocked with grayling. These lakes are at Mile 30, Mile 43.8, Mile 45.5 and Mile 47.9. In the river, grayling should be available at any point where you can reach the riverbank. Check fishing regulations carefully before fishing, however. Because this is the most popular grayling fishery in the state, bag limits are fairly low (two fish a day in 1989), and the area is carefully patrolled for violators.

Insider's Tip: The best time to catch Chena River grayling is usually late May (Memorial Day weekend) when the fish are moving upstream to spawning and summer feeding areas. Stand in one spot near the shore and every time a school of fish swims into view, cast to them. The schools of fish will come at fairly rapid intervals.

Two excellent trails are available for hikers, both suitable for either day hiking or overnight excursions. The first is the Granite Tors Trail, whose trailhead is at Mile 39.5. On this trail it's 6 miles to the first tors (a *tor* is a stark outcropping of rock) and 8 miles to the main grouping of tors—the latter a 16-mile round trip if you elect to do it in a single day. Be sure to carry water on this trail.

More ambitious hikers will want to check out the Chena Dome Loop Trail. The trailheads are at miles 48.9 and 50.5. In between, the trail takes a circuitous 29-mile route through the hills and valleys of this part of Alaska. Allow at least 2 days to do the whole loop; 3 days are even better. As with the Granite Tors Trail, plan to carry plenty of water.

Though the water in the Chena River and elsewhere in Alaska may look quite clear, it isn't suitable for drinking until you've boiled it for several minutes or pumped it through an adequate filter. Giardia ("beaver fever") is prevalent in most Alaskan watersheds. Those who have experienced the extreme abdominal discomfort of this disease will tell you it's nothing to fool with.

In August, berry pickers delight in vast fields of blueberries and cranberries at various points along the road. In Alaska's interior, blueberry bushes are low shrubs producing a profusion of tiny, tart, but oh-so-good berries. If you're not sure where to look, watch for cars parked at roadside and people stooped over in the open areas nearby—they're almost certainly picking blueberries.

Human berry pickers will occasionally bump into Mother Nature's most ardent berry picker, a black bear. Usually the bear is just as surprised as the people involved. Stay together in groups of two or more, make lots of noise talking and laughing and the odds are you won't have any unexpected encounters.

Insider's Tip: If you do meet a bear that doesn't run away when it realizes you are near, face it and back away slowly, all the while talking in a relatively normal voice. Turning to run may excite the bear into giving chase. If you are charged by a bear, climb a tree if one is available and if you have time. If the bear catches you, drop face forward onto the ground, curl up into a fetal position with your back in the air, and remain perfectly still.

Bears are extremely unpredictable, that much is known. The techniques noted here can never be considered 100 percent effective. Statistically, though, these have proven to be the best responses available. Another statistic to consider if you're nervous about bears is that most bear attacks happen to people who are alone or separated from the group. Stick close together with one or more companions and you'll almost certainly be left alone by the bears.

Most bear encounters, and there are thousands every year in Alaska, wind up as nonthreatening, even humorous, though they might not seem so at the time they happen. As an example, one of the funniest bear stories in Alaska came off of the Chena Hot Springs Road about 10 years ago. A young couple from the lower 48 was visiting relatives—the man's brother, who was stationed with the Army at Fort Wainwright near Fairbanks. One weekend they camped out in one of the Chena Hot Springs Road camp-grounds. The Alaskan relative offered space in his huge wall tent for his brother and the brother's wife. They declined, preferring instead to try out the tiny backpacking tent they'd purchased just for their Alaskan adven-ture.

With two people in this tight space, their fluffed-up sleeping bags were pressed lightly against the sides of the tent. Early in the morning a young black bear wandered into camp and sat down beside the small tent, fascinated by the rhythm of the tent wall rising and falling with the woman's breathing. She was sleeping on her stomach, so the most obvious bulge in the side of the tiny A-frame-shaped tent was over her rear end. After watching for a time, the bear leaned forward against the tent, placed his left front paw on the back of the woman's thighs, his right paw on the small of her back and nipped her in the behind through the tent fabric and the sleeping bag. Though pinched a little, she was unhurt.

As you might guess, some screaming ensued, which prompted the curious bear to scamper around to the doorway in front of the tent, where he plopped down to look inside. Since only the mosquito netting had been zipped closed, the bear could look in and the people could look out. The humans inside the tent wouldn't go out the door with the bear sitting there, so the bear stared at the people, and the people stared at the bear. Things continued in a standoff until the brother in the big tent stumbled outside to see what was going on. At that point the bear scampered away, and the couple in the small tent quickly moved into the big tent for the remainder of the night.

Bear stories aside, Chena Hot Springs Road is a pleasant outdoor playground with a special place at the end of the road, Chena Hot Springs Lodge. Lying back at the end of the day in the pool's naturally warmed water is good for the soul, and afterwards there is a great restaurant in the lodge as well as overnight accommodations. If you visit the restaurant, be sure to sample the home-baked pies.

The Steese Highway

Until the Pipeline Haul Road was completed in the mid-1970s, the Steese Highway offered one of only two routes to the shores of the Yukon River in Alaska. Then and now, it is still the most popular route.

When you pull into Fairbanks on the Alaska Highway, you come to a four-way intersection with a stoplight. To the left is downtown Fairbanks and the road to Anchorage; to the right is Fort Wainwright; the Steese Highway begins straight ahead. The Steese sweeps around the east side of Fairbanks and heads due north at first, gradually swinging to the northeast.

Arguably, gold was responsible for the Steese Highway. Felix Pedro's discovery claim, which resulted in part from the founding of Fairbanks, is just north of the city along the Steese. It's well marked and has a wide graveled area for stopping. Beyond that, about 127 miles from Fairbanks, lies Central, the town that grew up in a region where gold was being mined before it was discovered near Fairbanks. Gold is still mined in the hills and streams around Central, though little of this activity is visible to road travelers. However, the lower Steese Highway near Fairbanks offers several things of interest to those wanting to sample Alaska's golden past.

Near Fox and at intervals along the highway, the bottom lands are filled with mounded gravel. These are the tailings left by gold dredges that worked through area streams. A gold dredge is a metal mechanical monster designed to scoop gravel from stream bottoms, process it for gold and spit all the other stuff out the back. Even the smallest streams in gold-producing areas would get the gold dredge treatment. Dredges worked their way gradually downstream by digging a hole to float in and filling it in behind them. Though they floated, dredges can't be called boats. Before they could move, they had to dig out another place to float. The dredges gradually worked their way downstream crisscrossing the valley, trying to leave no stone or bit of bedrock unscraped in the quest for the precious yellow metal.

Today, environmentalists would have a fit were you to suggest reactivating an inland gold dredge. Without a doubt, these machines significantly alter the landscape. However, it is possible to visit gold dredges today, because when the gold ran out, these things were just left where they stopped. Little more than 9 miles from Fairbanks on the Steese Highway sits Gold Dredge #8. Guided tours are available and you can try your hand at panning for gold. There are also a restaurant, bar and hotel for those who want to stay a little longer.

Insider's Tip: If you tour the gold dredge, try to imagine yourself living and working on this monster. It ran 24 hours a day, every day during the season, and its job was processing rocks. The noise from the uninsulated conveyor system must have been deafening.

Officially, Gold Dredge #8 is a "National Historical Mechanical Engineering Landmark." (I'll bet that's a designation you've never heard before.) The dredge last operated in 1959. In the past few years, this five-story, 250-foot-long dredge has been restored and opened to the public, rapidly becoming one of the Fairbanks area's most visited attractions.

Insider's Tip: Probably the best spot along Alaska's road system for viewing the trans-Alaska pipeline is along the Steese Highway just prior to reaching Fox. The pipe is above ground and right next to the road. A turnout with an interpretive sign is located there.

From the dredge, the Steese Highway winds past Fox, past Pedro's discovery claim and up to Cleary Summit, a little less than 21 miles from Fairbanks. Atop Cleary Summit (2,233 feet) you look out over the Chatanika River valley, which the road follows upstream for about the next 45 miles. Like the Chena River, there is grayling fishing available in the Chatanika as well as canoeing. The Chatanika, though, is not as heavily used as is the Chena.

As far as fishing goes, the Chatanika does have one far-out thing that the Chena lacks—a spear fishery for whitefish, usually about the third week in September, just a few days before freeze-up. Most of the action takes place on a Saturday night at the Chatanika River Wayside, 39 miles from Fairbanks. Otherwise sane adults pull on hipboots, hoist a lighted gasoline lantern in one hand and a spear in the other and wade into the river. Amid much shouting, consumption of personal antifreeze and general revelry, these folks stand all night in freezing water trying to spear whitefish, which really aren't very big. Often this event coincides with the first snowfall of the year. If you've got a snug camper or motorhome to sleep in, it's certainly something to see. But, be careful: should you get bit by the whitefish bug, you just might find yourself standing in the middle of a rapidly freezing river, all the while trying to think up some believable story for the folks back home.

Seventeen miles or so past Chatanika Wayside a large pipe is visible to the left. This is part of the Davidson Ditch, built in the 1920s to move water down to the gold dredges. After the dredges shut down, the water flow was used to generate electrical power until 1967, when a major flood in Fairbanks flattened more than 1,000 feet of the pipe.

Insider's Tip: Fishermen will want to look closely for a one-lane dirt road on the right side of the pipe. It leads about 8 miles to Nome Creek. At Nome Creek, turn left on the dredge tailings, where you'll find a trail that winds back and forth across the creek for a couple more miles until the tailings end. Start fishing for grayling right there or in several of the clear pools among the dredge tailings. This is one of the hottest grayling streams in the Fairbanks area. This road cannot be recommended for any vehicle, but if you want to try it, your best bet is a powerful four-wheel-drive pickup truck.

Past the Davidson Ditch, the road continues to climb. When the climbing stops this time, drivers will find themselves well above timberline at Eagle Summit, 3,624 feet, 108 miles from Fairbanks. Timberline in this part of the world extends to between 2,500 and 3,000 feet. For folks used to the Colorado Rockies, where timberline starts above 10,000 feet, these numbers are pretty low. But they are handy. Using these numbers, travelers almost always have a means of estimating the heights of various mountains.

For example, say you note from a distance that timberline on a coastal mountain ends about one-third of the way up the mountain. Using that observation, you wouldn't be very far wrong to say that the mountain is about 7,500 feet high. You do, however, have to be a little careful and have some sense of where you start in relation to sea level. Say you're sitting at an elevation about 1,000 feet above sea level and you see another mountain where the timbered slopes run one-third of the way up. In this case, the summit would be only about 4,500 feet, because there are only 1,500 feet between you and the timberline.

At any rate, Eagle Summit is well above timberline. This is great country for ptarmigan hunting in August or September, but Eagle Summit is best known for the summer solstice.

Though it doesn't ever get completely dark during summer nights in Fairbanks, the sun does set at least briefly every night. But on June 21, if the sky is clear, the added elevation at Eagle Summit means watchers can see the sun that never sets. At midnight (true midnight, not daylight savings time), the sun dips against the northern horizon but never quite sinks below it. On any given June 21, several hundred Fairbanksans trek to Eagle Summit hoping that the weather will permit them a glimpse of the midnight sun. The weather cooperates about half the time.

Insider's Tip: If you are stuck in Fairbanks on June 21, take heart—there's another special event in this land of perpetual daylight. Fairbanks' semipro baseball team, the Goldpanners, plays its first home game on the night of June 21. Start time is somewhere between 10 P. M. and midnight, and the game is played without lights.

From Eagle Summit, the Steese Highway drops rapidly down to Central, one of the interior's oldest settlements—and, these days, one of the smallest. Central services various mining operations in the hills around town, though you won't see many of these folks in town during the summer. Those who make their living mining gold have only a few short summer months to extract a year's livelihood.

Just on the northern edge of Central there's a road junction. Straight ahead leads to Circle on the Yukon River. The road to the right leads to Circle

Hot Springs, possibly the finest hot springs resort in Alaska that is accessible by road. Circle Hot Springs is open year-round, though it's usually a fly-in resort during the snowbound months. There's a great pool, outdoors but sheltered from the wind, and a renovated lodge that has stood on this site for decades. Circle Hot Springs is less than 9 miles from the junction on the Steese Highway.

The last 35 miles of the Steese Highway, from Central to Circle (also known as Circle City), is mostly through lowland forests of spruce and birch. Circle, 162 miles from Fairbanks, was erroneously named by area miners in the late 19th century who thought the townsite was actually on the Arctic Circle. Unfortunately, the Arctic Circle is about 50 miles farther north.

Circle periodically floods in May. When the ice goes out on the Yukon River each year, ice jams form from time to time. When one of these jams occurs just downstream from Circle, the water quickly backs up into town. When the ice jam releases, usually within hours to a day or so, the town quickly drains. At the entrance to the campground on the riverbank in Circle is a large plywood sign welcoming visitors to the campground. The last time the Yukon River flooded the town during breakup, the water reached the bottom of this sign, about 4 1/2 feet above the ground.

The Elliott Highway

This road leads to some fairly wild and remote country. It also passes through active gold mining areas where owners are often adamant about their private property signs. Specific regions of gold-mining activity include the settlement of Livengood (no services available) at 71 miles from the road's start at Fox, and Eureka, 131 miles from Fox.

There are few services available at any point on this road except at the start and finish. Therefore travelers should start this trek with a full gas tank.

These liabilities aside, this is a beautiful drive through the heart of interior Alaska. Most of the route is forested with scraggly black spruce and stands of birch. There is some fairly open country at roadside about 100 miles into the route, country heavy with extensive fields of blueberries.

At the start of the road is a picnic area by Fox Spring. Area residents have long cherished the sparkling water that comes from the ground year-round at this point. Many make regular trips to the spring for drinking water, ignoring the relatively pure water delivered to the taps in their homes. It's well worth a stop to fill water bottles or just for tasting the water.

From the spring, it's little more than 4 miles to Hilltop, a cafe and gas station on the left side. This is a favorite stop for Haul Road truckers and at any given time there will likely be several rigs parked out front. This is also the last gas available before reaching Manley at the end of the road, some 147 miles distant.

The first 73 miles of this road is an extension of the Haul Road, and truck traffic can be particularly heavy at times. Be exceedingly careful during dry periods, because these 18-wheelers kick up blinding clouds of dust. The majority of the northbound truckers turn off on the Dalton Highway 73 miles from Fox, leaving the second half of the Elliott Highway relatively free of traffic.

Prior to reaching the Dalton Highway junction, the Elliott crosses both the Chatanika and Tolovana rivers. There's a splendid campground and picnic area next to the Chatanika River bridge (11 miles), though fishing here is mediocre at best, except for a few brief days just after breakup when grayling are moving upstream to summer spawning and feeding areas.

The Tolovana River, 57 miles from Fox, offers slightly better fishing for small grayling as well as opportunities to catch northern pike. Pike are thrilling sport, particularly on light tackle. Minto Flats, the extensive region of lakes and marsh to the south of the road, regularly produces pike in excess of 30 pounds. River fish will likely be smaller. As a general rule, it takes big water to hold big pike.

Minto Flats is also the favorite region for interior waterfowlers. Best access is usually a 15-minute charter flight from Fairbanks, though it can be reached by road from the village of Minto, accessed by an 11-mile side road that begins at mile 110 of the Elliott Highway. Minto and the surrounding lands are private property belonging to the Native village. Strangers are often looked over critically by local residents. Should you elect to drive to Minto and put a boat into the flats to sample the waterfowl hunting or the fishing, be careful out on the water. Native fishermen set gill nets throughout the area, and these are sometimes difficult to spot as you speed through the lakes or marshes in a power boat. A line of cork floats, usually white, just barely breaking the surface of the water is the only indication of a gill net.

Insider's Tip: Should you wish to stop at Minto just to observe village life or to sample the fishing and waterfowling, it would be good to inquire at the Tanana Chiefs' office in Fairbanks prior to setting out. This organization, listed in the phone book, serves various villages throughout interior Alaska and can make several suggestions as to timing and activities.

Beyond the Dalton Highway junction, this is a fairly narrow road and not nearly as well maintained. Though it is open year-round and maintained by the state of Alaska, parts of it can be exceedingly rough.

Probably the best fishing available along the entire road is at Baker Creek, 137 miles from Fox. All summer long this creek is capable of producing grayling to 20 inches in length.

Probably no other fish symbolizes the purity of arctic waters more than the grayling. It's generally found in only the clearest streams. Fresh from the water, there is no finer eating available. The flesh is white, delicate and smells faintly of thyme. When first pulled from the water the skin shimmers in rich purple hues, though these colors recede to a dark gray with the death of the fish. Prime grayling lures are small silver spinners and various small flies.

Approaching Manley, a side road leads 16 miles to a former mining area known as Tofty. Though there is still some mining around Tofty, the situation is more congenial, though visitors should scrupulously obey private property signs. Inquire locally in Manley before driving to Tofty.

Just prior to entering Manley, Manley Hot Springs is to the right. The lodge there offers a great hot springs pool and tours to fish camps, gold mines and sled-dog kennels.

Four-time Iditarod champion Susan Butcher lives and maintains her kennel on the outskirts of Manley. She dominated this 1,049-mile endurance race from Anchorage to Nome in the late 1980s. It's probably best not to drop in unannounced, but local inquiries in Manley should produce information on whether or not Susan or her husband Dave Monsen are available and willing to provide kennel tours.

Susan's archrival on the Iditarod Trail, and the Iditarod's only other four-time champion, used to live and train his teams near Manley. Rick Swensen, however, moved closer to Fairbanks several years ago, leaving Susan as the undisputed champion musher in the Manley area.

Manley itself rests on the banks of the Tanana River, with about 90 full-time residents. Residents here live a largely self-sufficient lifestyle with few of the amenities most other people take for granted. Some of the vegetable and berry gardens surrounding well-kept homes must be seen to be believed. It takes a fair amount of work to produce these kinds of crops in interior Alaska.

For a real taste of the past, stop in at the Manley Roadhouse, a great place to meet the local citizens—mostly miners, trappers and mushers—over refreshments. Try the blueberry pie, a house specialty, for a real treat.

Fishermen will find pike to 3 feet long in the Manley Hot Springs Slough. A campground on the slough offers a boat launch for those who have the equipment to get away from the immediate shoreline.

Northern pike prefer big pieces of bright hardware—red-and-white or black-and-white spoons being favorites. Best to use a steel leader in front of the lure, as these fish have mouths filled with jagged teeth that make short work of most fishing line. Fly fishermen will find that big, bright streamers will take pike. On a flyrod, catching a pike best correlates to that old cliché about having a tiger by the tail.

Insider's Tip: Pike fishermen should carry long-nosed pliers for removing hooks from a pike's toothy jaws. You risk your fingers otherwise.

The Dalton Highway

Of the various roads described in this guide, the Dalton Highway is far and away the most remote and potentially the most rugged trek available. It is also the one road where having a second spare tire makes sense. In the entire 211 miles of this road available for public travel (summer only), there are but two facilities offering limited repairs or services.

Also, travelers should carry extra food and a complete first aid kit. Help can be a long time coming along this road. Being prepared is the key phrase. Breakdowns will cost you money. Towing services along the Dalton Highway commonly cost in the range of $5 per mile.

From its junction with the Elliott Highway, the Dalton Highway is open year-round to general travel as far as the Yukon River bridge, about 56 miles. From the Yukon River north to Disaster Creek, the road is open to the public from June 1 to September 1. North of Disaster Creek to Prudhoe Bay, the road is closed to all but industrial traffic. All these closures, however, may change in the years ahead. The Dalton Highway is partially maintained by federal funds, and there is pressure to open the entire road to the public on a year-round basis.

Insider's Tip: Stop only where there are pullouts available off the road. The Dalton Highway is fairly narrow and used mostly by truckers driving 18-wheelers, many with extra trailers. Truckers tend to "make time," which means that they are often unwilling to slow down and that they raise tremendous clouds of dust during dry periods. If you are engulfed in a cloud of dust at roadside, another trucker approaching may not be able to see your vehicle.

Along the Dalton, the speed limit is 45 mph. The road is patrolled by the Alaska State Troopers. If you need police assistance, there is a trooper permanently stationed at Coldfoot, 175 miles from the Elliott Highway junction.

At intervals along the road, you will see one-lane trails leading up to the trans-Alaska pipeline. These trails are generally barricaded and are not open to public travel. The trans-Alaska pipeline and its access roads are private property.

Grades along this road are steep, at times exceeding 10 percent. Again, this road was built for industry by industry, and general vehicle travel was not a factor in its construction.

All the cautions aside, this is a spectacular trip, a trip that offers the only road access to the Brooks Range, Alaska's northernmost mountain range. Many Alaskans consider the mountains of the Brooks Range to be the most beautiful in the world, and with good reason. Jagged peaks, stunning valleys and endlessly varying terrain leave no time for boredom. Unfortunately, travelers cannot cross the range; private vehicles are stopped just prior to climbing over Atigun Pass. Fortunately, the south side of the Brooks Range offers the best scenery and the most breathtaking vistas for travelers.

Northbound from the Elliott Highway junction, the terrain is mostly rolling hills with small creeks. The largest of the creeks, Hess Creek, 24 miles from the junction, offers good fishing for whitefish and grayling. You can camp here, if you wish; there is a gravel bar alongside the creek on the north side of the bridge. There are no facilities in terms of tables or outhouses.

From Hess Creek, it's about 32 miles to the Yukon River. The bridge here offers the only vehicle crossing of the Yukon in Alaska. One of North America's mightiest rivers, the Yukon's drainage includes nearly half of Alaska and much of Yukon Territory, Canada.

In July and August it may be possible to obtain fresh-caught salmon from commercial fishermen on the Yukon. Much of the catch is carried upriver to the bridge and shipped by vehicle to Fairbanks. These salmon are the most protein-rich fish in the world, many of them heading all the way to Canada to spawn. No other salmon in North America make such a tremendous journey (1,500 or more miles) after leaving salt water, so these fish must be stronger than most others. Even at the Dalton Highway bridge, hundreds and hundreds of miles from salt water in the Bering Sea, these are bright, shiny fish showing little evidence of the decay that usually begins when salmon enter fresh water.

The north side of the Yukon River bridge also offers one of only two places to purchase gas or get your car repaired along the Dalton Highway. Here you'll find a restaurant and other travelers' facilities. Best to fill up here. It's 120 miles to the next gas station at Coldfoot.

Insider's Tip: Carry plenty of water. Drinking water is available only at the Yukon River bridge, Coldfoot and from an artesian well 5 miles north of the bridge. Water from streams, no matter how clear it appears, must be boiled for several minutes before drinking.

North of the Yukon, fishermen should start thinking of limbering up their rods. An assortment of streams offer possibilities for burbot, pike, grayling and Dolly Varden. Of all the streams at roadside in Alaska, these are the least visited. Good spots to try (and distances from the Yukon River) include: Ray River (15 miles), No Name Creek (24 miles), Kanuti River (50 miles), Fish Creek (59 miles), South Fork Bonanza Creek (69 miles), North Fork Bonanza Creek (70 miles), Prospect Creek (80 miles), Jim River (bridges at 85, 86 and 89 miles) and the South Fork of the Koyukuk River (101 miles).

Insider's Tip: Though the water is open in June, good fishing north of the Yukon River usually doesn't occur until July and August. In June, most rivers are high and muddy from melting snows.

Campgrounds along the Dalton Highway are sparsely furnished if furnished at all. Most good camping spots are simply level areas near the fishing streams that have been used by others. As such, no litter barrels or maintenance are provided. An exception is a campground right on the Arctic Circle, 60 miles north of the Yukon River bridge. This campground is about half a mile to the right of the road if you are northbound, and the turnoff is marked. A large, colorful sign denotes the Arctic Circle for travelers. There is a litter barrel in this campground. When you camp in other areas, burn all combustible trash in a safe campfire and carry your noncombustible garbage with you until you reach a suitable disposal site.

Insider's Tip: Be extremely careful when planning a campfire. Most of the ground along the Dalton Highway is either tundra or muskeg, both of which are mostly vegetation susceptible to catching fire. Riverbank gravel bars, or areas cleared to bare soil/gravel during road construction, are often the only sure places to have a safe campfire. Forest fires are expensive to fight in Alaska, and government agencies have begun presenting bills for fire-fighting services when the cause can be traced to a person or group of people.

Sixty miles north of the Arctic Circle is Coldfoot, a small community more or less at the base of the Brooks Range. Travelers' services here are owned by Dick and Cathy Mackey. Dick, one of the North's more colorful characters, won the Iditarod Trail Sled Dog Race from Anchorage to Nome in 1977 and still runs the race occasionally. He also organized the Coldfoot Classic sled-dog race, which takes place in April in and around the western edge of Gates of the Arctic National Park. The Coldfoot Classic has become one of Alaska's better-known middle-distance races for mushers and their dogs. It's also the last big race of the season for distance mushers.

Also at Coldfoot, the National Park Service has established an information center for Gates of the Arctic National Park, whose eastern boundary is just to the west of the road. One of Alaska's remotest national parks, Gates of the Arctic is accessible only via chartered airplane or on foot from the road. The hiking is strenuous, and there are no maintained trails.

From Coldfoot north to Disaster Creek, where nonindustry travelers must turn around, the cliffs surrounding the road offer opportunities for viewing Dall sheep. Look among the rocks and open alpine areas for flashes of pure white. Binoculars are usually required for best viewing.

Bears, both black and grizzly, are frequently seen along the Dalton Highway. Highest concentrations of black bears are found at lower elevations and in wooded regions. Grizzlies generally inhabit the more open tundra in alpine areas.

Insider's Tip: Do not feed the bears. Over the years a number of "road bears," both blacks and grizzlies, have been created along the Dalton Highway by people unthinkingly providing handouts. Some bears, particularly grizzlies, will occasionally lie down in the center of the road and force you to stop, then saunter up to the driver's door looking for a handout. Feeding bears in Alaska is punishable by fines and jail time. It also endangers bears and people. If a bear approaches your vehicle, drive on, then stop and watch from a distance.

At Disaster Creek, a manned check station ensures compliance with regulations prohibiting general travel farther north on the Dalton Highway.

Those who believe they have a necessary reason for continuing to Prudhoe Bay can contact the Director of Maintenance and Operations, Alaska Department of Transportation, 2301 Peger Rd., Fairbanks, AK 99701, (907) 451-2209, and apply for a permit to drive to Prudhoe Bay. Be forewarned: Few requests are approved.

For additional information about the trans-Alaska pipeline, write to Public Affairs Department, Alyeska Pipeline Service Co., 1835 South Bragaw St., Anchorage, AK 99512.

Author's note: Although it is technically forbidden to drive north of the Disaster Creek checkpoint without a permit, the state has not staffed the checkpoint for the past several years. Thus, anyone who has wanted to drive to Prudhoe Bay has done so. If you elect to try this—and this is not a recommendation that you do—you are on your own in terms of services—it's about 250 miles from Coldfoot to the next gas station in the Deadhorse–Prudhoe Bay complex. To my knowledge, no one has been prosecuted for driving to Prudhoe Bay without a permit these past few years, but the possibility of prosecution does exit.

Dall sheep can be seen along the Dalton Highway.

Fairbanks to Anchorage

The Parks Highway

LENGTH: 360 miles (600 km)

GAS AVAILABLE: **Cripple Creek Tire Store,** 3 miles (5 km); **Monderosa,** 49 miles (82 km); **Nenana,** 54 miles (90 km); **Healy,** 109 miles (182 km); **Healy Roadhouse,** 113 miles (188 km); **Cantwell,** 148 miles (247 km); **The Igloo,** 170 miles (283 km); **Chulitna River Lodge,** 202 miles (337 km); **Trapper Creek,** 243 miles (405 km); **Willow,** 289 miles (482 km); **Houston,** 301 miles (502 km); **Meadow Wood Shopping Mall,** 306 miles (510 km); **Wasilla,** 316 miles (527 km); **Peters Creek,** 336 miles (560 km)

LODGING: **Cripple Creek Resort** (Esther), 6 miles (10 km); **Nenana,** 54 miles (90 km); **Rochester Lodge,** 78 miles (130 km); **Clear Sky Lodge,** 78 miles (130 km); **Healy Hotel,** 109 miles (182 km); **Healy Roadhouse,** 113 miles (188 km); **McKinley Chalet Resort,** 119 miles (198 km); **Harper Lodge,** 119 miles (198 km); **Crow's Nest Log Cabins,** 120 miles (200 km); **McKinley Village Inn,** 127 miles, (212 km); **Houston,** 301 miles (502 km); **Wasilla,** 316 miles (527 km)

CAMPGROUNDS: **Skinny Dick's Halfway Inn** (RV parking only), 30 miles (50 km); **Tripod RV Park,** 54 miles (90 km); **Tatlanika Trading Co.** , 82 miles (137 km); **McKinley KOA Kampground,** 110 miles (183 km); **Mt. McKinley Pioneer RV Park,** 111 miles (185 km); **Lynx Creek Campground,** 119 miles (198 km); **Denali Grizzly Bear Cabins and Campground,** 127 miles (212 km); **East Fork Rest Area,** 172 miles (287 km); **Byers Lake Wayside,** 211 miles (352 km); **Big Susitna River Bridge,** 254 miles (423 km); **Montana Creek,** 262 miles (437 km); **Willow Island Resort,** 287 miles (478 km); **Nancy Lake Recreation Area,** 291 miles (485 km); **Rainbow Acres,** 309 miles (515 km); **Green Ridge Camper Park,** 319 miles (532 km)

WILDLIFE: Black bears, moose, Dall sheep (rare), caribou (late May to early June only)

FISHING: Grayling, rainbow trout, king salmon, silver salmon, chum salmon, pink salmon

===== Section 2 =====

Fairbanks to Anchorage

Of all the major roads in Alaska, the George Parks Highway joining Fairbanks and Anchorage, Alaska's two largest cities, is the newest, having opened for general vehicles in the early 1970s. In less than 20 years, it has become Alaska's most-used road, and it is continually upgraded and maintained. Only near the cities, where people use the ends of various highways for commuting to and from work, are any roadways used by more vehicles in the course of a year.

Though this is an all-weather road kept open year around, winter travelers may occasionally need to wait out blizzards in Broad Pass, where the road crosses the Alaska Range. Complete white-out conditions occur a couple of times a year, making travel exceedingly dangerous.

Probably the greatest reason for the Parks Highway's popularity is that it makes road travel to Denali National Park convenient. The Parks Highway cuts across the park's eastern boundary.

Denali National Park is far and away the most visited of Alaska's 11 national parks. In fact, more travelers stop at Denali than at all the other national parks in Alaska combined.

The negative side to this is that the small part of Denali National Park that is readily available to visitors has become extremely crowded. For the most part, visitors to this Maryland-size park are restricted to a narrow ribbon of roadway penetrating about 70 miles into the park. And, with a few exceptions, visitors are not even permitted to drive their own vehicles on the park road. To hold traffic to a minimum, in hopes of keeping the park's varied wildlife near the road, a limited number of buses carry visitors into the park.

Two sets of buses operate in Denali National Park. The most popular are school buses leased by the Park Service. Visitors can board and reboard regularly for a week for payment of a modest $3 fee (subject to change). The other buses belong to a concessionaire and charge $50 or more per person for a ride to the end of the road and back. Reservations can be made on the latter buses. For the Park Service buses, it's pretty much first-come, first-served, though in early 1990 the Park Service announced plans to allow at least a limited number of reservations to be available in advance.

Camping in Denali National Park is similarly complicated because of the dedicated effort at crowd control. There are only about 200 campsites within the park. Again, it's pretty much first-come, first-served. As with the buses, however, the Park Service is going to try making a few campsites available on a reservation basis.

As for campsites, the news is not good for RV drivers. Most of the campsites available within the park are for tent campers. This, again, is an effort to limit road traffic. Tent campers can carry their gear onto Park Service buses and be dropped off without using their own vehicles.

However, as driving and camping requirements have become more restrictive within the park during the past decade, a number of businesses have opened up at the edge of the park, including hotels, cafes and campgrounds for RVs. A few miles from the park entrance there now exists a thriving "mini-city" every summer to serve travelers. It is, for the most part, a well-maintained community performing a very satisfactory service. Costs, because of demand and the short tourist season, are somewhat higher than normal, though not unfairly so.

In a sense, the sudden growth of visitor services near the park entrance has taken away some of the magic of visiting Denali National Park for old-timers in Alaska. Just a few short years ago locals wanting to weekend in the park would often spend Friday night camped in a large graveled area near the park entrance, waiting to dash into the park the next morning and sign up for campsites. These impromptu RV gatherings often turned into the most memorable part of the weekend, with spontaneous, shared good times. The mini-city of services that has since grown up in the area took over the gravel pullout. Thus the impromptu gatherings so many looked forward to are pretty much a thing of the past, replaced by the stricter formalities of individual campsites rented in a private campground—almost certainly a necessity as more and more visit Denali National Park, but a necessity that brings with it a certain nostalgia.

To increase your chances of getting a campsite within Denali National Park, leave Fairbanks very early in the morning for the 3-hour drive to the park. You'll want to time your arrival at Denali for between 8 A.M. and 10 A.M. As campers from the previous night depart their sites, those waiting at the park Information Center will be granted permits as they become available. Most days you must literally be standing in the Information Center as campsites become available. While you're in the center, you can also sign up for the Park Service buses departing the center at regular intervals for the interior of the park.

Leaving Fairbanks this early, however, is not without advantages. Wildlife is most active in the early morning, and there are good opportunities to see moose and black bear between Fairbanks and Denali Park. The highway will be less crowded, as well. You may, in fact, have much of the road to yourself.

Insider's Tip: As with the Alaska Highway, buy your gas in Alaska's larger cities, like Fairbanks, whenever possible. It's almost always cheaper in the cities than at more remote locations along the road.

From Fairbanks, the road leads through low, rolling hills of spruce and birch forests to Nenana at the confluence of the Nenana and Tanana rivers. Nenana is a river shipping port accessible to the Alaska Railroad. As you drive across the bridge over the Tanana River, the barge-loading docks are immediately on your left. With luck you may see a tug pushing a load of barges downstream toward the Yukon River communities served by the barge company. The Tanana, particularly where it joins the Yukon, is a shallow, braided river that requires the utmost skill by tug pilots and their crews. The deepwater channel changes almost daily, which means boat operators must have a keen sense of the rivers and their many moods.

Often visible from the bridge are fish wheels used by subsistence and commercial fishermen. The current slowly turns a double-basket-and-paddle rig through the water, scooping up salmon and dropping them into a box built as part of the contraption.

If you take time out to explore Nenana, down near the riverfront, you'll see a large black-and-white tripod. This is the tripod for the Nenana Ice Classic, Alaska's biggest and most rewarding annual guessing game. Over the winter, the tripod is placed on the Tanana River ice with a cable connecting it to a large clock. When the ice goes out sufficiently to move the tripod enough to stop the clock, ticket holders who guessed the exact day, hour and minute the ice goes out share a prize that can exceed $180,000. Usually there are several winners each year. Ice has gone out as early as mid-April and as late as mid-May.

South from Nenana the countryside is fairly flat for the next 50 miles or so, until you approach Healy. For the most part, the ground is fairly soggy—almost marshy—and the undergrowth quite thick.

Healy, on the northern edge of the Alaska Range, is a coal-mining town. Off in the mountains to your left is Alaska's primary source of coal for power and for export, the Usabelli Mine. No mining activity is visible from the road. Occasional tours of the mining area are available; inquire in Healy.

From Healy, the road quickly winds into the heart of the Alaska Range, through a narrow notch in the mountains, then into the wider expanse of Broad Pass near timberline. As you enter Broad Pass, Denali National Park is to the right. Shortly before reaching the turnoff for park headquarters you will pass the collection of businesses that have grown up to serve area visitors.

Insider's Tip: Between Healy and Denali Park, the road bridges a deep chasm carved out by the Nenana River. Though not quite up to Grand Canyon standards, it is impressive nonetheless. A turnout on the south side of the bridge allows you to stop and walk back to take a lingering look into the gorge. Winds on this bridge can be quite fierce—there's a windsock at the bridge's midpoint to give you some idea of how hard the wind is blowing.

The turnoff for Denali Park along the Parks Highway is the start of the Denali Park Road, or Mile 0 of the Park Road, as it's most often called. If you turn into the park, a short drive, well-marked, leads to the park Information Center. This should be your first stop. If you want a campsite or space on one of the park services buses, this is where you wait in line.

The Denali Park Road

If you want to see wildlife, the Denali Park Road is far and away your best bet in Alaska. During a day-long bus trip in summer, passengers will almost certainly see caribou and moose, Dall sheep, probably several grizzly bears and, with luck, a wolf. Smaller animals like martens and fox are common.

Most day-visitors to the park board Park Service shuttle buses at the Information Center near the park entrance. Inside the center, tokens are provided on a first-come, first-served basis for boarding the buses. The best buses to take with the most chance of seeing wildlife are the early morning buses (starting at 6 A. M.) or the last buses in the evening.

Pack a small cooler full of lunch materials, ideally snack-type food that you can eat at intervals during the day. There is no opportunity to purchase food on the trip, and the bus ride to Wonder Lake and back will last 8 hours or longer.

The habitat at roadside, as you move through the park, tends to dictate the type of wildlife you will see. At lower (forested) elevations near the start of the trip and about 30 miles into the trip, near Teklinika Campground, moose sightings are more likely than at any other part of the road.

Past Teklinika, in the mountains near Igloo Creek, Dall sheep should be visible on the steep mountains near the road. Opportunities for seeing grizzlies are best above timberline, particularly after passing Igloo Creek. Caribou and wolves, as well, will most likely be seen in the open tundra.

On board the Park Service school buses, things are pretty informal. Anyone seeing wildlife should immediately speak out. The bus driver will stop the bus for viewing whatever animal is spotted and will allow plenty of time for pictures. Most pictures will have to be taken through open bus windows, as passengers are not generally permitted to disembark except at rest stops.

If you wish to get off the bus and hike around in the tundra for a while, advise the bus driver. He will stop wherever you want, let you out, then drive away. When you've finished your hike, flag down the next bus in either direction (depending on which way you want to go) and reboard to complete your trip. Those wishing to be dropped off for day hikes or overnight treks should check in at the Information Center for suggestions and to let the rangers know the area you want to explore.

Be sure to take plenty of film. Binoculars should also be in your daypack.

Past the park entrance, the Parks Highway passes several more tourism-related businesses, among them several companies offering raft trips on the Nenana River, which shares this valley with the road. This is whitewater rafting at its best, and those with a few hours or a day to spare should consider signing up for one of these trips. Denali Raft Adventures is probably the best known and most experienced of the whitewater rafting operators.

A few miles after leaving the park you'll come to two road junctions. The first, to the left, is the Denali Highway, which leads about 135 miles (mostly gravel) through the Alaska Range to Paxon on the Richardson Highway. Much of this road is above timberline.

Insider's Tip: The Denali Highway is a spectacular drive, albeit a fairly slow one. There are few facilities along the road other than state or BLM (Bureau of Land Management) campgrounds. It is, however, a wonderful opportunity to penetrate the heart of Alaska's most dominant range of mountains. Allow at least a full day for one-way travel on the Denali Highway; you'll want to stop often to admire the view or wander through the tundra. Wildflowers are at their best in early July; blueberries peak in mid-August.

The second junction, with a road leading to the right, is Cantwell Junction. The tiny town of Cantwell is a couple of miles off the main road. Several gas stations, a gift shop and a convenience store are scattered along the Parks Highway at Cantwell Junction.

Heading south out of Cantwell, the road stays right on the edge of the timberline for quite a few miles. Assuming the weather is clear, as you proceed south, Mount McKinley and Mount Foraker will be visible to the right, about 75 miles away. For the next 100 miles or so, McKinley will drift in and out of view to the right. Turnouts are provided at many prime viewing spots to allow time out for observation and for taking pictures.

As the road begins dropping out of the Alaska Range into the broad Matanuska-Susitna Valley, fishermen should start rubbing their hands in anticipation. Between Broad Pass and Anchorage are the biggest runs of salmon anywhere along the road system in Alaska. Many of these same streams hold large populations of native rainbow trout, though the big 'bows are hard to reach when salmon choke the streams.

Insider's Tip: Salmon are generally available throughout the summer; however different species of salmon are available at different times. The big kings (chinooks) arrive first, in June, followed at intervals by pinks, chums and silvers (cohoes), the latter most prominent in August and into September. Those seeking rainbows should fish before the salmon arrive, or in September, just before freeze-up.

Several streams crossed by the Parks Highway offer splendid fishing opportunities, among them Montana Creek, Sheep Creek and Willow Creek. Even more opportunities are available just off the road system via river charters or fly-in charters. Your best bet to finding good charter fishing is to inquire at the Visitors Center in Wasilla, a roadside town about 45 miles from Anchorage. The center is right alongside the highway. Be prepared for the fishing adventure of a lifetime if you take one of these charters during the height of the king or silver salmon runs.

Before reaching Wasilla, a short spur road leads left to Talkeetna, another source of good charter fishing on area rivers. As well, Talkeetna is the jump-off point for climbers heading for Mount McKinley and other nearby peaks. The climbing season is late April through mid-June. If you're in Talkeetna then, it's well worth the time to drive out to the airport and watch the almost frantic activity involved in getting climbers and their equipment to and from the mountain.

The air services that handle the climbers are run by some of the finest bush pilots in Alaska. Besides serving the climbers, they also offer flightseeing trips in and around Mount McKinley. These are great trips in light planes, offering up-close views of the tallest peak in North America. Depending on the air service and your own goals for flightseeing, you can stop off on a mountain glacier (usually Ruth Glacier) for a few minutes of wandering around in an icy wonderland. Most people who take a Talkeetna-based flightseeing trip agree that it's the finest part of their Alaskan adventure.

South of Talkeetna, the road moves ever closer to Anchorage and Alaska's population center. Wasilla, in fact, is more or less Anchorage's northernmost bedroom community, with several thousand area residents commuting 45 miles or more to work in Anchorage each morning and back again in the evening.

Insider's Tip: If at all possible, avoid driving to Anchorage from the Wasilla area between 6:30 and 8:30 A. M. on weekday mornings. Only one road leads to Anchorage, and it's crowded during the rush hours. The same holds true for leaving Anchorage between 4 and 6:30 P. M. on weekday afternoons if you are headed north to Wasilla.

In the Wasilla area and near neighboring Palmer are many small lakes stocked with trout. These are all pleasant places to spend an afternoon picnicking and fishing. Most are well suited to canoes or other small boats. Again, inquire at the Wasilla Visitors Center for ideas if you want to sample some of these.

The final leg of the drive to Anchorage from Wasilla takes an hour or a little less, much of it on four-lane highway. If it's late in the day, you may want to consider staying in a campground or hotel in the Wasilla-Palmer area unless you have a reservation in Anchorage. There are a fairly limited number of campgrounds in Anchorage and most hotels are booked pretty solid during the summer months. Those wanting either a hotel room or a campsite in Anchorage should plan to arrive fairly early in the day.

Caribou can be seen in the open tundra along the Denali Park Road.

The Kenai Peninsula

The Seward Highway
(Anchorage to Seward)

LENGTH: 127 miles (212 km)

GAS AVAILABLE: **BJ Gas, Grocery & Camper Park,** 26 miles (43 km); **Girdwood Junction,** 37 miles (62 km); **Moose Pass,** 98 miles (163 km); **Seward,** 127 miles (212 km)

LODGING: **Seward,** 127 miles (212 km)

CAMPGROUNDS: **BJ Gas, Grocery & Camper Park,** 26 miles (43 km); **Bertha Creek** (USFS), 62 miles (103 km); **Granite Creek** (USFS), 64 miles (107 km); **Tenderfoot Creek** (USFS), 81 miles (135 km); **Tern Lake** (USFS), 90 miles (150 km); **Trail River** (USFS), 103 miles (172 km); **Ptarmigan Creek** (USFS), 104 miles (173 km); **Primrose** (USFS), 110 miles (183 km)

WILDLIFE: Dall Sheep, beluga whales, black bears, moose

FISHING: Pink salmon, silver salmon, hooligan, rainbow trout, Dolly Varden, grayling

The Sterling Highway
(Mile 89 Seward Highway to Homer)

LENGTH: 137 miles (228 km)

GAS AVAILABLE: **Sunrise Inn,** 9 miles (15 km); **Kenai Lake,** 12 miles (20 km); **Cooper Landing,** 13 miles (21 km); **Hamilton's Place,** 14 miles (23 km); **Sterling,** 46 miles (77 km); **Soldotna,** 60 miles (100 km); **Treasure Cache,** 67 miles (112 km); **Clam Gulch,** 83 miles (138 km); **Ninilchik,** 99 miles (165 km); **Happy Valley,** 110 miles (183 km); **Anchor Point,** 121 miles (202 km); **Homer,** 137 miles (228 km)

LODGING: **Sunrise Inn,** 9 miles (15 km); **Kenai Lake,** 12 miles (20 km); **Alpine Inn Motel,** 13 miles (21 km); **Cooper Landing,** 13 miles (21 km); **Hamilton's Place,** 14 miles (23 km); **Gwin's Lodge,** 16 miles (27 km); **Sterling,** 46 miles (77 km); **Soldotna,** 60 miles (100 km); **Clam Shell Lodge,** 83 miles (138 km); **Beachcomber Motel,** 99 miles (165 km); **Happy Valley,** 110 miles (183 km); **Anchor Point,** 121 miles (202 km); **Homer,** 137 miles (228 km)

CAMPGROUNDS: **Sunrise Inn,** 9 miles (15 km); **Quartz Creek,** 9 miles (15 km); **Cooper Creek** (USFS), 15 miles (25 km); **Russian River** (USFS), 17 miles (28 km); **Knowlton's,** 43 miles (72 km); Bing's **Landing,** 45 miles (75 km); **Sterling,** 46 miles (77 km); **Scout Lake,** 50 miles (83 km); **Soldotna,** 60 miles (100 km); **Tustumena Lake,** 74 miles (123 km); **Clam Gulch,** 82 miles (137 miles); **Ninilchik**

Recreation Area, 99 miles (165 km); **Deep Creek**, 102 miles (170 km); **Stariski Creek**, 116 miles (193 km); **Anchor River**, 122 miles (203 km); **Homer**, 137 miles (228 km)

WILDLIFE: Moose, black bears, brown bears (rare), caribou, Rocky Mountain goats

FISHING: Rainbow trout, king salmon, red salmon, pink salmon, silver salmon, steelhead, razor clams, halibut

Section 3

The Kenai Peninsula

This peninsula is relatively small when drawn on a map of Alaska, but it's physically larger than several other states. It has become Anchorage's playground, and not without reason. Here the largest king salmon in the world come to spawn, campers have any number of options, and the U.S. Forest Service maintains the finest system of wilderness hiking and canoeing trails anywhere in Alaska.

Insider's Tip: Travelers visiting the Kenai Peninsula should time their trips for weekdays. Avoid the weekends whenever possible. Starting midafternoon every summer Friday, an endless stream of Anchorage weekenders heads south to favorite Kenai Peninsula destinations. Bumper-to-bumper traffic for 50 or more miles is not unusual at the start and finish of the weekend. All Kenai Peninsula facilities are packed during weekends, especially in June and July when the king and red salmon are running.

The Seward Highway

Starting in Anchorage, only one road leads south, the Seward Highway. Those entering Anchorage from the north, Anchorage's only other road out of town, intercept the Seward Highway as they pull into town. Where these highways join, 5th and Gambell streets, is the starting point for Seward Highway mileages given here. Within Anchorage proper, both Gambell Street and Seward Highway signs refer to the same road.

Anchorage, like similar-sized cities throughout the nation, has its share of pluses and minuses. Urban sprawl is one of the problems; veiled references by residents to "Los Anchorage" are not made without reason.

This town does spread out and requires some sort of vehicle for getting around in conveniently.

On the plus side, there are a first-class performing arts center, plenty of green space and good museums. Finally, there's the setting. On clear days, mountains are visible whichever way you turn. To the east are the Chugach Mountains; the city edges upward on their lower slopes to the boundary of Chugach State Park, one of the largest state parks in the nation. Across Cook Inlet to the west and around to the north of town is the Alaska Range. Even Mount McKinley, nearly 200 miles away, is visible on the clearest days. Finally, to the south, are the Kenai Mountains of the Kenai Peninsula, certainly not a large mountain range, but the most accessible in Alaska.

Those who want to stay in Anchorage hotels during the summer months should make reservations ahead of time if at all possible. During July and August, it is almost impossible to find a room on short notice. Information on hotels, motels, lodges and bed-and-breakfast lodging can be obtained from the Anchorage Convention and Visitors Bureau, listed in Appendix A of this book.

Turning south on the Seward Highway at 5th and Gambell, the first few miles are fairly typical city driving, complete with traffic lights and specific lanes for left and right turns at many intersections. The distance between exits begins to stretch out as you enter south Anchorage, primarily a residential area. Suddenly, you crest a small hill and you're out of town, looking down onto Potter's Marsh, a state wildlife refuge, on the left side of the road and Cook Inlet to the right. Winding around to your front is Turnagain Arm of Cook Inlet. Southbound travelers drive completely around Turnagain Arm.

The famed British explorer, Captain Cook, named Turnagain Arm during an 18th-century exploration of Cook Inlet. He entered the arm in seeking the Northwest Passage, but the shallow waters forced him to turn his ship time and again to avoid grounding.

Potter's Marsh is worth a stop, particularly in June. Waterfowl are the most obvious critters in this park, and in June nesting birds bring their down-covered offspring right up to the boardwalk for close viewing. A parking area is provided, though it's not very large.

South of Potter's Marsh, the road twists and turns on a narrow strip of land between the Chugach Mountains and Cook Inlet for about 30 miles. In spring, avalanches are frequent, as are traffic delays while the road is cleared. In summer, Dall sheep ewes and their lambs are readily visible on the cliffs near the road, often wandering down to the shoulder of the road. Several turnouts are provided near areas frequented by the sheep.

In Cook Inlet during July and August, beluga whales (small white whales) can be spotted in the inlet chasing salmon as they approach spawning streams. Best whale viewing is at high tide; otherwise the water's edge is quite far from the road.

Cook Inlet tides are the second-highest in the world, exceeded only by those of the Bay of Fundy in Nova Scotia. During full-moon periods, water levels between high and low tides may vary by 35 feet or more. Of particular interest is the bore tide, a moving wall of water that may be as high as 6 feet rolling across Turnagain Arm as the tide changes from low to high.

Insider's Tip: The broad, mud-colored beaches exposed during Cook Inlet's low tides are extremely hazardous. This mud has been likened to quicksand. People stuck in this mud are often unable to free themselves before a high tide returns and drowns them. Avoid walking out on these mudflats at all costs. If you see anyone stuck in the mudflats, contact state troopers immediately, before attempting to render assistance.

The best place to watch for both beluga whales and bore tides is, appropriately, Beluga Point, a well-marked turnout with plenty of parking. Also, viewers looking inland can often see Dall sheep from this point. Beluga Point is about 17 miles from Anchorage.

Along the shores of Turnagain Arm, about 35 miles from Anchorage, the Seward Highway passes a turnoff to Girdwood, the town that serves Alaska's premiere skiing area. A dirt road from Girdwood leads to the historic Crow Creek Mine.

Continuing south, 48 miles from Anchorage, another side road leads to Portage Glacier, one of the most-visited attractions in Alaska. At the end of this short road, travelers will find a splendid interpretive center built and managed by the U.S. Forest Service. The center overlooks iceberg-choked Portage Lake, with Portage Glacier visible at the far end of the lake. Well worth seeing. Ask one of the rangers about iceworms—believe it or not, they're real.

Insider's Tip: In and around the Portage Glacier turnoff is considerable evidence of the Great Alaska Earthquake of 1964. The ground in this region sank several feet as a result of the shifting earth. Abandoned homes and dead spruce trees on the right are all victims of this earthquake.

From the Portage Glacier turnoff, the Seward Highway bends around the eastern tip of Turnagain Arm, runs along its south shore for a short distance, then begins to climb Turnagain Pass through the Kenai Mountains. In winter, this is among the snowiest roadways in Alaska, with snow packs often exceeding 8 to 10 feet. In summer, the route offers dense forests, clear streams and a profusion of wildflowers in the open areas. Southbound, the ascent from sea level is rather rapid. Once on top, the descent is gentler, though the road twists and turns through an assortment of narrow river valleys.

A few miles past the summit, a turnoff to the left leads to the Johnson Lake Trail, one of the Kenai's lesser-used hiking trails, but a good one. The trail runs for about 21 miles through the mountains, exiting at Moose Pass, also on the Seward Highway. On the north side of the trail's summit, at about the halfway point, is Bench Lake, with excellent grayling fishing. Little more than a mile south across the pass is Johnson Lake, offering great fishing for rainbows to about 16 inches in length.

Insider's Tip: Because it is relatively unknown, the Johnson Lake Trail offers a perfect Kenai Peninsula getaway during crowded weekends. The last time I hiked this trail was a July 4th weekend, the most crowded weekend of the year on the Kenai Peninsula. In four days on the trail, I saw fewer than 10 other people.

About 70 miles from Anchorage, a turnoff to the right leads 18 miles to Hope, founded as a mining community in 1896. Evidence of this activity, which continued well into the 20th century, exists throughout the area. An oldtimer or two can frequently be found drinking coffee in Hope's Discovery Cafe and will talk about the heyday of gold mining in Hope.

Just before the entrance to Hope is the trailhead for the Resurrection Pass Trail, the Kenai Peninsula's most popular hiking route. Thirty-eight miles long, this trail leads south to the Sterling Highway. Eight Forest Service cabins along the route can be rented as shelters by hikers traversing the trail, though reservations should be made as early as possible. Write to the Chugach National Forest, 201 E. 9th Ave., Suite 206, Anchorage, AK 99501, for trail maps and information necessary for cabin reservations. Cabins cost $20 per night, and reservations can be made up to 6 months in advance.

Eighteen miles past the Hope junction, the Sterling Highway takes off to the right from the Seward Highway. Just past the junction, a marshy lake to the right is often a great place to see moose early in the morning or late in the evening. During June and July, most of the Anchorage weekend traffic will turn off on the Sterling Highway, lessening the crowds on the remaining 39 miles of the Seward Highway.

Along the final miles of the Seward Highway is an assortment of Forest Service campgrounds. Just prior to entering Seward, the highway levels out and all travelers' facilities are available there.

Seward is the gateway to Kenai Fjords National Park, a wilderness preserve along the rugged south shore of the Kenai Peninsula. The best way to see the park is via one of the commercial operators offering day-long boat trips from Seward through Resurrection Bay and into some of the glacier-headed fjords. En route, there is an excellent chance of seeing killer whales. Almost certainly, passengers on the boats will see sea lions, sea otters, bald eagles and tens of thousands of various birds in rocky rookeries at the water's edge.

Seward offers two major events each summer: the Mount Marathon race on the 4th of July, a rugged scramble up and down the mountain that looms over the town, and the Seward Silver Salmon Derby in August. The latter is probably Alaska's biggest and best-attended salmon derby, with large cash prizes and an assortment of related activities. Fishing is done from a boat in Resurrection Bay. Party boats are available, or private boats can be launched in Seward's harbor for access to the fishing grounds. Small-boat operators should watch the weather carefully. Resurrection Bay's winds can quickly generate heavy waves, making things extremely hazardous on the water.

Insider's Tip: The most productive bait for salmon derby fishermen is usually herring trolled slowly behind a boat. During August, virtually every store in Seward seems to have frozen bait herring for sale. Troll at varying depths until you find fish. Then rig every pole to troll at the depth the fish was caught. If you're going to enter the derby, you must buy a derby ticket prior to fishing, and every fisherman aboard the boat must have a derby ticket.

The Sterling Highway

The Kenai Peninsula is Alaska's most famous fishing area, and the bulk of that fame comes from the streams and shoreline found along the Sterling Highway. There are several reasons for this. The road makes these streams accessible, a relative rarity in Alaska. The king salmon in the Kenai River are the largest of this species in the entire world; the same holds true for the halibut caught from party boats in Homer at the end of the road. In between are hefty runs of red, silver and pink salmon; razor clams; and rainbow trout. Along this 137-mile route is more fishing adventure than almost anyone can imagine, the only liability being the crowds of people that compete for these fish. For the most part, fishing along this stretch of road is not the wilderness experience that most people think of when they dream of fishing in Alaska. However, most of those thoughts are quickly put aside with the first ferocious lunge of an 80-pound king salmon or 200-pound halibut.

It takes about an hour and 45 minutes (depending on traffic) to drive the Seward Highway from Anchorage to the start of the Sterling Highway. From there, another 2 1/2 hours will take you to the end of the road in Homer, should you not wish to stop. But few people can resist a stop or two in what are some of Alaska's most popular campgrounds or favorite fishing holes.

Westbound, on the Sterling, the first obvious chance for fishermen is Kenai Lake, though it's illegal to fish for salmon in the lake or its tributaries. Try instead for lake trout or Dolly Varden. The brilliant green color of this lake is caused by silt from nearby glaciers suspended in the water.

The road parallels the north shore of the lake, then cuts across the Kenai River at the outlet of the lake. In the Kenai River are the big kings in May, June and July; red salmon in July and August; pinks in August; silvers in August and September; and rainbows to 18 pounds year-round. Usually, though, it's difficult to reach the rainbows during salmon runs. Best rainbow fishing is usually late September or early October, just before the river freezes.

Insider's Tip: The best Kenai River fishing is usually from a boat, either a drift boat or a powered boat. A wide variety of operators offer day charters, usually two or three fishermen to a boat for half days or whole days. Boat operators generally furnish necessary tackle and bait. The world record king salmon came from the Kenai River in 1985, all 97 pounds, 4 ounces of it. In 1989, a visiting fisherman from Minnesota fought a king believed to be larger for nearly 48 hours before the fish broke the line and got away.

The best bait on the Kenai River for all salmon and rainbows is usually a glob of salmon roe rigged with some sort of attractor and bounced slowly along the bottom with the current. Fishermen should expect to lose a lot of terminal tackle to snags on the river bottom. If you are not regularly snagging on the bottom, you are not fishing deep enough.

In 1987 a couple of Kenai River guides took time out to hook onto and pull up the most famous snag in the river, a sunken log in one of the hottest fishing holes. When they wrestled this monster to the surface, stuck to it were thousands of lures and a complete rod-and-reel outfit. The total value of the lost tackle on the log has been estimated at $10,000 or more.

The Sterling Highway pretty much follows the Kenai River from the lake to the town of Soldotna. At Soldotna, the river turns north and the road turns south. South from Soldotna, the road crosses several other streams with opportunities for salmon fishing, among them the Kasilof (*ka-SEE-loff*) and Anchor rivers and Deep Creek. Off the mouth of Deep Creek, fishermen can also troll for kings from a boat or jig for halibut.

Prior to reaching Soldotna, the Russian River joins the Kenai. The Russian is Alaska's premiere red salmon fishery in July, and it gets crowded at the few points of public access to the river. Fishing here is flies only, but this is also combat fishing. Riverbanks will be jammed, and there's little opportunity to practice the delicate art of true fly fishing. Almost everybody uses a spinning rod with 20-pound test line and ties a fly to the end just below a large weight. When a fish is hooked, it is dragged quickly from the water to avoid tangling with the hundreds of other lines in the water. At the height of the red salmon run, this fishery must be seen to be believed.

Insider's Tip: A premiere Kenai Peninsula attraction is often overlooked by anglers: the Swanson River and Swan Lake canoe trails in the Kenai Wildlife Refuge. The canoe trails are laid out through chains of lakes, some joined by narrow sloughs, others by short portages. Rainbow fishing in this water system can be fantastic, particularly in June and September. Inquire locally in Soldotna for canoe rentals and access points. This is strictly a paddling adventure; no motors are allowed.

South of Soldotna, past the Kasilof River, Cook Inlet beaches are famed for the availability of razor clams. Clam digging is best at periods of minus tides, in other words during the 3 or 4 days each month a full moon exerts its strongest pull on the oceans. The most obvious clamming beach is at a place known as Clam Gulch, though the Deep Creek area offers good clamming as well. Hit the beach an hour or so before low tide and dig for 2 to 3 hours until the rising tide covers the beaches. Small dimples in the sandy mud indicate the presence of razor clams. Locate one of these, dig quickly with a shovel or your hands, reach into the water-filled hole, grab the clam and pull. Clamming is a wonderful excuse for covering yourself with mud from head to foot. On almost any good clamming beach, an hour or so of frantic digging should easily provide the daily limit of 60 razor clams. Then all you have to do is clean them. You must have a valid Alaska sport fishing license in your possession to dig for clams.

Insider's Tip: As a general rule, the farther south you do your clamming, the bigger the clams. At the northern edge of the clam beaches, just below the outlet of the Kasilof River, clams are plentiful in places but pretty small, 3 to 4 inches long being about the largest. Near Clam Gulch, Ninilchik and Deep Creek to the south, clams as large as 10 inches long have been uncovered, with an average clam being between 5 and 7 inches long.

Past the salmon streams and the clam beaches, the Sterling Highway drops down to Homer near the outer edge of Kachemak Bay. Homer is Alaska's favorite halibut fishing site, and a plethora of party boat operators offer day trips for about $135 per person. The limit is two fish per fisherman. Fish weighing more than 300 pounds are caught almost every year. The rod-and-reel record for halibut, a 440-pounder, came from the Homer area.

When selecting an operator for halibut fishing, spend some time asking around the docks when fishermen return in the afternoon and evening. The rapid growth of this industry has resulted in some skippers providing less service than others. Book your trip on boats that deliver the happiest clients to shore. All bait and tackle should be provided, but fishermen must generally bring their own lunches. Medication for motion sickness is also recommended for those with queasy stomachs.

One of Homer's most famous attractions is the Homer Spit, a 5-mile-long mini-peninsula jutting into Kachemak Bay. Throughout the summer, a large transient population camps along the spit, and various businesses have grown up near the small boat harbor at the end. Driving out on the spit can be a visual feast during a spectacular sunset.

Also in Homer, you can board a boat for a short trip across Kachemak Bay to Seldovia on the south shore. Seldovia is a small, tightly knit community, mostly made up of fishermen. It makes for a pleasant 1-day outing.

11

HEADING BACK

If getting there is supposed to be half the fun, followed by lots of fun while you're there, what's left for the trip back? In the case of a drive to and from Alaska, plenty. This alternate routing, starting from Anchorage, will take you deep into British Columbia. You can do this by repeating only about 25 miles of your journey north on the original Alaska Highway.

As an overview, this routing, broken down by days, is as follows:

- Anchorage to Tok: Glenn Highway
- Tok to Dawson City, Yukon: Taylor and Top of the World highways
- Dawson City to Carmacks: Klondike Highway
- Carmacks to Watson Lake: Campbell Highway
- Watson Lake to Yellowhead Highway 16 in British Columbia: Cassiar Highway (2 days)

Once past Tok, this routing offers long legs through remote regions. A couple of the side trips available will really take you into the wilds. Be sure of your fuel status and the distance to the next gas station at all times.

Finally, this is a much longer route south, taking about 6 days if you don't stop to explore Dawson City or sample the fishing. If you've dawdled longer than planned on your way north or in Alaska and need to hurry home, the Alaska Highway offers the fastest route.

Anchorage to Tok

STARTING MILEAGE:_____

MILEAGE: 328 miles (545 km)

DRIVING TIME: 7 to 8 hours

TOWNS EN ROUTE: **Palmer**, 42 miles (70 km); **Glennallen**, 187 miles (312 km); **Tok**, 328 miles (545 km)

GAS AVAILABLE: **Palmer**, 42 miles (70 km); **Pinnacle Mountain RV Resort**, 70 miles (116 km); **Sheep Mountain Lodge**, 114 miles (190 km); **Eureka Lodge**, 128 miles (213 km); **Glennallen**, 187 miles (312 km); **Gakona**, 205 miles (342 km); **Chistochina Lodge**, 236 miles (393 km); **Sinona Creek Trading Post**, 238 miles (397 km); **Mentasta Lodge**, 281 miles (468 km); **Tok**, 328 miles (545 km)

CAMPGROUNDS: **Palmer**, 42 miles (70 km); **Moose Creek State Recreation Site**, 55 miles (92 km); **Coyote Lake Recreation Area**, 61 miles (101 km); **Pinnacle Mountain RV Resort**, 70 miles (116 km); **King Mountain State Wayside**, 76 miles (127 km); **Long Lake**, 85 miles (142 km); **Matanuska Glacier State Campground**, 101 miles (168 km); **Sheep Mountain Lodge**, 114 miles (190 km); **Little Nelchina State Campground**, 138 miles (230 km); **Kamping Resorts of Alaska**, 153 miles (255 km); **Tolsana Creek State Campground**, 173 miles (288 km); **Dry Creek State Campground**, 192 miles (320 km); **Porcupine Creek State Wayside**, 267 miles (445 km); **Eagle Trail State Wayside**, 312 miles (520 km); **Sourdough Campground**, 326 miles (541 km); **Tok**, 328 miles (545 km)

LODGING: **Palmer**, 42 miles (70 km); **Glacier Park Resort**, 102 miles (169 km); **Sheep Mountain Lodge**, 114 miles (190 km); **Eureka Lodge**, 128 miles (213 km); **Tolsana Lake Resort**, 171 miles (285 km); **Glennallen**, 187 miles (312 km); **Gakona**, 205 miles (342 km); **Chistochina Lodge**, 236 miles (393 km); **Mentasta Lodge**, 281 miles (468 km); **Tok**, 328 miles (545 km)

MAJOR TERRAIN FEATURES: Chulitna Pass (Chugach Mountains), Mentasta Pass (Alaska Range), muskeg, boreal forest, tundra

WILDLIFE: Black bears, caribou, moose, grizzly bears, Dall sheep, Rocky Mountain goats (rare)

FISHING: King salmon, red salmon, grayling, lake trout, Dolly Varden, northern pike

======= Section 1 =======

Anchorage to Tok

From Anchorage, the only way to go south to a lower-48 state or a home in Canada is to first drive north for several hundred miles to intercept the Alaska Highway or the Taylor Highway at Tok. And, if you wind up taking the Taylor Highway as recommended in this chapter, you'll drive even farther north before turning south.

But just getting to Tok from Anchorage is one of Alaska's most breath-taking drives, through two major mountain ranges and across broad expanses of Alaska's interior.

From Anchorage, you'll retrace your route into Anchorage for about 35 miles on the Glenn Highway to its junction with the Parks Highway. Keep to the right on the Glenn Highway, following the signs to Palmer. An alternative route to Palmer, now known as the Old Glenn Highway or the Palmer Alternate, turns off the Glenn Highway 28 miles from Anchorage. This is a fairly scenic but winding road along the base of the Chugach Mountains. In August, at about Mile 13 of the Old Glenn, sockeye salmon in full spawning color (brilliant red) can be seen in the creek at roadside.

In a sense, Palmer is fairly unique in terms of American communities. During the depression of the 1930s, President Franklin Roosevelt's admin-istration colonized the region with farmers from the Midwest, transporting several hundred farming families to the Mat-Su Valley in an attempt to make Alaska self-sufficient in terms of food production. Families were given 160 acres of land to clear, and homes and barns were built under government contract. Many of the old barns, locally called Colony Barns, still stand. Essentially, a midwestern-style barn was erected on top of a lower story of logs to create these buildings.

Whichever route you take to Palmer, there are several attractions here worth checking out. First is the Musk-Ox Farm, actually on a side road about 2 miles out of town along the route to Tok. Musk-oxen are shaggy beasts of about 600 pounds normally found in the most extreme arctic regions. They were wiped out in Alaska by meat hunters around the turn of the century, and the musk-oxen now in Alaska—both wild and at the farm—are descend-ants of animals imported from Canada. The underfur of these animals, carefully combed from them each spring, is a warm wool (*qiviut*) suitable for spinning into yarn then weaving into a host of winter clothing such as stocking caps, mittens and scarves. Various items are for sale at the farm and a downtown Anchorage store, the latter also named Qiviut. Since this wool is in rather short supply, these garments are fairly expensive.

Near the turnoff to the musk-ox farm is a hybrid wolf kennel offering tours. Most of the animals here range from 75 percent to 95 percent pure wolf and exhibit wolf behavior. If you're lucky, there'll be a litter of pups available to play with.

Probably Palmer's premiere annual attraction is the Alaska State Fair, held the 10 days in late August and early September leading up to Labor Day. On display will be the massive vegetables that the Mat-Su Valley has become famous for—like cabbages in excess of 80 pounds. Most of the usual state-fair-type activities are on the menu as well, but most have a decidedly Alaskan twist.

Insider's Tip: The state fair's biggest crowds show up on Labor Day weekend. Come early in the fair to take advantage of the less-crowded days and before the big vegetables (judged the first day of the fair) begin to wilt.

Also in the Palmer area is the Hatcher Pass road, leading through a gold-mining area to an abandoned mine site high in the mountains. The mine is a state historic site, and tours are available. The last few miles of this road are extremely narrow. Signs to Hatcher Pass, the Musk-Ox Farm and the wolf kennels are prominent along the Glenn Highway.

For winter travelers, Hatcher Pass offers tremendous cross-country skiing and great sledding adventures. Snowmobilers also find great tracts of land to explore at length.

Insider's Tip: In and around Palmer (the Mat-Su Valley) are more than 140 known hiking trails. Those who want a day hike, an overnight or an expedition of several days can investigate the possibilities by inquiring at the Mat-Su Borough natural resources office in the Borough Administration Building in downtown Palmer.

From Palmer, the Glenn Highway twists through the Chugach Mountains with few opportunities to pass slow-moving vehicles for about 70 miles. If a line of cars builds up behind your vehicle, Alaska law requires that you pull over at one of the plentiful turnouts and allow them to pass.

This is rugged but beautiful country, climbing from Alaska's south coastal climatic zone into the drier interior climate. The Matanuska Glacier can be seen from roadside, and a turnoff at Glacier Park Resort leads to the face of the glacier. This is a private road, and there is usually a fee for driving up to the glacier.

The animals most frequently seen between Palmer and Glennallen (187 miles from Anchorage) are Dall sheep and caribou, though occasionally a black bear crosses the road. The sheep are usually visible, appropriately enough, on Sheep Mountain, on the left side of the road near Sheep Mountain Lodge, about 114 miles from Anchorage. The road is fairly narrow and winds around quite a bit at the foot of Sheep Mountain; if you want to spend time observing the sheep, be sure to find a pullout that enables you to stop well off the road. Best times for sheep viewing are in June and July. In August, when the sheep-hunting season opens, the sheep go deeper into the hills.

But, in August, chances are good for seeing caribou, once you cross the summit of Chulitna Pass. The fairly flat land from the summit to Glennallen hosts the Nelchina caribou herd each fall, almost certainly the most accessible herd to overland travelers. The animals will be mostly in scattered bands of from 2 or 3 to about 10 animals, and they're not above standing in the road trying to stare down passing cars.

Between Palmer and Glennallen, the clear streams along the route offer fair opportunities for grayling and Dolly Varden throughout the summer months, as do some of the lakes at roadside. Most fish caught near the road won't be very large, but diligent nimrods should be able to catch enough for a meal or two.

Glennallen, the largest community between Palmer and Tok, is primarily a service center for this portion of Alaska's interior. Full services are available. Also, Glennallen hosts the headquarters for Wrangell–St. Elias National Park, the largest national park in the United States. Approaching Glennallen on a clear day, drivers can get some idea of the scope of this park by looking at the eastern skyline. Three major peaks—Mount Sanford, Mount Drum and Mount Wrangell—dominate the horizon, though still many miles in the distance. And these are not the tallest peaks in the park. Mount St. Elias, on the Canadian border and too distant to be visible, rises to 18,001 feet, making it the second-highest summit in both Alaska and Canada.

Past Glennallen the Glenn Highway joins the Richardson Highway, which runs from Valdez to Fairbanks. Turn left at the stop sign to continue on to Tok; turn right for Valdez on Prince William Sound.

Northbound, for 16 miles from the junction, the Glenn and Richardson highways are the same road. At Gakona Junction, Tok-bound travelers turn right to continue on the Glenn, and Delta- or Fairbanks-bound travelers continue straight ahead on the Richardson.

Those who wish to view the most spectacular mountain pass in Alaska should alter their route to Tok and take the Richardson Highway to Delta, then turn right on the Alaska Highway for Tok. Isabel Pass, on the Richardson, can be spectacular when the weather's good. But, when the weather's bad, it can be very bad, with frightening winds and wind-driven rain, snow or sleet at any time of the year.

Valdez

Valdez, made infamous by the 1989 grounding of the tanker *Exxon Valdez*, offers much more than just an oil terminal—or an oil spill. In fact, despite many assumptions to the contrary, Valdez itself and the broad bay to its front, were untouched by the spilled oil.

Salmon fishing can be tremendous in and near Valdez, and the protected waters of Valdez Arm and Prince William Sound make the fish fairly easy to get at, though boaters should keep a weather eye out—things can blow up fast in this country. In July, pink salmon can be caught one right after the other just by fishing from the shore near town. In August, silver salmon are available from a boat or from selected spots along the shore (try some of the rocky areas along the road leading to the trans-Alaska pipeline terminal).

From the Glenn-Richardson highways junction just outside of Glennallen, it's 115 miles to Valdez on a good road. The route takes you over Thompson Pass—a gentle slope upward for southbound travelers, but almost a plunge from the summit to the small coastal plain where Valdez sits. Worthington Glacier comes almost to roadside near the summit of the pass, and visitors can walk up to the face of it and chip ice for the cooler if they desire. Try chilling your evening cocktails with a bit of clear glacier ice—if you listen closely, you can hear it fizzle and pop as air trapped centuries ago escapes from the melting ice.

Thompson Pass holds one distinction that summer travelers probably won't notice—it's the snowiest place in Alaska, receiving as much as 1,000 inches of snow or more a year.

Probably Valdez's major attraction, besides the fishing, is Columbia Glacier, the largest of the few tidewater glaciers in Alaska that are reasonably accessible. Several charter operators in the harbor offer day trips to the glacier in large, comfortable boats, the best-known and most experienced probably being Stan Stevens Charters. These trips last 8 hours or more, and besides the glacier, passengers will almost certainly see bald eagles, seals, sea lions and—with a little luck—killer whales.

Lodging can be a problem in Valdez during the summer months. If you need a room for the night, have a travel agent in Anchorage make you a reservation before you head for Valdez. Campground space is usually not too much of a problem, though the RV park near the small boat harbor fills up very quickly on most summer days.

Chitina–McCarthy Road

About 30 miles south of Glennallen en route to Valdez there's a turnoff to the left and a sign noting a road leading 26 miles to Chitina. More than that, however, this road leads another 65 miles beyond Chitina to McCarthy— sort of.

The final bridge across the Kennicott River into McCarthy washed out more than 20 years ago, so the road gets just as far as the river. To get the magnificent dose of scenery and Alaska history offered by the McCarthy area and neighboring Kennecott mine complex, you have to pull yourself across the raging Kennicott River on a small hand tram. (For reasons no one can remember, the mine complex is spelled Kennecott and the river and glacier are spelled Kennicott.)

However, before you get to the tram, the 65 miles of road may give you cause to pause. It will take you three hours or more to drive this narrow gravel lane. It's nothing more than an old railroad bed with the rails removed and gravel dumped on it to even out the surface. Most of the bridges are only one-lane wide. If you're careful and take your time, even a large RV can make the trek, and there's plenty of places to park at the end of the road. There's good tent camping near the tram.

The railroad bed you drive on was the original route of the Copper River and Northwestern Railroad, which ran from Cordova on Prince William Sound to the Kennecott mine, just a few miles past McCarthy. When the high-grade ore ran out in 1938, the owners of the mine put everybody on the last train out of town and locked the doors. Save for the ravages of weather and time, everything in Kennecott is pretty much as it was more than 50 years ago. The blacksmith's tools are still in place near the forge, records are scattered about the administrative office and the old hospital, despite a creek that periodically flows through it, still smells like a hospital.

With Kennicott Glacier just a short walk from the mining complex, the scenery is spectacular. Most who visit this little known site come away feeling it was the best part of their Alaska trip.

Mentasta Pass, on the Glenn Highway to Tok, is quite beautiful, though it falls short of the rugged magnificence that is Isabel Pass. The terrain is much gentler through Mentasta Pass, and the road stays well within the timberline.

Approaching Tok, one of the best campgrounds in the area is the Sourdough Campground, about 2 miles before you reach the junction with the Alaska Highway in downtown Tok. A small restaurant adjoining the campground office puts on a wonderful feed of sourdough hotcakes every morning. This is one breakfast well worth trying—besides, even for motorhome travelers, the cook needs a break every so often.

If you don't stop at Sourdough Campground, there are several suitable facilities for RVs in Tok, as well as an assortment of lodges and motels. Travelers continuing north on the Taylor Highway to Dawson City, Yukon, or back down the Alaska Highway to Beaver Creek, Yukon, should be sure to top off their gas tanks in Tok. What little gas is available beyond Tok is often frightfully expensive.

Tok to Dawson City, Yukon

STARTING MILEAGE:_____

MILEAGE: 187 miles (312 km)

DRIVING TIME: 5 to 6 hours

TOWNS EN ROUTE: **Chicken**, 79 miles (132 km); **Boundary**, 118 miles (197 km); **Dawson City,** 187 miles (312 km)

GAS AVAILABLE: **Tetlin Junction**, 12 miles (20 km); **Chicken**, 79 miles (132 km); **Boundary**, 118 miles (197 km)

CAMPGROUNDS: **Tetlin Junction**, 12 miles (20 km); **Walker Fork** (BLM), 94 miles (157 km)

LODGING: **Tetlin Junction**, 12 miles (20 km); **Boundary**, 118 miles (197 km)

MAJOR TERRAIN FEATURES: Low, rolling, forested hills gradually giving way to alpine tundra

WILDLIFE: Moose, black bears, grizzlies (rare), caribou (in the fall)

FISHING: Grayling, sheefish

================ Section 2 ================

Tok to Dawson City, Yukon

Though driving distance on this day is fairly short, allow plenty of time. The road is narrow in places, twists like a snake in other places, and sometimes suffers both problems. Also, it's mostly gravel road—hot and dusty when dry, cool and gooey when wet.

Leaving Tok, head south on the Alaska Highway for 12 miles to Tetlin Junction. At the junction, turn left (north) onto the Taylor Highway. This highway, originally a trail that over time has evolved into a road, leads into the heart of active gold mining country. In fact, the Fortymile Country, as it's called, was the scene of a thriving gold-mining economy almost two decades before the Klondike Gold Rush of 1898. The small Yukon River town at the end of the Taylor Highway, Eagle, was the judicial and military center of interior Alaska before gold was discovered in Fairbanks.

Except for miners and a few others, mostly hunters in the fall and tourists in the summer, the country along the Taylor Highway is pretty well deserted these days. Chicken, about 90 minutes' driving time from Tetlin Junction, is the only town along the route, and some would say describing this collection of a few residents as a town is being charitable. But these are fine folks, and the party/picnic they throw on July 4 is well worth attending if you're in the area. Most of the miners come in from the creeks for this event, the only time off that they allow themselves during the summer.

A rather delightful story surrounds the naming of Chicken. The miners in the area during the 1880s wanted to name the town after the ptarmigan (grouse-like birds) that lived throughout the area. However, none of them could spell ptarmigan. Thus they settled on *chicken* as the closest word for describing an edible bird.

A great way to get a feel for Chicken's history is a book by Ann Purdy, *Tischa*. Purdy came to Chicken as a young school teacher in the 1920s, reaching the town after an arduous horseback ride of several days. She fell in love with the region, married and spent the rest of her life living in Chicken. She died just a couple of years ago, but her book lives on. Many of the people she wrote about are still in the area. The title of her book comes from the way the young Indian children struggled to pronounce the word *teacher*.

Before reaching Chicken and after passing it, the road crosses various forks and tributaries of the Fortymile River, an excellent stream for canoeists. Most popular is putting in at one of the Fortymile River access points, floating downstream into Canada, then floating into the Yukon and downstream to Eagle. It's a great 4- or 5-day trip with occasional Class III water, but mostly Class II.

Fishermen can pull grayling from the Fortymile and its tributaries at breakup in the spring and just before freeze-up in the fall. Sheefish to 10 pounds are occasionally caught in July and August—try the slower stretches of water.

Past Chicken, the surrounding country becomes a bit more rugged, and evidence of bygone mining days is all around if you look closely: old log cabins, a gold dredge abandoned right next to the road and various pieces of equipment left lying around, mostly near the streams. Avoid trespassing on posted mining claims. Area miners can be extremely protective of their rights to a piece of ground. If you want to try your hand at gold panning, there are plenty of places along the streams that are accessible and not part of any active mining claim.

A gold dredge along the Taylor Highway between Tok and Eagle.

After winding through the river valleys for a short distance, the road begins to climb up to Jack Wade Junction. At the junction, the Taylor Highway goes left (north) to Eagle; the Top of the World Highway turns east to Dawson City, Yukon.

The road to Eagle is even narrower and less traveled than the lower stretches of the Taylor Highway. However, if you have time, Eagle is worth a visit. Several clear streams meet the road close to Eagle; almost all have hungry grayling to about 17 or 18 inches in length. These fish are rarely bothered, so it should be fairly easy to entice a few to a hook.

In Eagle, there's an excellent museum, a campground near the old Army barracks, a gas station, a restaurant and a lodge. John McPhee spent considerable time living and observing life in Eagle for his book *Coming into the Country*. Though things have changed to some extent in the nearly two decades since McPhee was in residence, his book offers an interesting portrait of the town and its people that is still relatively accurate.

Those electing not to go to Eagle continue on the Top of the World Highway to Dawson City, Yukon, 79 miles from the junction. You'll quickly see why this is called the Top of the World Highway—much of it is above timberline or right on the edge of it, and on clear days you can see for miles and miles. Plenty of blueberries along this road in August.

Boundary, just inside the Alaska border, is not so much a town as it is the reflection of a man who died a few years back. Action Jackson was the only name anyone ever knew him by, and his bar—the Boundary Lodge, more popularly known as Action Jackson's—was a riotous frontier establishment. Jackson tended the bar with a six-shooter on each hip, and he wasn't above pumping a round or two into the ceiling when things got a little out of hand.

A lot of folks from Dawson City used to drive to Boundary looking for action on Friday and Saturday nights. Things are quieter these days, but that quiet is often a minor distinction.

Leaving Boundary, the U.S. customs station is on your left. Those leaving Alaska are not required to stop. Across the border, however, those leaving Alaska are required to stop at the Canadian customs station. Clearing customs in either direction should take no more than a minute or two for U.S. and Canadian citizens.

These customs stations are normally open from about May 15 to September 15 and closed during the rest of the year. Hours are usually 8 A.M. to 8 P.M. on the Alaska side and 9 A.M. to 9 P.M. on the Canada side, which reflects the fact that this is a time-zone change at the border; 9 A.M. in Canada is 8 A.M. in Alaska.

The road seemingly stays on the ridgeline until the last possible minute, when it drops steeply to the Yukon River and Dawson City. There is no bridge at Dawson, but a free ferry hauls people and vehicles across the river to Dawson.

Campers should check out the Yukon Territorial Campground on the Alaska side of the river, across from Dawson. This is an excellent site laid out along the banks of the Yukon. After camp is set up, take a walk to the riverbank beside the campground and walk downstream a short distance. You'll suddenly come upon the graveyard of several of the old sternwheelers that used to ply their trade on the Yukon. When they had outlived their usefulness, these boats were just abandoned where they were put up for the winter. There's not much left of them these days, but it's still interesting to look them over. Climbing aboard these boats is definitely not recommended; they are in an advanced state of deterioration, and you risk injury by doing so.

Looking across the river to Dawson, try to imagine the steep hill behind the town covered with log cabins, as it was less than 100 years ago. Brush has overrun these sites since, and you almost have to walk the ground to find these old areas of habitation.

---

*Insider's Tip:*Two great events highlight the summer season in Dawson: Canada Day on July 1 and Discovery Days in mid-August. The latter features a parade, dances, even an outhouse race. It's a rollicking good time.

Dawson itself is enjoying a rebirth as a historic park. City ordinances require anyone building within the city limits to erect false fronts and generally give their structures a turn-of-the-century appearance. Many of the surviving old buildings have been restored, some are under restoration and at least one or two have been rebuilt from the ground up using the original plans.

Great 1900-era theater with a professional cast can be found each summer night in the Palace Grand Theatre. Legalized gambling, complete with can-can show, is on every night at Diamond Tooth Gertie's, and a wide variety of other attractions tempt visitors at all hours of the day. Dawson City is well worth some walking-around time.

If you are in Dawson on June 21, drive to the top of the Dome (the mountain behind the town) to watch the midnight sun. Though Dawson sits just south of the Arctic Circle, the elevation atop the Dome is such that the sun never completely sets on June 21 and 22. Also, a drive to the Dome provides several opportunities to look down on Dawson and the Klondike River valley.

Dawson City to Carmacks

STARTING MILEAGE:_____

MILEAGE: 225 miles (375 km)

DRIVING TIME: About 5 hours

TOWNS EN ROUTE: **Pelly Crossing**, 158 miles (263 km)

GAS AVAILABLE: **Klondike River Lodge,** 25 miles (42 km); **Moose Creek Lodge**, 98 miles (163 km); **Stewart Crossing Lodge**, 113 miles (188 km); **Pelly Crossing**, 158 miles (263 km); **Midway Lodge**, 183 miles (305 km); **Carmacks**, 225 miles (375 km)

CAMPGROUNDS: **GuggieVille**, 3 miles (5 km); **Klondike River Territorial Campground**, 11 miles (18 km); **Moose Creek Territorial Campground**, 98 miles (163 km); **Stewart Crossing Lodge**, 113 miles (188 km); **Ethel Lake Territorial Campground**, 121 miles (202 km); **Minto Territorial Campground**, 179 miles (298 km); **Tatchum Territorial Campgrounds**, 208 miles (347 km); **Carmacks Territorial Campground,** 225 miles (375 km)

LODGING: **Klondike River Lodge**, 25 miles (42 km); **Moose Creek Lodge**, 98 miles (163 km); **Stewart Crossing Lodge**, 113 miles (188 km); **Midway Lodge**, 183 miles (305 km); **Carmacks**, 225 miles (375 km)

MAJOR TERRAIN FEATURES: Low, rolling hills, mostly forested; Yukon River valley

WILDLIFE: Black bears, moose

FISHING: Grayling, lake trout, northern pike

==================== Section 3 ====================

Dawson City to Carmacks

Dawson City, created by the Klondike gold rush (mistakenly called the Alaska gold rush by many), sprung into being just downstream of the confluence of the Yukon and Klondike rivers. Within a couple of years of the discovery of gold in August 1896, this previously barren stretch of riverfront became the North's largest city. In its heyday, it was called the "Paris of the North" and the "largest city north of San Francisco."

The Klondike Highway leading south from Dawson retraces the steps of the argonauts who rushed to the gold fields on the "Trail of '98." However, there wasn't much of a road or even a trail in those days. Most came to Dawson by boat, floating down the Yukon River in craft built from lumber hastily whipsawed from green trees. The boats leaked, were dangerously unstable, and were often sawed in half when partners began to argue. But most of them eventually made it to Dawson,

The SS *Keno,* restored on the Yukon River waterfront in Dawson City, Yukon.

The Dempster Highway

Twenty-five miles south of Dawson, heady adventurers with a taste for the remote can turn north on the Dempster Highway, which runs 466 miles to Inuvik at the apex of the Mackenzie River delta. This road leads as far north as it's possible to drive in North America without a permit.

Be absolutely certain you can go halfway (234 miles) without refueling before setting out for Inuvik. There are no fuel or auto repair facilities for the first half of the drive.

At Peel River and Arctic Red River, free ferries carry you and your vehicle across. However, early and late in the season, during breakup and freeze-up, respectively, there is no way to cross these rivers. It's best not to try to cross prior to June 15 and after September 1. Also, these ferries do break down occasionally, and it's not unusual for travelers to have to wait for a day or longer while they are repaired. Be prepared for cold weather, high winds and limited visibility at all times.

Insects can also be a severe problem—black flies, mosquitoes and gnats. Carry plenty of repellent; there are few places to purchase it en route.

Early and late in the season, a caribou herd migrates across the highway. Other wildlife is abundant as well—grizzlies, moose, fox, wolves and all manner of birds. If caribou are in the area, look carefully for wolf packs hovering on the fringes of the herd hoping to pick off injured animals or those that stray too far from the herd. Few things can compare with watching this fundamental part of nature, as a wolf pack assaults and brings down prey.

There is good to excellent grayling fishing available in several streams crossed by the Dempster, simply because few travelers tackle this road. It's not unusual to drive for hours without seeing another vehicle.

Allow a minimum of 2 days each way for driving the entire length of the Dempster. Slow way down during rainy periods. Much of this gravel road is surfaced with a material rich in clay. It becomes extremely slick when wet. Dry, it generates intense clouds of dust from every vehicle that passes.

where the lumber used to build the boats was recycled into cabins and furnishings.

The Yukon River, the transportation artery that carried these fortune hunters, is the primary terrain feature visible along the Klondike Highway. It's a fairly gentle stream, though the current is respectable. Downstream from Whitehorse en route to Dawson, the only major river obstacle is Five Finger Rapids, visible from a highway turnout. The rapids upset a number of the home-built boats and later contributed to the destruction of some of the sternwheelers plying this water road.

As you leave Dawson, the highway crosses the Klondike River. Evidence of the region's golden past is all around, including tailings from the gold dredges that worked through area streams. Several businesses and govern-ment agencies offer activities near the Klondike River bridge to provide a glimpse of the past.

After passing the Klondike River, the road swings to the east of the Yukon River, and doesn't come within sight of it again until near Minto, 3 to 4 hours' driving time from Dawson. This is pretty country, though it can be hot and dry during the summer months, with only occasional thunderstorms providing relief. A few years back, I spent a long, hot July 4th weekend in Dawson, with daytime temperatures exceeding 100 degrees F. At the time, the most popular activity was waterskiing on the Yukon River.

A good bet for lunch while driving south is Moose Creek Lodge, about 98 miles from Dawson. You can almost describe this place as a deli, with home-baked breads and other options beyond the usual hamburgers and other hot sandwiches.

Fishermen will want to check out Ethel Lake for lake trout, 121 miles from Dawson. Fish from a boat, trolling slowly at different depths until you find the fish. The lake and campground with a boat launch are about 17 miles off the highway. Good fishing for grayling is available at Crooked and Moose creeks. Crooked Creek also holds northern pike.

Travelers planning to overnight in or near Carmacks will have to backtrack about 3 miles the next day if they want to drive the Campbell Highway to Watson Lake. Those wishing to continue south to Whitehorse, there to intercept the Alaska Highway, have an additional 103 miles to go on the Klondike Highway. En route, the road passes Lake Laberge (la-BARGE) made famous by one of Robert Service's best-known poems, *The Cremation of Sam McGee*. "Twas on the marge of Lake Laberge . . . "

Those planning on taking the Campbell Highway to Watson Lake should figure on getting an early start if they want to drive the entire route in a single day. Little, if any, of this road is paved, and there are few facilities along the 365-mile route.

Carmacks to Watson Lake

STARTING MILEAGE:_____

MILEAGE: 365 miles (608 km)

DRIVING TIME: 8 to 10 hours

TOWNS EN ROUTE: **Faro**, 106 miles (177 km); **Ross River**, 139 miles (232 km); **Miner's Junction**, 300 miles (500 km)

GAS AVAILABLE: **Faro**, 106 miles (177 km); **Ross River**, 139 miles (232 km); **Miner's Junction**, 300 miles (500 km)

CAMPGROUNDS: **Frenchman's Lake Territorial Campground**, 25 miles (42 km); **Salmon Lake Territorial Campground**, 51 miles (85 km); **Drury Creek Territorial Campground**, 72 miles (120 km); **Fisheye Lake Territorial Campground**, 104 miles (173 km); **Lapie Canyon Territorial Campground**, 138 miles (230 km); **Frances Lake Territorial Campground**, 260 miles (433 km); **Simpson Lake Territorial Campground**, 316 miles (527 km)

LODGING: **Faro**, 106 miles (177 km); **Ross River**, 139 miles (232 km); **Miner's Junction**, 300 miles (500 km)

MAJOR TERRAIN FEATURES: **Pelly River**, many large lakes

WILDLIFE: Black bears, moose

FISHING: Grayling, lake trout, cutthroat trout, northern pike

======= Section 4 =======

Carmacks to Watson Lake

This road should prove an absolute delight to fishermen. It offers probably the best roadside fishing in all of Yukon Territory, simply because so few travelers drive this route.

Coffee Lake, 146 miles from Carmacks, holds big, tackle-busting Kamloops cutthroat trout to 25 pounds or more. Lake trout lurk in the depths of Frenchman's Lake (25 miles), Little Salmon Lake (Drury Creek Campground, 72 miles), Frances Lake (260 miles) and Simpson Lake (316 miles). Other streams and lakes along the way offer fishing for stocked rainbows and kokanees, northern pike and grayling. This is truly a road where a fisherman could invest a week or more without getting bored.

But the fishing is not what brought this road into being. Like most northern roads, mining led to its creation. Much of that mining is still going on today, and all of the towns along the Campbell Highway are supply points for mining activities.

For the first 106 miles to Faro, there will be heavy truck traffic—ore trucks carrying rock to Carmacks. This lead, silver and zinc ore is trucked from Faro to Carmacks, to Whitehorse and finally to Skagway, where it is loaded aboard ship for transport to processing sites.

Ross River, though situated near coal fields, offers more in the line of visitor services, particularly to big-game hunters. Several outfitters are active in the region, all offering hunts deep into Yukon and Northwest territories. Also, canoeists interested in floating the Pelly River often start their trips in Ross River and float downstream to where the river intersects the Klondike Highway at Pelly River. Officials recommend camping on islands and gravel bars to avoid bears and the dense hordes of mosquitoes that can descend without warning. Usually there's a breeze in the open areas to help keep the bugs away. There are two sets of rapids en route. Inquire locally for river conditions before setting out.

Tamarack, a type of larch, can be seen near the Watson Lake end of the road. Though a member of the pine family, this tree loses all its needles in winter. For the most part, tamarack is fairly rare in the Yukon.

The Campbell Highway joins the Alaska Highway in Watson Lake at the sign forest. Travelers following the route recommended here will turn north on the Alaska Highway for a few miles to intercept the Cassiar Highway. Alternately, the Alaska Highway leads southeast to Fort Nelson and Dawson City.

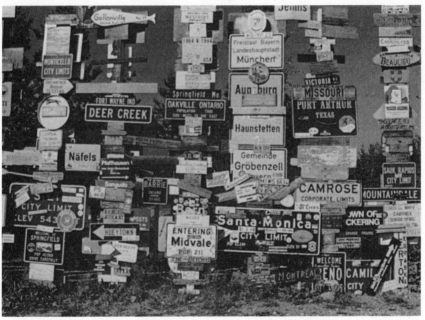

Small part of sign forest, Watson Lake, Yukon.

Watson Lake to Yellowhead Highway 16

STARTING MILEAGE:_____

MILEAGE: 476 miles (793 km)

DRIVING TIME: 2 days

TOWNS EN ROUTE: **Cassiar**, 88 miles (147 km); **Dease Lake**, 160 miles (266 km)

GAS AVAILABLE: **Cassiar Highway Junction**, 13 miles (22 km); **Good Hope Lake**, 74 miles (123 km); **Cassiar**, 97 miles (10 miles from highway) (162 km); **Dease Lake**, 160 miles (266 km); **Forty Mile Flats**, 203 miles (338 km); **Iskut**, 211 miles (352 km); **Tatogga Lake Resort**, 220 miles (367 km); **Meziadin Lake Junction**, 375 miles (625 km); **Kitwanga**, 468 miles (780 km); **Highway 16 Junction**, 476 miles (793 km)

CAMPGROUNDS: **Boya Lake Provincial Park**, 66 miles (110 km); **Mighty Moe's Place**, 107 miles (178 km); **Forty Mile Flats**, 203 miles (338 km); **Tatogga Lake Resort**, 220 miles (367 km); **Kinaskan Lake Provincial Park**, 236 miles (393 km); **Meziadin Lake Provincial Park**, 376 miles (627 km)

LODGING: **Dease Lake**, 160 miles (266 km); **Iskut Valley Inn**, 213 miles (355 km); **Tatogga Lake Resort**, 220 miles (367 km); **Meziadin Lake Junction**, 375 miles (625 km)

MAJOR TERRAIN FEATURES: Rugged mountains with glaciers to west, mostly rolling terrain along roadway

WILDLIFE: Black bears, moose

FISHING: Lake trout, rainbows, grayling, Dolly Varden

Section 5

Watson Lake to Yellowhead Highway 16

Though more remote and much less traveled, the Cassiar Highway offers the shortest route to and from Alaska. Using Watson Lake on the Alaska Highway as a base, it's several driving hours shorter to use the Cassiar than to go via Dawson Creek and the regular Alaska Highway.

There are some liabilities, though. Most of the midsection of the Cassiar is gravel, and this part of the road quickly becomes nasty in heavy or prolonged rains. Potholes develop quickly and the road surface becomes very slick. Services, too, are few and far between. Most of the long-haul truckers headed for Whitehorse or Alaska tend to prefer the Cassiar because it cuts down their driving time.

But many travelers believe the scenery along the Cassiar is superior to that along the Alaska Highway, with the Coast Range looming to the west and several glaciers distantly visible. There's probably a better chance of seeing black bears along this road than on most other northern roads. Of several trips on the Cassiar, I have never failed to see at least one black bear each time.

Fishermen will find much to interest them, though it's best if each has some sort of boat available. Much of the fishing is fairly tough to get to, requiring some walking off the road or negotiating narrow, twisting, rutted and unmaintained trails to reach a lakeshore. Car-top or other easily transportable boats are probably best. There is good fishing for rainbows in several spots and for lake trout in most of the large lakes along the way.

Insider's Tip: Though the Cassiar Highway from Watson Lake to Yellowhead Highway can be done in 1 very long driving day (12 to 15 hours), it's far better to take 2 days. Major portions of this drive are slow-going and extremely fatiguing for drivers.

From Dease Lake, about midway along the Cassiar Highway, a gravel road leads 74 miles to Telegraph Creek on the Stikine River. Charter boat trips are available on the Stikine, and hardy souls may want to float the river all the way to its mouth near the southeastern Alaska town of Wrangell. Access in and out of Wrangell is via Alaska Airlines or the Alaska Marine Highway ferries. No roads lead to Wrangell. From the mouth of the river, there's an open-water crossing of several miles to reach Wrangell. Kayaks are much better than canoes for this trip.

A second great side trip along the Cassiar leads from Meziadin Lake Junction, 375 miles from Watson Lake, to Stewart, British Columbia, and Hyder, Alaska. Hyder is unique for a U.S. community in that the medium of exchange is Canadian currency. There are no banks in Hyder, thus the few local businesses keep their accounts in Stewart, a couple of miles away. The road dead-ends in Hyder, though travelers have the option of boarding an Alaska Marine Highway ferry on its weekly trip to Stewart. The ferry runs to Ketchikan, where it is possible to board a ferry headed south to either Prince Rupert, B.C., or Bellingham, Washington.

Of particular interest on the Stewart Highway Access Road is Bear Glacier, which terminates in a lake a few hundred yards away from the highway. It's possible to sit at roadside and watch the glacier calve icebergs into the lake at almost any time during the summer. Several other hanging glaciers in the mountains above the road can be seen along this route. Only at Worthington Glacier near Valdez can travelers drive this close to a glacier anywhere on their trips to and from Alaska.

Insider's Tip: Mail postcards to friends and relatives from Hyder. Dare the recipients to find this place on a map.

Just south of Meziadin Lake Junction, Meziadin Lake Provincial Park offers one of the most beautiful settings for a campground anywhere in northwestern Canada or Alaska. Campsites are right on the lake's shore, and a summer sunset here must be seen to be believed.

Both north and south of Meziadin Lake Junction are extensive regions of clear-cut forest. These deforested lands are not, however, just meant to line the pockets of the logging industry or to create an eyesore. In recent years, area spruce trees have suffered from a heavy infestation of spruce bark beetles, which kill virtually every tree they touch. As the dead trees dry, they become major forest-fire hazards. Rather than accept the hazard or allow a resource to go to waste, local authorities have allowed extensive clear-cutting of the forests. Current hopes are that the extensive cutting will drastically reduce or even eliminate the beetle infestation.

On the plus side, these clear-cuts absolutely burst into vibrant colors in July when the fireweed flowers. Whole mountainsides turn a reddish lavender. From high ground, these brilliant fields of flowers can be seen extending for miles. The best time to see the fireweed is the latter half of July.

Bear Glacier on Stewart–Hyder Cutoff from Cassiar Highway.

Insider's Tip: Several of the logging roads used in the clear-cutting lead into the relatively treeless hillsides. These offer excellent access for those who want a close look at the fireweed. Be very careful, however, as these roads are not maintained and are likely to be very narrow in spots.

Near the southern end of the Cassiar Highway, several small Indian communities offer for viewing a broad assortment of totem poles. Gitwangak, off on a side road less than half a mile from the end of the highway, has the most-visited and accessible totems.

Once you complete your trip on the Cassiar, you are on Yellowhead Highway 16, which leads 307 miles east to Prince George. From Prince George you can either turn south on B.C. 97 toward Washington or continue east on the Yellowhead Highway to Jasper and Edmonton, both in Alberta. Except for isolated areas of road construction, the Yellowhead Highway is paved.

Fort Nelson, British Columbia, to Grimshaw, Alberta, via Fort Simpson and Enterprise, Northwest Territories

STARTING MILEAGE:_____

MILEAGE: 875 miles (1,458 km)

DRIVING TIME: 3 to 4 days

ROUTING: **Fort Nelson, B.C., to Fort Simpson, N.W.T.**, Alaska Highway, 17 miles (28 km); to Liard Highway, 244 miles (406 km); to Mackenzie Highway, 40 miles (67 km); **Fort Simpson to Enterprise**, Mackenzie Highway, 245 miles (408 km); **Enterprise to Grimshaw, Alberta**, Mackenzie Highway, 346 miles (577 km)

GAS AVAILABLE: **Fort Liard Junction**, 126 miles (182 km); **Fort Simpson**, 301 miles (473 km); **Yellowknife Junction**, 466 miles (777 km); **Enterprise**, 528 miles (880 km); **Steen River**, 581 miles (968 km); **High Level**, 701 miles (1,168 km); **Manning**, 824 miles (1,373 km); **Grimshaw**, 875 miles (1,458 km)

CAMPGROUNDS: **Blackstone Territorial Park**, 196 miles (327 km); **Fort Simpson**, 284 miles (473 km); **Whittaker Falls**, 378 miles (630 km); **Lady Evelyn Falls**, 476 miles (793 km); **Louise Falls**, 534 miles (890 km); **NWT/Alberta Border**, 581 miles (968 km); **Steen River**, 611 miles (1,019 km); **Meander River**, 651 miles (1,085 km); **Hutch Lake**, 678 miles (1,130 km); **High Level**, 701 miles (1,168 km); **Boyer River**, 749 miles (1,248 km); **Twin Lakes**, 786 miles (1,310 km); **Notikewin Provincial Park**, 800 miles (1,333 km); **Hotchkiss Provincial Park**, 814 miles (1,357 km); **Manning**, 824 miles (1,373 km); **Grimshaw**, 875 miles (1,458 km)

LODGING: **Fort Simpson**, 284 miles (473 km); **Enterprise**, 528 miles (880 km); **High Level**, 701 miles (1,168 km); **Manning**, 824 miles (1,373 km); **Grimshaw**, 875 miles (1,458 km)

WILDLIFE: Deer, black bears, raptors

FISHING: Limited grayling and northern pike

12

THE MACKENZIE LOOP

Why drive this route? No "great" scenery is obvious; most of the roads described in this chapter wind through some fairly flat country. Perhaps the best excuse is simply that it's there, and few others have even attempted this swing through the southern edge of Northwest Territories.

There are some awesome sights, though you'll have to do a little extra work to seek them out. Specifically, this otherwise flat terrain hides some of the most magnificent waterfalls in the North Country.

Most of the ground is soft limestone, a prehistoric coral reef that has been uplifted into a plateau over thousands and thousands of centuries. Rivers coursing through the region cut deep into the soft stone, gouging out canyons. In these canyons, below the level of the surrounding terrain, roaring rivers cascade over towering cliffs. For the most part, you'll have to drive a short distance off the main road to find these; most are marked with some sort of sign indicating where to turn. Follow these signs and the rewards are many, as are the opportunities for photographs.

Plan well your drive for this loop from British Columbia into Northwest Territories and south into Alberta. Gas stations and lodging—even campgrounds—are spaced at lengthy intervals for most of the route. And at least one gas station listed in another popular guide has been closed for years. However, the gas stations listed in the book you are reading were confirmed as open in 1992, and all have been in business long enough to provide at least minimal insurance that they can be expected to remain operational in the years ahead.

Leaving Fort Nelson, drive 17 miles westbound on the Alaska Highway and turn north at the sign for the Liard *(leerd)* Highway. From this point on, you will be on a gravel road until approaching the Northwest Territories–Alberta border some 575 miles farther on. It is a good, well-maintained road, though exceedingly dusty during hot, dry periods.

Just out of Fort Nelson on the Alaska Highway, you will immediately

Limestone escarpment, Northwest Territories, along the Mackenzie Highway.

begin to climb over the Rocky Mountains, but once on the Liard Highway, the Rockies gradually recede to the northwest. After a hundred miles or so, mountains can no longer be seen, and from the higher points along this gently rolling terrain you can see for miles and miles on clear days.

The highway generally parallels the path of the Liard River, though the river can rarely be seen from the road—it's just a little too far to the west. The Liard is the major tributary of the Mackenzie River, the largest drainage system in northwestern Canada.

The first major tributary of the Liard River is the Fort Nelson River, crossed about 30 minutes' driving time after starting north from the Alaska Highway. The Fort Nelson River bridge is the longest Acrow bridge in the world, a bridge type better known to some as a Bailey bridge in honor of Sir

Donald Bailey, the British engineer who designed it. The steel truss panels it features have been in use on various northern bridges since World War II. As the other bridges were rebuilt or replaced, the salvageable panels were stored until needed for bridging the Fort Nelson River.

On the north side of the bridge is a turnout with a picnic table and an excellent view of the bridge structure, if you want to study it more closely.

Fifty-five miles past the Fort Nelson River crossing, the road crosses the Petitot River, reputed to have the warmest water in British Columbia. From here, canoeists might want to attempt the 10-hour trip to Fort Liard—down the Petitot to the Liard River; the village is at the confluence of the two rivers. Sheer rock canyons and rapids make this an adventurous trip, but one that's easily done in a day. Freshwater clams, pike and pickerel provide limited offerings for those wanting a meal from the wild.

Past the river, the road climbs rapidly with a 10 percent grade for about a mile and a half. A mile past the crest, you cross the border into Northwest Territories, far and away Canada's largest province, almost three times as large as the state of Alaska, with a population of about 20,000.

The only community along the Liard Highway, Fort Liard, is accessed by a side road that runs to the west 125 miles from Fort Nelson. The gas station at this junction offers the only fuel available between Fort Nelson and Fort Simpson, Northwest Territories. Fort Simpson is nearly 200 miles from this junction. If in any doubt about your fuel supply, fill up before proceeding north. There is a campground in Fort Liard.

The only campground on the actual Liard Highway is at Blackstone River, about 194 miles from Fort Nelson. This is an attractive site offering access to the Liard River. A caretaker at the campground runs a small visitors center and usually has time to talk about the area. Like all the relatively few facilities along this road, his sees little business in the course of an average day.

From Blackstone River, it's about 107 miles to Fort Simpson, 67 miles to the junction with the Mackenzie Highway, then 40 miles west. To reach Fort Simpson, Northwest Territories provides a free vehicle ferry across the Liard River. However, when water levels are low, usually in late August and early September, the ferry may not be able to make the crossing.

The best part of the ferry crossing is the boat's skipper, Earl Settee. By all means find the time to chat with him about his job, about the local folks, or whatever. He's got a story for every occasion, most with a superb punch line.

Fort Simpson is well worth a visit. Primarily a community of Dene (an Indian word meaning "the people"), the region is rich in history. The name comes from the Royal Canadian Mounted Police post that was established here in the 1800s. Now, the people in the area are taking an active interest in Native rights and sovereignty. They are organized and active in local and national politics.

Probably the best place to stop is at the newspaper office, which also doubles as a visitors center. The large man behind the counter is the editor and chief booster for the region. He'll fill you in on local affairs and insist that you visit the spot where Pope John Paul II spoke several years ago. The Dene are intensely proud that the Pope singled out Fort Simpson for a visit, and they go to great lengths to keep the site attractive. You'll see the newspaper office to the right as you pull into town.

Leaving Fort Simpson, you'll have to retrace your route for 40 miles back to the Liard Highway junction. From there, the road runs due east to Enterprise, where it turns south toward Alberta. However, along the way are some of the spectacular waterfalls mentioned earlier. Some of the best of these, in order as you are eastbound, are Whittaker Falls, Lady Evelyn Falls and Louise Falls. Photographers should visit Lady Evelyn Falls in the early morning hours. Then the angle of the sun creates a fabulous rainbow in the mists engendered by the falling water.

Campgrounds, though still relatively few, are more readily available along this stretch of road leading to Enterprise. There are four campgrounds along this 245-mile stretch of road. Gas is available 180 miles from Fort Simpson, near the junction where a separate road leads to Yellowknife, capital of Northwest Territories on the north shore of Great Slave Lake.

Detouring off the Mackenzie Highway to Yellowknife is at least a 2-day affair. Driving time one way from the junction to Yellowknife is about 6 hours and includes another free ferry trip, this time across the Mackenzie River. Yellowknife is a modern city in every sense of the word, with full facilities for travelers and many new buildings. As the center of government for this massive province, it is primarily a service center—and probably the only town in the whole region where one regularly sees men in jackets and ties and women in skirts and dresses suitable for office wear.

For those who want to see Great Slave Lake (the sixth largest lake in the world) and don't want to drive to Yellowknife, turn left and follow the signs to Hay River when the Mackenzie Highway reaches Enterprise. Hay River is a shipping port and railhead on the south shore of the lake. Here, goods for Yellowknife and other points in the interior are brought by rail and transshipped across the lake in ocean-sized freighters. There's also a great swimming beach, complete with white sand, just outside the port. And, if you're traveling with kids, Hay River offers the first opportunity in several days to buy a pizza or an ice cream cone—important for the mental health of adults, too, on hot summer afternoons.

At Enterprise, the Mackenzie Highway turns south for Alberta, gradually leaving the wilderness behind as you drive deeper and deeper into one of Canada's prairie provinces.

Alberta is one of the world's great duck factories. The potholes in the northern part of the province provide some of the finest waterfowl nesting areas in the world. However, in recent years drought has severely lowered water levels, drying up some of these nesting sites. Still, though, there will be a lot of waterfowl near the road if you look carefully. For the most part these birds won't take flight at your approach and will attempt to hide in the

Wood Buffalo National Park

Leading to the east from the road to Hay River is NWT 5, which leads to Fort Smith and Wood Buffalo National Park. The park is named for the last survivors of this particular strain of bison, which are slightly larger than the plains buffalo so familiar to most people.

Wood Buffalo National Park also offers one other distinct claim to fame—snakes, the most northern population of common garter snakes known in North America. The only snakes in Alaska, Yukon or Northwest Territories are found in Wood Buffalo.

Park biologists will probably be reluctant to direct visitors to the snake habitat. The population is fairly limited, and it's believed that the survival of these reptiles is best ensured by keeping disturbances to a minimum.

They will, however, gladly direct you to the buffalo, if they are accessible—and also to what might be the park's major attraction: the whooping crane. Wood Buffalo is the last natural nesting ground for this endangered species. Again, biologists aren't too keen on these birds being disturbed. But keep a sharp eye out; you may get lucky and catch sight of this very rare bird.

At the Salt River, about 150 miles from Hay River, fishermen can try for inconnu (sheefish), one of the few places in the North where road travelers get a chance at this spectacular game fish, often called the "tarpon of the North." If the sheefish aren't biting, there are pike and walleye available as well.

Headquarters for Wood Buffalo National Park is in Fort Smith, a town of about 2,400 people approximately 167 miles from Hay River. All travelers' services are available at Fort Smith.

From Fort Smith, two narrow roads lead deep into Wood Buffalo National Park. Be certain to carry enough gas for a round trip if you attempt either of these drives.

Lady Evelyn Falls along the Mackenzie Highway, Northwest Territories.

reeds at the edge of the water. Look closely and you should be rewarded by frequent sightings of ducks and ducklings.

As the road runs deeper into Alberta, much of the swampy land turns into fields of hay, wheat and other grains. In a sense, Alberta and parts of neighboring Manitoba are Canada's breadbasket. The economies of farming in this day and age, however, are such that few of the "typical" family farms exist anymore. Most of the acreage under cultivation is in the hands of large conglomerates or huge private tracts created by the acquisition of smaller, neighboring farms over the past several decades. During harvest time in the fall, watching these operations is awe-inspiring. Huge phalanxes of combines sweep through fields of grain whose borders are measured in miles. That, combined with the colors of fall, makes for unforgettable photographs.

The end of the Mackenzie Highway (or the beginning if you choose this route to start your trip) is at Grimshaw in central Alberta. From Grimshaw you can turn west for Dawson Creek or southeast for Edmonton. Dawson Creek is less than a 2-hour drive from Grimshaw; Edmonton is about 5 hours away.

13

THE ALASKA MARINE HIGHWAY

One of Alaska's most scenic regions cannot be reached by vehicle, but if you can get your vehicle to southeastern Alaska, you can explore to your heart's content. And, the state of Alaska subsidizes a system of ocean-going ferries to allow vacationers to do just that.

Ferry travelers can bring their vehicles to the densely forested fjords of Alaska's panhandle, or use them to speed and ease the drive to Fairbanks or Anchorage. Frankly, there's so much to do and so many places to visit that a ferry-hopping vacation in southeastern Alaska should be separate, rather than combined as part of a we'll-do-it-all-this-summer-or-else trip.

Northbound travelers can board Alaska Marine Highway ferries in Bellingham, Washington (about an hour's drive north of Seattle), or in Prince Rupert, British Columbia, the western end of Yellowhead Highway 16 described elsewhere in this book. Those wishing to use a ferry to speed their way to Fairbanks or Anchorage should book passage to Haines, the northernmost community in southeastern Alaska served by the ferry system. From Haines, it's a little over 600 miles—2 fairly easy days—to Fairbanks and about 700 miles to Anchorage.

Typically, there are two ferries northbound from Bellingham each week during the summer season (May 1 to September 30). On the 65-hour trip to Haines, these ships stop briefly at Ketchikan, Wrangell, Petersburg and Juneau.

Sample costs for ferry transportation from Bellingham to Haines in 1989 were as follows:

- Adult: $230 (meals and berth not included)
- Vehicle, 19 to 21 feet long: $847
- Cabin (two-berth, shared washrooms): $218 per person

Thus, two adults and a typical pickup/camper vehicle would travel to Haines from Bellingham for about $1,525. The 2 1/2 days spent on the ferry would cut about 5 driving days out of a trip to Fairbanks or Anchorage.

However, it is possible to do this trip for even less money. Cabins are not really necessary unless you desire complete privacy. Sheltered upper decks on the larger ferries (which include the ships on the Bellingham schedule) offer room to erect free-standing tents for those who want to "boat-camp." Shower and toilet facilities are available. Also, the observation lounges aboard the ships are equipped with reclining chairs, much like airline seats only better, and many people choose to sleep in these when traveling by ferry.

It is also possible simply to walk on the ferry with only your luggage and pay just the per-person fare; one does not need to bring a vehicle aboard to utilize the ferries. Every summer, many young people enjoy cheap vacations in southeastern Alaska doing just that. They hop from town to town as the mood strikes them. At the end of the summer, most have had an experience beyond compare. As they travel, these young men and women, college students for the most part, while away the hours planning their futures, staging singalongs on the decks where their tents are pitched—there's always at least one with a guitar—and, in the manner of youngsters the world over, make the first struggling attempts at correcting the imperfect world that surrounds them. Perhaps some of the most pleasant evenings of an Alaskan vacation can be spent sitting with these folks as they explore southeastern Alaska on their limited budgets.

From Prince Rupert, there are generally daily departures northbound to Alaska ports of call, though not all of these ships take the most direct routing to reach the northern terminal at Haines. Prices from Prince Rupert to Haines in 1989 were as follows:

- Adult: $118 (meals and berth not included)
- Vehicle, 19 to 21 feet long: $407
- Cabin (two-berth, shared washrooms): $118

It is significantly cheaper to drive the extra 2 days to Prince Rupert and ferry north from there.

However, the ferries from Bellingham or Prince Rupert to Haines are just a small part of a very big story. Besides these northbound conveniences, a host of ships continually work routes throughout southeastern Alaska. One of the best of these is run by the M/V *Aurora*, which calls several times a week at Hollis on Prince of Wales Island.

Prince of Wales Island offers a driving vacation in southeastern Alaska. Over the past several decades, roads built by the logging industry have been joined throughout the island, ultimately producing a network of several hundred miles of roads. These roads are rarely traveled, they pass some of the finest fishing streams in Alaska, bald eagles by the score nest in tall, stately Sitka spruce and large numbers of black bears and deer travel barely discernible trails through the rain forest.

Though Prince of Wales Island can be explored by tent campers with a car, the wet climate makes a camper or travel trailer more desirable. For those without an RV, however, tents are not the only means of getting out of the elements. The U.S. Forest Service maintains about 160 cabins in scenic spots throughout southeastern Alaska. Dozens of these are on Prince of Wales Island and can be rented for $20 a day—bring your own food and sleeping bags.

Most cabins are on a lake or stream teeming with fish, most lakeside cabins have rowboats available and all can be reserved up to 6 months in advance. On Prince of Wales Island, a couple of cabins can be reached by vehicle, others require a short hike and the rest are best reached by floatplane chartered out of either Ketchikan or Craig, the latter the largest community on Prince of Wales Island. For an affordable wilderness experience that you'll remember for the rest of your life, these cabins can't be beat. For details on renting a cabin on Prince of Wales Island, or for anywhere in southeastern Alaska for that matter, write to Tongass National Forest, Ketchikan Ranger District, 3031 Tongass Ave., Ketchikan, AK 99901. The Forest Service will send you a packet of information that includes instructions for reserving a cabin, a map of cabin locations and information on fishing and other attractions. Reservations are on a first-come, first-served basis and can be made up to 6 months in advance. If you have a special cabin in mind, make your reservations as early as possible—the more popular cabins tend to fill up fast.

Besides Prince of Wales Island, the ferries in southeastern Alaska serve several other communities, including Sitka, Wrangell, Juneau (Alaska's capital reachable only by air or by ship), Skagway, Petersburg, Angoon and Tenakee. All of these communities offer a particular charm and a slice of Alaska's history.

Sitka was the capital of Russian America at the time the United States purchased Alaska from the czar in 1867. On the beach in Wrangell, petroglyphs etched in the rocks suggest ancient cultures. Juneau offers monolithic government buildings in an unparalleled setting of mountains, glaciers and rain forests. Skagway, the jumping-off point for the Chilkoot Trail and the Klondike gold rush, also connects to the Alaska Highway near Whitehorse. Petersburg is a fishing town, best known as Alaska's Little Norway, and offers a fine celebration of its Scandinavian heritage every year during the third week in May. Angoon, on Admiralty Island, is the only port of call on a large island famed for both its wilderness and its timber industry. Finally, Tenakee has been known for decades for the therapeutic hot springs located in town. It was long a winter haven for miners escaping the severe cold of interior winters.

Those wishing to use the southeastern Alaska ferries should do so with reservations, particularly northbound travelers who want to start in either

Bellingham or Prince Rupert. Southbound travelers can often find space available during the summer months, but for northbound travelers, it's rare. For information and reservations, write to Alaska Marine Highway, P.O. Box R, Juneau, AK 99811, or call 1-800-642-0066. If the 800-number is busy (quite common in January), you can call (907) 465-3941 during business hours. Reservations for each summer season are taken beginning on January 1 of that year. Exact schedules and pricing information are normally available in early December. Prices for ferry travel have increased steadily for the past several years and likely will continue to do so.

Besides the ferries in southeastern Alaska, a separate, smaller system serves southwestern Alaska, specifically communities in Prince William Sound, on the southern edge of the Kenai Peninsula, Kodiak Island and Dutch Harbor in the Aleutian Islands. The two ferry systems do not connect; in other words, it is not possible to board in Bellingham and sail to Homer, just a few hours' driving time from Anchorage. Reservations and information for the southwestern Alaska ferries can be had from the same address and phone number as given above.

Alaska Marine Highway ferry M/V *Taku* at Skagway dock.

14

THE ALASKA HIGHWAY BY AIR

For years you've devoured stories about the mystique and glamor of bush pilots in the far reaches of Alaska and the Canadian Northwest. Finally, as an aircraft owner and pilot you decide it's time to join in the fun and begin making plans accordingly.

First and foremost, forget about the mystique and the glamor. Bush flying is hard, precise work that utilizes skills developed over years of flying over uninhabited terrain and dealing with the worst weather in the world. The old saying that "there are no old, bold pilots" is more true in Alaska than anywhere else on earth. If nothing else, the aviation accident statistics from Alaska make this glaringly apparent.

Flying your own light plane to Alaska, through Alaska and back takes more time and effort in planning than any other flight you're likely to make in your lifetime. Margins for error are razor thin, and waiting for help in the wilderness can test all of your existing survival skills—and make you wish you had a few more on which to draw.

Sometimes the strangest things can turn out to be a piece of survival gear. Back in 1980, a wind-up alarm clock helped save my neck.

It was early winter on the North Slope, and I had been hauling sling loads by helicopter all day at the aptly named settlement of Lonely, about 100 miles west of Prudhoe Bay on the North Coast. The original plan was for me to stay there the night and fly back to Prudhoe in the morning. I finished a few minutes early, and thought I had time to get back.

Dusk found me out over the Beaufort Sea in a whiteout blizzard with no horizon and very few immediate prospects. Using my radar altimeter, I eased down to about 50 feet above the surface and turned due south toward land. A few minutes later I spotted the frozen mud above the tide line and gratefully landed on the snowbank above it. I was out of radio range and nobody knew where I was. I had to keep that aircraft from freezing up through a 14-hour night so I could start it in the morning to get back, and there was less than two hours fuel in the tanks.

Sifting through my personal gear and survival gear, I came across the alarm clock. Bingo! I'd set it for two hours of sleep in an Arctic bag, then get up and run the helicopter for 10 minutes or so to warm everything up and charge the battery. Two hours was just long enough to keep the oil from thickening too much in the cold. Five times that night I crawled out of my bag and fired up the engine—once scaring the dickens out of several caribou that had come by to investigate (and me as well when I saw them move suddenly in the glare of the landing light). When the new day brought a firm horizon to the featureless landscape, I took off and flew back to Prudhoe Bay and a warm bed.

PILOT QUALIFICATIONS
A private pilot with little or no training in instrument flying has no business flying in Alaska. Even if you plan to make your trip strictly under VFR (Visual Flight Rules) conditions, avail yourself of the opportunity to qualify for an instrument rating before you head for Alaska. Weather in the North's remote areas is extremely variable and exceedingly difficult to predict. Look on an instrument ticket as insurance. While you may not need it, it is sure nice to have it if conditions deteriorate, as can happen with little warning.

Besides an instrument ticket, training and practice in mountain flying are essential for flying to Alaska. You will be flying around, through and near the most extensive mountain ranges in North America on this trip, and knowing how to deal with mountainous terrain and the weather it can generate is imperative.

AIRPLANE EQUIPMENT
At a minimum, your aircraft should carry sufficient fuel for 350 miles of flight with an adequate reserve. More is better.

Your instrument panel should include all basic flight instruments, a radio compass (magnetic compasses are notoriously unstable and often unreliable in northern latitudes), an operational ADF receiver, an operational VOR receiver (ideally one with DME) and a first-rate attitude indicator as a minimum. Other nice-to-have features include either LORAN or GPS, a vertical-speed indicator and a radar altimeter. Two VHF radios for voice communications are better than relying on one.

An ELT (emergency locator transmitter) with fresh batteries should be properly mounted to the airframe so that it transmits upon impact in a crash or can be easily switched on by the pilot or a passenger. If something does go wrong, an ELT is the best possible insurance that you will be found quickly. Test the ELT frequently to make certain it is operating.

Survival gear is required by law for flights in Alaska and Canada, and sufficient quantities should be carried to adequately serve each person on board in the event of a mishap. At a minimum, food for several days and a sleeping bag should be included for each occupant of the aircraft. An ax, lightweight shovel, a water container (an unlubricated condom contained in a sock makes a nice, lightweight water bag and can hold a pint or more of liquid), insect repellent, wire for small-animal snares, fishing lures and line, fire-starting materials, shelter (a tent) and warm clothing should be included. Other nice-to-have items include rain gear, a warm hat and gloves.

A firearm and ammunition are required in Alaska to be on board, and most pilots operating only in Alaska carry some sort of handgun. It is, however, illegal for foreigners to transport a handgun through Canada. Thus you should carry some sort of long gun and ammunition for it. Several breakdown survival rifles are available (usually .22 caliber) and these will do nicely as long as they can only be operated as a rifle. Any firearm that can be fired with a single hand will likely be questioned by Canadian authorities.

PUBLICATIONS

In addition to the charts and publications you routinely carry in your aircraft, you should obtain all VFR and IFR charts for Canada and Alaska as appropriate to your flight, an Alaska Supplement, IFR approach plates for western Canada and Alaska and one or more of the various booklets listing aerodromes and related facilities. A particularly handy VFR chart covers the Alaska Highway in Canada as a single map. This is essentially a strip map covering the highway itself and terrain 50 or more miles on either side of the road. It can be ordered wherever you purchase your charts, as can any of these other publications. Never has the term "flying bookkeeper" been more appropriate than for a pilot setting out for Alaska.

ROUTES

Essentially there are two air routes leading to Alaska. One follows the coast north from Seattle through British Columbia and Alaska's Panhandle; the other essentially follows the Alaska Highway through British Columbia and Yukon Territory.

The coastal route can be a real bother because of weather. This is very wet country with at least one coastal community, Port Alexander, receiving upward of 300 inches of rain a year. All that rain means lots of low clouds and poor visibility in a region famed for its towering mountains and narrow fjords.

For single-engine airplane pilots there's another hazard—there are virtually no suitable forced-landing areas along the coastal route for wheeled planes. Any pilot attempting to fly this route to Alaska in a single-engine aircraft is best advised to use a floatplane or amphibian in lieu of a wheeled plane.

For obvious reasons, then, the route following the Alaska Highway is the preferred course for most who fly to Alaska. And, with a little common sense and application of the basic rules learned early in ground school, a competent pilot should be able to fly to Alaska in just a couple of days, given decent weather.

When flying along a road, treat it just as if you were driving that road. Stay to the right side. Northbound, choose an altitude of even thousands of feet plus 500 feet (2,500, 4,500, etc.) just as you learned in ground school when your heading is in the western half of the compass rose (180 degrees to 359 degrees). Southbound, use odd thousands plus 500 feet (1,500, 3,500, etc.) for the same reason (headings of 000 degrees to 179 degrees). Within reason, higher altitudes offer more options in the event of an emergency than lower altitudes, particularly in the mountains.

Whatever you do, don't push the weather on either route. If you experience the slightest doubt, land at the earliest opportunity, even if it means turning back. Thunderstorms, severe turbulence, high winds, icing conditions and other weather hazards are all possible in any summer month in the North. With the exception of thunderstorms, all these conditions can occur in the winter months as well.

For those with limited mountain flying experience, the mechanical turbulence associated with winds blowing over mountains is perhaps the most difficult condition to understand and overcome. On a clear day there may be few visual clues, although any time you're flying near mountains on a windy day you should be particularly alert. The one primary visual clue that should send you scurrying to the nearest landing strip is a lenticular cloud clinging to the top of the mountain or in the sky just downwind of a peak. When you see these clouds, the wind is really howling near the summit, for these clouds are made up of tiny ice crystals blown off the mountain. Mechanical turbulence associated with the winds causing these clouds can be experienced 50 or more miles downwind of the mountains.

One particular bit of sage advise I received from an old pilot early in my flying career had to do with mountain turbulence. He told me that whenever he approached a mountain range and hit an updraft, he immediately applied power and climbed even higher, because he knew that as soon as he crossed the ridge line he would hit a down draft of equal or even greater intensity. Nothing is quite so frightening as a severe downdraft when you're flying along very close to the ground.

My own worst turbulence experience in Alaska came on New Year's Eve, 1972. I was flying a large Army helicopter out of Fairbanks and had gone to Anchorage to pick up the Army band for that night's party in the officers' club. The weather wasn't great—it was clear and windy for the return trip. But, you know how it is: This was one of those "must-do" missions, and we finally got the weather-briefer to admit that there might be only moderate turbulence at intermediate altitudes (6,000 to 9,000 feet) through Broad Pass in the Alaska Range.

We blasted north out of Anchorage at dusk (about 3 P.M.) for the two-and-a-half-hour flight to Fairbanks. Things were going great, until we approached the first major ridgeline near Talkeetna. Heading across the ridge, we were flying at 6,500 feet and the ground was about 2,000 feet beneath us.

A massive updraft seized the helicopter and shot us upward at an unbelievable rate. Even putting the aircraft into a screaming dive (I hadn't yet learned about climbing in updrafts) had no effect on our upward progress. Seconds later the updraft spit us out at more than 12,000 feet. In the clear night we could see the lights of Fairbanks some 200 miles distant. And, at 12,000 feet, the air was smooth as silk. We stayed there for another half hour or so to cross the mountains, then eased down to 10,000 feet to complete the trip.

Taking the band back to Anchorage the next day was a snap. The air was absolutely calm all the way, though it was a trifle cold in Fairbanks (66 degrees below zero) when we took off.

INSURANCE

Check carefully with the agent that insures your airplane before departing for Alaska. Insurance rates are higher in Alaska, and you may have to pay a little extra for suitable coverage on the trip. Also check if your policy has a clause about crossing the Arctic Circle. Some aircraft policies are void north of this latitude.

FLIGHTSEEING AND FLIGHT PLANS

In a nutshell, common sense and prior planning will make a flying trip to Alaska a success. And, having a plane in Alaska opens up possibilities that most people in a vehicle can't even dream about.

For example, Lake Minchumina on the north side of the Alaska Range is about 150 miles southwest of Fairbanks. It offers an excellent gravel landing strip, one end of which is just a few steps from the lake. Park off this end of the strip, unlimber your fishing rod and start catching northern pike weighing 10 pounds or more. Or, fly west to Nome, inaccessible by road and an excellent place to spend a few days soaking up a little of Alaska's gold-rush history (and revelry).

If salmon fishing's your goal, try King Salmon or Iliamna southwest of Anchorage near the head of the Alaska Peninsula. Be real careful with weather here, as you'll probably fly through Rainy Pass, one of Alaska's more unpredictable places insofar as weather is concerned. The fishing at either spot is grand.

Other flightseeing possibilities include Denali National Park, Wrangell–St. Elias National Park, a variety of glaciers and wilderness of every description.

Finally, never take off without filing a flight plan. And make it as specific as possible. Controllers in Alaska are well used to maintaining and following flight plans for people flying over remote areas and probably know the landmarks better than anyone. Don't be afraid to list your route of flight as a river or stream, or from mountain peak to valley. Pilots do it all the time in Alaska, and for good reason. We want somebody, somewhere, to know when and where to start looking for us if something goes wrong.

===== Appendix A =====

Visitor Information

ALASKA
STATEWIDE
  Alaska Division of Tourism
  P.O. Box E-101, Juneau, AK 99811

ANCHORAGE
  Anchorage Convention and Visitors Bureau
  201 E. Third Ave., Anchorage, AK 99501
  (907) 276-4118

  Whittier Convention and Visitors Bureau
  810 E. Ninth Ave., Suite 200, Anchorage, AK 99501
  (907) 272-4445

DELTA JUNCTION
  Delta Convention and Visitors Bureau
  P.O. Box 987, Delta Junction, AK 99737
  (907) 895-5068

FAIRBANKS
  Fairbanks Convention and Visitors Bureau
  550 First Ave., Fairbanks, AK 99701
  (907) 456-5774

HAINES
  Haines Convention and Visitors Bureau
  P.O. Box 518, Haines, AK 99827
  (907) 766-2234

HOMER
  Homer Visitor and Convention Bureau
  P.O. Box 541, Homer, AK 99603
  (907) 235-5300

JUNEAU
  Juneau Convention and Visitors Bureau
  76 Egan Dr., Suite 140, Juneau, AK 99801
  (907) 586-1737

KENAI
Kenai Convention and Visitors Bureau
P.O. Box 497, Kenai, AK 99611
(907) 283-7989

KETCHIKAN
Ketchikan Convention and Visitors Bureau
131 Front Street, Ketchikan, AK 99901
(907) 225-6166

KODIAK
Kodiak Island Convention and Visitors Bureau
100 Marine Way, Kodiak, AK 99615
(907) 486-4782

NOME
Nome Convention and Visitors Bureau
Box 251, Nome, AK 99762
(907) 443-5535

PALMER/WASILLA
Matanuska-Susitna Convention and Visitors Bureau
HC01 Box 6166 J21, Palmer, AK 99645
(907) 746-5000

SITKA
Sitka Convention and Visitors Bureau
330 Harbor Dr., Sitka, AK 99840
(907) 747-5940

SKAGWAY
Skagway Convention and Visitors Bureau
Box 415, Skagway, AK 99840
(907) 983-2854

VALDEZ
Valdez Convention and Visitors Bureau
Box 1603, Valdez, AK 99686
(907) 835-2984 or (907) 835-INFO

WRANGELL
Wrangell Visitors Center
P.O. Box 1078, Wrangell, AK 99929
(907) 874-3770

ALBERTA
PROVINCEWIDE
1-800-661-8888

BANFF
Banff/Lake Louise Chamber of Commerce
Box 1298, Banff, AB T0L 0C0 Canada
(403) 762-3777

CALGARY
Calgary Tourist and Convention Bureau
237 Eighth Ave., SE, Calgary, AB T2G 0K8 Canada
(403) 263-8510

CAMROSE
Battle River Tourist Association
Box 1515, Camrose, AB T4V 1X4 Canada
(403) 672-8555

DRUMHELLER
Big Country Tourist Association
170 Centre St., Box 2308, Drumheller, AB T0J 0Y0 Canada
(403) 823-5885

EDMONTON
Edmonton Convention and Tourism Authority
#104, 9797 Jasper Ave., Edmonton, AB T5J 1N9 Canada
(403) 426-4715

EDSON
Evergreen Tourist Association
Box 2548, Edson, AB T0E 0P0 Canada
(403) 723-4711

GRANDE PRAIRIE
Game Country Travel Association
9932 111 Ave., Grande Prairie, AB T8V 4C3 Canada
(403) 539-4300

JASPER
Jasper Park Chamber of Commerce
Box 98, Jasper, AB T0E 1E0 Canada
(403) 852-3858

LETHBRIDGE
   Chinook Country Tourist Association
   2805 Scenic Dr., Lethbridge, AB T1K 5B7 Canada
   (403) 329-6777

MEDICINE HAT
   South-East Alberta Travel and Convention Bureau
   Box 605, Medicine Hat, AB T1A 7G5 Canada
   (403) 527-6422

PEACE RIVER
   Land of the Mighty Peace Tourist Association
   Box 3210, Peace River, AB T0H 2X0 Canada
   (403) 624-4042

RED DEER
   David Thompson Country Tourist Council
   4836 Ross St., Red Deer, AB T4N 5E8 Canada
   (403) 342-2032

ST. ALBERT
   Midnight Twilight Tourist Association
   #1, Sturgeon Rd., St. Albert, AB T8N 0E8 Canada
   (403) 458-5600

ST. PAUL
   Lakeland Tourist Association
   Box 874, St. Paul, AB T0A 3A0 Canada
   (403) 645-2913

BRITISH COLUMBIA
PROVINCEWIDE
   Ministry of Tourism
   Parliament Buildings, Victoria, BC V8V 1X4 Canada
   (604) 387-1642

CENTRAL BRITISH COLUMBIA
   Cariboo Tourist Association
   Dept. #003, P.O. Box 4900, Williams Lake, BC V2G 2V8 Canada
   (604) 392-2226

DAWSON CREEK
Travel Infocentre Dawson Creek
900 Alaska Ave., Dawson Creek, BC V1G 4T6 Canada
(604) 782-9595

FORT NELSON
Town of Fort Nelson
Bag Service 399, Fort Nelson, BC V0C 1R0 Canada
(604) 774-6400 (seasonal)

FORT ST. JOHN
Peace River Alaska Highway Tourism Association
Dept. #009, Box 6850, Fort St. John, BC V1J 4J3 Canada
(604) 785-2544

KAMLOOPS
High Country Tourism Association
Dept. #004, P.O. Box 962, Kamloops, BC V2C 6H1 Canada
(604) 372-7770

KIMBERLEY
Rocky Mountain Visitors Association of British Columbia
Dept. #007, P.O. Box 10, Kimberley, BC V1A 2Y5 Canada
(604) 427-4838

KOOTENAY
Kootenay Country Tourist Association
610 Railway St., Nelson, BC V1L 1H4 Canada
(604) 352-6033

OKANAGAN
Okanagan Similkameen Tourist Association
Dept. #005, 104 - 515 Highway 97 South, Kelowna, BC V1Z 3J2 Canada
(604) 769-5959

SMITHERS
North by Northwest Tourism Association of British Columbia
Dept. #008, P.O. Box 1030, Smithers, BC V0J 2N0 Canada
(604) 847-5227

VANCOUVER
Tourism Association of Southwestern British Columbia
Dept. #002, Box 48610, Bentall P.O., Vancouver, BC V7X 1A3 Canada
(604) 688-3677

VANCOUVER ISLAND
Tourism Association of Vancouver Island
Dept. #001, Suite 302 - 45 Bastion Square, Victoria, BC V8W 1J1 Canada
(604) 382-3551

NORTHWEST TERRITORIES
PROVINCEWIDE
Tourism Association of the Northwest Territories
Box 506, Yellowknife, NWT X1A 2N4 Canada
1-800-661-0788

INUVIK
Western Arctic Visitors Association
Box 1525, Inuvik, NWT X0E 0T0 Canada

YELLOWKNIFE
TravelArctic
Yellowknife, NWT X1A 2L9 Canada
(403) 920-4944

YUKON
PROVINCEWIDE
Tourism Yukon, Government of Yukon
P.O. Box 2703, Whitehorse, YT Y1A 2C6 Canada
(403) 667-5340

DAWSON CITY
Klondike Visitors Association
P.O. Box 389, Dawson City, YT Y0B 1G0 Canada
(403) 993-5575

MAYO
Silver Trail Tourism Association
P.O. Box 268, Mayo, YT Y0B 1M0 Canada

WATSON LAKE
Alaska Highway Interpretive Centre
(403) 536-7469 (summer) or (403) 667-5340 (winter)

WHITEHORSE
Tourism Industry Association of the Yukon
302 Steele St., Whitehorse, YT Y1A 2C5 Canada
(403) 668-3331

=====   Appendix B   =====

Currency Exchange

I once asked a youngster in Whitehorse which currency she preferred, Canadian or U.S. She pondered the question for a moment, then replied, "I like U.S. money because it spends better, but I think the Canadian money is prettier."

Canadians measure their wealth just as do U.S. citizens, in terms of dollars and cents. And the youngster was right, bills of various denominations in Canada are printed in different colors and could be described as prettier, or at least not as boring as having everything green.

And, she was right about the spending power. In recent years, a Canadian dollar has been worth about $0.85 in U.S. currency. What that means is that a U.S. dollar will buy more goods than a Canadian dollar.

Canadian business will gladly accept U.S. currency on a one-for-one exchange if you so offer. However, you'll be cheating yourself if you do. Stop at a national bank, either before leaving the United States or as soon as you get into Canada, and exchange your money. Depending on the exact rate of exchange at the moment, you should get about $115 in Canadian currency for every $100 of U.S. currency you exchange.

Businesses in Canada will make the exchanges at their cash registers for you as well, though often they assess a penalty of from 2 percent to 5 percent. You're almost always ahead if you exchange your money at a national bank where no penalties are assessed.

Credit card users can freely charge to VISA, MasterCard, Discover, American Express, Diners Club and gasoline cards. The companies issuing the cards will adjust for the differences in exchange rates prior to sending you a billing statement. VISA and MasterCard are the most frequently accepted cards in western Canada.

================ Appendix C ================

Border Crossings

Though U.S. and Canadian citizens can travel freely across each other's borders without a passport, travelers are still required to clear through customs each time they enter one country or the other.

For most people, border crossings are completed through the car window by answering a few questions. Occasionally, one of these answers will result in a customs inspector asking to examine certain items. Cooperation is the key to any border crossing. Customs officers do have the authority to completely search you, your vehicle and all your possessions should your answers be unsatisfactory.

Items that cause the most problems at border crossings include:

- **Firearms**: Foreigners may not possess handguns or fully automatic rifles and shotguns in Canada. Do not even attempt to cross into Canada with these items in your possession; they will be seized.
- **Alcoholic beverages**: Up to 1.2 liters of hard liquor, 1.2 liters of wine and 8.5 liters of beer can be transported legally across the border. More than that is subject to seizure.
- **Items for resale in Canada**: Items carried across the border for sale to Canadian citizens are subject to duty.
- **Tobacco**: Up to a carton of cigarettes per person for personal consumption can be carried into Canada. Larger amounts are subject to duty.
- **Insurance**: Be prepared to demonstrate proof that your automobile insurance is valid in Canada. Most auto insurance companies will send a statement to you just for the asking. You must carry at least $200,000 of third-party liability insurance.
- **Identification**: Ensure that each member of your party carries proper identification. Birth certificates or passports, which show proof of citizenship, are usually acceptable. Driver's licenses may or may not be acceptable.

Travelers bound for Alaska may also be asked how much cash they are carrying. Canadian authorities are concerned that people not run out of money en route, particularly in the event of an emergency.

====== Appendix D ======

Pets

The family dog or cat is certainly welcome to join you on your vacation to and from Alaska. However, out of consideration for your pet, and for the citizens of the states and provinces you will be passing through, certain things should be done in advance.

Within 10 days of your departure, take your pet to a veterinarian and ask that all its shot records be brought up to date and a health certificate prepared. Customs officers may ask to see this health certificate and can, if uncertain about the health of your pet, place it in quarantine. The key item of interest on an animal's health certificate will be a current vaccination for rabies.

Be sure to allow sufficient time for your pet to get exercise. And, remember, courtesy requires that your pets be leashed in public areas such as campgrounds or parks.

Provide plenty of water at regular intervals for your animals. Traveling on hot, dusty days can be dehydrating for animals just as it is for people.

Those traveling via the Alaska Marine Highway should note that pets are not permitted in passenger areas aboard ship. Pets are confined to their owners' vehicles except for twice-daily exercise periods on the vehicle deck. Take along the equipment necessary to clean up after your pet on these excursions.

Finally, keep your pet under control at all times. Wildlife officials have a special distaste for dogs that chase wild animals and, in many cases, may shoot any dog found doing so. Your pet is your responsibility.

===== Appendix E =====

Firearms and Ammunition

For whatever reason, driving trips to and from Alaska inspire people to carry guns, usually in the name of personal protection from bears or whatever. For the most part, these weapons are unnecessary.

Bear problems in campgrounds generally are not fatal for either the people or the bear. Most are avoided simply by keeping a clean camp. Officials work hard to keep bears away from campgrounds, often trapping and relocating bears that are a problem.

For those venturing to remote areas far from any assistance, a firearm may be of some value, though, again, a clean camp and traveling with a group will almost always eliminate any problems with wildlife.

If you do choose to carry a gun on your trip to Alaska, be completely familiar with its operation. Probably the most dangerous weapons anywhere are those in the hands of people who don't know how to use them.

In your vehicle, keep guns and ammunition separate, so a child or an intruder can't easily get hold of both together. For safety's sake, do not, under any circumstances, travel down the road with a loaded gun in your vehicle.

Hunters traveling to Alaska or any of the Canadian provinces should keep their firearms packed away until the time has arrived to take part in the hunt. After a lengthy road trip, all rifles should be test-fired in a safe area to ensure that the sights were not jarred during transit. Most guides and outfitters can recommend a nearby rifle range or other safe area for this activity.

In general, when traveling with a firearm, think in terms of safety and the peace of mind of the people you might meet. Few things cause more unnecessary excitement than someone walking around a campground carrying a loaded rifle or shotgun.

On a personal note, the only time my family was bothered by a bear in camp en route to Alaska, the family dog, a miniature Dachshund, leashed to a picnic table, sent the bear packing before anybody could get a good look at it. Heidi still thinks of herself as the meanest 11 pounds on four feet.

Appendix F

Time Zones

Geographically, Alaska spans five time zones. However, in the early 1980s, Alaska's politicians decided that two were sufficient. Virtually all of the populated parts of the state now run 1 hour earlier than the Pacific Coast. Only the extreme western part of the Aleutian Islands runs on a clock that is 2 hours earlier than the Pacific Coast.

Thus, noon in New York City is 11 A.M. in Chicago, 10 A.M. in Denver, 9 A.M. in Los Angeles and 8 A.M. in Anchorage, Fairbanks or Juneau.

Canadian provinces operate with a little more knowledge of functional geography. Both Yukon Territory and British Columbia keep to Pacific Coast time; Northwest Territories runs on Rocky Mountain time, the same as Denver.

Daylight savings time is observed in Alaska.

=========== Appendix G ===========

Camping:
Public and Private Campgrounds

Private campgrounds are those on private land operated as a business serving the traveling public. Fees for usage are generally higher than for public campgrounds, but usually there are more facilities available, such as showers, coin-operated washers and dryers, electrical service and water and sewage hookups for RVs.

Public campgrounds are those operated by a national, state, provincial or local government. Samples of these would be the USDA Forest Service, the Bureau of Land Management, the National Park Service, British Columbia's provincial parks, Yukon's territorial campgrounds and Parks Canada facilities. Usually these are in more remote areas well away from towns, and facilities are usually limited to picnic tables, level parking sites and pit toilets.

Fees for public campgrounds range from a low of about $5 per night to a high of about $12 per night, depending on the location. Fees for private campgrounds generally start around $10 for a tent site and go up to more than $20 for a site with hookups for electricity, water and sewage. Showers and laundromats are almost always coin-operated in private campgrounds, though some operators will provide tokens for showers.

Dump stations for RVs are usually found in private campgrounds or in some service stations. Drinking water may or may not be available in public campgrounds, or if available it may require boiling before drinking.

Appendix H

Fishing

Some of the most fabulous fresh- and saltwater sport fishing on earth is available in northwestern Canada and Alaska. However, each state and province has its own regulations governing the take of fish from various waters. In many cases, these regulations are stream- or lake-specific. Be absolutely certain you have with you a valid fishing license for the particular state or province you are in, and that you understand the regulations governing that body of water. For additional information and a synopsis of pertinent fishing regulations, write to the following:

ALASKA
> The Alaska Department of Fish and Game
> P.O. Box 3-2000, Juneau, AK 99802

BRITISH COLUMBIA
> Ministry of Environment
> Recreational Fisheries Branch
> Parliament Buildings, Victoria, BC V8V 1X5 Canada

NORTHWEST TERRITORIES
> Northern Frontier Visitor's Association
> P.O. Box 1107, Yellowknife, NWT X1A 2N8 Canada

YUKON TERRITORY
> Tourism Yukon
> 302 Steele St., Whitehorse, YT Y1A 2C5 Canada

===========   Appendix I   ===========

Hunting

Alaska and northwestern Canada offer unmatched opportunities for hunting a wide variety of big-game animals, including Dall sheep, Stone sheep, caribou, moose, black bear, brown bear, grizzly bear, mountain goat and wolf. As with the fishing, however, the taking of these animals is carefully regulated by each state and province.

In Alaska, out-of-state or foreign hunters must be accompanied by a state-licensed guide or master guide while hunting Dall sheep, brown bear or grizzly bear. U.S. citizens hunting big-game animals in Canada must, in almost every case, be accompanied by an outfitter or guide.

Guided hunts, however, are no assurance of success. It is, for example, illegal for an Alaska guide to guarantee that clients will collect a trophy or fill their game tags. Guided hunts are also expensive, with fees typically averaging $500 a day or more while afield. Finally, guided hunts are usually booked a year or more in advance.

Beyond big-game hunting, there are spectacular opportunities for small-game hunts in Alaska and northwestern Canada, specifically for waterfowl in September and October, and for grouse or ptarmigan—usually with an August to March season. Bag limits are liberal, up to as many as 20 ptarmigan and 15 grouse per day.

For additional information on hunting opportunities and for information on pertinent regulations, write to:

ALASKA
>The Alaska Department of Fish and Game
>Box 3-2000, Juneau, AK 99802

BRITISH COLUMBIA
>Ministry of Environment, Wildlife Branch
>Parliament Buildings, Victoria, BC V8V 1X5 Canada

NORTHWEST TERRITORIES
>Northern Frontier Visitor's Association
>P.O. Box 1107, Yellowknife, NWT X1A 2N8 Canada

YUKON
>Tourism Yukon
>302 Steele St., Whitehorse, YT Y1A 2C5 Canada

 Appendix J

Gas Prices/Converting Liters to Gallons

Gasoline in Canada is measured and sold by the liter. It takes approximately 3.7 liters to equal 1 U.S. gallon.

To obtain a figure on the price paid per U.S. gallon of gasoline, multiply the per-liter price displayed on the pump by 3.7. To determine the number of gallons purchased, divide the number of liters measured out by the gas pump by 3.7.

To determine the price paid per gallon in U.S. funds, first multiply the cost per liter by 3.7 to obtain the cost per gallon in Canadian funds. Then multiply the cost per gallon in Canadian funds by the conversion rate obtained when you exchanged your money.

For example, if you pay $0.56 (Canadian) per liter of fuel and the conversion rate is 0.85, the math works like this:

$0.56 x 3.7 x 0.85 = $1.76 (U.S.) per U.S. gallon.

INDEX

195

ABOUT THE AUTHOR

Ron Dalby, award-winning former editor of *Alaska*™ magazine, has authored four books on his native state, including the *Insight Guide to Alaska*. Born in Skagway, he first traveled the Alaska Highway at 13 months of age; since then he has experienced high points and low in more than twenty years of vacationing along the route. He and his wife, Jennifer, live in Palmer.